Re-Forming the Narrative

Re-Forming the Narrative

TOWARD A MECHANICS OF MODERNIST FICTION

DAVID HAYMAN

Cornell University Press

ITHACA AND LONDON

First published 1987 by Cornell University Press.

International Standard Book Number 0-8014-2005-9
Library of Congress Catalog Card Number 87-47546
Printed in the United States of America
*Librarians: Library of Congress cataloging information
appears on the last page of the book.*

*The paper in this book is acid-free and meets the guidelines for
permanence and durability of the Committee on Production Guidelines
for Book Longevity of the Council on Library Resources.*

For Loni

Contents

Preface

The title of this book emphasizes my central concern, the isolation of operative functions that set off the literature of what has been called modernism from that of earlier periods. Operating within a "mechanics" perspective, I have devoted one chapter to each of five devices foregrounded, if not innovated, by advanced writers in our century. My aim in highlighting such tools is to indicate how modernist writers reshaped their tools in response to the demands both of the text and of evolving tastes. To this end each of my chapters, after exploring the traditional roots of a device, establishes range and function in general terms in conjunction with a study of applications within a variety of specific literary contexts.

My concern is less with the discovery and use of new expressive means than with the change in priorities occasioned by shifts in the aesthetic sensibility and the manner in which such shifts alter the way narrative (even conventional narrative) performs and is performed and received. The focus is on how these five tactics contribute to an impressive number of fresh formulations, whose import and potential we have only begun to understand.

This approach is designed in part to reveal how certain particularly demanding texts function. It is also intended to make such texts more accessible by interpreting even the most radical-seeming departures in terms of a broadly defined modernist mindset. It shows, for example, that though there is nothing new about illusionism per se, our reading habits give particular poignancy to techniques that disconcert us by their unabashed manipulation of the machinery of display in the service of desire and the toying with belief and engagement. The same may be said of the tendency to foreground the disjunction inherent in all discourse, the deliberate unmasking and redefinition of distancing procedures, and the declaration of textual autonomy through the thematic and formal promotion of autogenerative procedures. Such revisionist tactics, instituted separately and in an unprogrammatic fashion by a significant number of narratives in a variety of western cultures, help define the literary climate of postsymbolist, postrealist modernism. If they do not establish a new rationale for literary developments that are still current after a century and a half of turbulence, they may at least help situate our speculations in the texts themselves. More important, our study of a selection of seemingly subversive devices within a broader literary historical frame may help us understand and appreciate the internal dynamics of change.

Over the years I have amassed debts to the students who participated in seminars taught in Iowa, Paris, Wisconsin, and most recently Frankfurt; to dissertators who have become colleagues, such as Eric Rabkin, Susan Lanser, and Gregory Lucente; to friends and colleagues Lawrence Dembo, Reinhold Grimm, Melvin Friedman, Bernard Benstock, Shari Benstock, Hugh Kenner, Tzvetan Todorov (whose suggestion inspired the form of this study), Gérard Genette, Julia Kristeva, Robert Scholes, Philippe Sollers (as thinker even more than as novelist), and the sorely missed Michel Benamou, Merle Brown, and Robert Champigny. Much stimulation came from friends not professing or writing literature, who were engaged in a different sort of study, or who cared enough to disagree usefully and even violently with the positions I was advancing. The former include Paul and Anne van Buren, who always listened and argued with tact and insight and whose questions touched on problems I was still far from solving; in the second category is Glyn Norton, whose hard philological scholarship and sympathetic ear helped much during the damp Mediterranean spring of Cassis. Also in that category is my Spanish friend, penpal, and editor, Julián Ríos, who encouraged me through dry periods by asking me to write essays that refreshed my perspective. Stephen Heath was particularly helpful when he advanced arguments that made me elaborate and expand my positions. His objections (and those of Ihab Hassan) confirmed my view of nodality and inspired me to investigate distancing procedures. Such challenges have made this effort worthwhile in unpredictable ways. Finally, Marianne Hirsch and Khachig Tololyan, as readers of an earlier version of this volume, obliged me to deepen, broaden, and modify many of my positions, greatly increasing my own satisfaction with the book.

The time needed to pursue this study was given me by a series of grants and fellowships. The Graduate School of the University of Wisconsin gave me two invaluable summers. With the help of a fellowship from the National Endowment for the Humanities, a fellowship at the Wisconsin Humanities Institute, and a semester spent at the Camargo Foundation in Cassis, I was able to eke out the year needed to think my way through and draft the major chapters.

Quotations from *Ezra Pound Speaking: Radio Speeches of World War II*, copyright © 1978 by The Ezra Pound Literary Trust, are reprinted by permission of New Directions Publishing Corporation. Selections from Witold Gombrowicz, *Cosmos*, are reprinted by permission of Grove Press, Inc. Selections from Alain Robbe-Grillet, *Project for a Revolution in New York*, translated by Richard Howard; Samuel Beckett, *Molloy*, translated by Samuel Beckett and Patrick Bowles; and Samuel Beckett, *The Unnamable*, translated by Samuel Beckett, are reprinted by permission of Grove Press, Inc., and of John Calder (Publishers) Ltd. For permission to quote from Raymond Roussel, *Locus Solus*, translated by Rupert Copeland Cuningham, I thank the University of California Press. Permission to quote from the "corrected edition" of James Joyce, *Ulysses*, comes from the copyright holders: copyright © 1986 by Random House, Inc.; reading text copyright © 1984 by The Trustees of the Estate of James Joyce; preface copyright © 1986 by Richard Ellmann; afterword copyright © by Hans Walter Gabler; The Bodley Head, and The Society of Authors acting on behalf of the Executors of the James Joyce Estate. For permission to quote from James Joyce, *A Portrait of the Artist as a Young Man*, copyright © 1916 by B. W. Huebsch, copyright renewed 1944 by Nora Joyce, definitive text copyright © 1964 by The Estate of James Joyce; and for permission to quote from James Joyce, *Finnegans Wake*, copyright © 1939 by James Joyce, copyright © renewed 1967 by George Joyce and Lucia Joyce, I thank Jonathan Cape, Viking Penguin, Inc., and The Society of Authors acting on behalf of the Executors of the James Joyce Estate. For permission to quote from the

James Joyce archives, I thank The Society of Authors acting on behalf of the Executors of the James Joyce Estate. For permission to translate excerpts from Philippe Sollers, *H;* copyright © 1973 by Editions du Seuil; from Philippe Sollers, *Nombres*, copyright © 1968 by Editions du Seuil; and from Maurice Roche, *Maladie mélodie*, copyright © 1980 by Editions du Seuil, I thank the copyright holder. Quotations from Jorge Luis Borges, *Labyrinths*, copyright © 1962, 1964 by New Directions Publishing Corporation, and Louis-Ferdinand Céline, *Death on the Installment Plan*, are reprinted by permission of New Directions. Quotations from Ezra Pound, *The Cantos of Ezra Pound*, copyright © 1934 by Ezra Pound, are reprinted by permission of New Directions and Faber and Faber Limited.

Though a few passages from this book have already appeared in periodicals, relatively few traces of those early efforts remain. The central pages of "Double-Distancing" are all drawn from an essay originally published in *Escandalar* 3 and *Novel*, Fall 1978. A small portion of my treatment of Beckett and Joyce in "Self-Generation" has been published under the title "Joyce—Beckett Joyce" in *Beckett Studies* 7 (Spring 1982) and reprinted in *Seventh of Joyce*, edited by Bernard Benstock (Bloomington: Indiana University Press, 1982). I have published three essays treating different applications of paratactics, but only one of them, "Parataxis and the Shape of Joyce's Fiction," published in *Scripsi*, vol. 1, no. 2 (November 1982), and excerpted in *Europe* 657/658, contains an early version of material included in the Joyce portion of my chapter. An earlier and much longer version of my discussion of Joyce's use of nodality appeared as "Réseaux infrastructurels" in *Poétique* 26 (1976), before being translated into Spanish as "La infraestructura nodal de *Finnegans Wake*" in *Espiral*, revista 3 (1977), and published in English as "Nodal Infrastructure in *Finnegans Wake*," in *James Joyce Quarterly*, vol. 16, nos. 1/2 (Fall 1978–Winter 1979). A more elaborate treatment of Sollers's use of nodality, from which material has been taken for my chapter, originally appeared in *sub-stance*, Fall 1984, as "Nodality or Plot Displaced: The Nodality of Sollers' *H*."

DAVID HAYMAN

Madison, Wisconsin

Re-Forming the Narrative

Introduction

A culture intent on the production of individualized expression puts special demands on both the writer and the reader, demands that eventuate willy-nilly in formal conventions, even in conventions of difference. Indeed, our age has elevated difference to the status of an operative myth, calling it progress and fetishizing it to the point where it demands critical attention, if not demystification. The best way to confront this result of modernity is to isolate the tactics so brazenly displayed, to study their applications in the light of an awareness that every tool has antecedents somewhere in the literary midden of the past. By illuminating the history, currency, and applications of a given set of tactics and simultaneously exploring the divergent roles they play in various texts, perhaps we can establish how individual uses of a device repeatedly "make it new" while contributing to the evolution of a properly "modern" style.

To be convincing, such a demonstration must follow a reasonably disinterested "mechanical" approach, one that reflects judgment used nonjudgmentally and employs close practical readings of a wide range of innovative texts within a framework that is historical only in relation to shared tactics. Whatever conclusions can be drawn from such a study, the real goal is to understand some of the procedures that continue to shape modern awareness.

Fiction in the post-Flaubertian, post-Mallarméan era, unlike writing in the era that Roland Barthes posits for the "readable" text, does not embed its devices in the texture of the experience. Instead it routinely displays them on or near its surface. Thus we may see certain novels as "transparent bodies" or as something analogous to the Plexiglass medical mannequin that, by featuring the body's inner organs, obscures their container and effectively reverses the priorities of perception.

Implicit in this metaphor is a proposition: during a period with uncertain boundaries, one that can be identified as the modernist epoch, the postromantic moment, or even Foucault's modern episteme, a significant number of writers have unconsciously mimicked the post-Encyclopédiste, Linnaean scientific establishment. They have studied, catalogued, mounted, and displayed first the human condition and then, and increasingly, the concealed procedures of their predecessors in the service of a more precise statement. Our own century has seen ever bolder and more technically proficient artists exhibit against the grain the operation of their desacralized muse. Secure perhaps in the awareness that, even when flayed, the literary body retains traces of traditional glories, they have capitalized on that exposure to institute a fresh range of mysteries, demanding of their overinformed and textually trained reader greater efforts and providing fresh rewards. Before proceeding with our dissection, however, we should note, after Roland Barthes, that even the less exposed texts of the eminent predecessors are more revealing, more open about their processes than critics have hitherto suspected or wanted to understand.

For the poetics of form, Edgar Allan Poe's contribution to the craft-consciousness of the writer was crucial in mid-century, as were Flaubert's letters toward the end and Henry James's introductions at the turn of our century. Still, in terms of novelistic practice, a more vital, if discreet, foreshadowing is discernible even in the least overtly experimental of Flaubert's fictions. *Madame Bovary* contains in germ much that Flaubert accomplished, so much in fact that we can approach even it from the perspective of the projected "text about nothing," the one sustained "by style alone." In fact, that meticulous delineation of a minimal instance of provincial life may well mark the first stage in the dissolution of the literary subject by virtue of its "serious" treatment of material more appropriate to either the traditional bedroom farce or the moral tract.

Flaubert's challenge in *Bovary* and elsewhere was how to make the trivial circumstance aesthetically viable and engaging. True, he managed to interest his readers in the predicaments and characters of his main protagonists, but one should not be surprised that his major accomplishment was the discovery of other, fresher sources of interest. The record of his struggle to do so is available in his correspondence, but it has also been woven into the very fabric of his discourse. Despite his vaunted self-awareness, he was probably never fully conscious of the implications or nature of his tactics, any more than were those writers who instinctively responded to the welcome signals by reshaping and accentuating them.

Madame Bovary itself testifies how, in the service of reader interest and authorial detachment, Flaubert evolved (1) a system of modal difference, (2) procedures for ironic and guarded but still potent authorial commentary, and (3) strategies of simultaneity. Such innovations may well be just as original as his other, more emphatically self-announced achievements. The second set of devices, which includes signifying images, systems of echoes and oppositions, and highlighting procedures, no longer seems quite as fresh after significant modernist exploitation and New Critical exposure. Though generally slighted by theorists,[1] simultaneity has also been widely exploited. In *Bovary* its locus classicus is the courtship of Emma by Rodolphe during the agricultural fair, or *comice*, in part 1, chapter 8, but we can identify other instances in the less spectacular group scenes. Repeatedly, Flaubert attempted to achieve interest by conveying the illusion that several activities were being pursued simultaneously within the novelistic moment. (These procedures reflect a narrative program that has existed at least since Homer struggled to convey the total moment of the Trojan War.) Since Flaubert, the novel has found ways, generally paratactic, to expand, vary, and extend the illusion of true or lived simultaneity. Indeed, we have already reached and perhaps passed the point where writers can cavalierly toy with the very illusion earlier novelists struggled to achieve.

The central item in our short list, modal juxtaposition in *Bovary*, has been neglected, perhaps because it seems too natural. The practice of bringing together contrasting modal materials is also as old as Homer, but it is most striking in the traditions of farcical dislocation, the

---

[1]The major exception is still Joseph Frank in his ground-breaking essay "Spatial Form in the Modern Novel," in his *The Widening Gyre* (Bloomington: Indiana University Press, 1968), pp. 14–16 and passim.

carnivalisque, and Menippean satire. If in such contexts it is highly paratactic and strongly manipulative of reader distance, in Flaubert's novel it constitutes an early (muted) instance of what I will be calling macroparatactic discourse. The difference is that Flaubert has applied it to a nondisruptive and quasi-serious context in a high literary form. Its function is almost too clear in relation to the internal dynamics of the comice sequence: how better to motivate and categorize the conventionally comic seduction than by setting it against patently farcical behavior, how better to cool the erotic than by juxtaposing it with the banal public utterance!

Viewed in a larger perspective, the central procedure of the chapter as well as the passage may be read as the most radical of Flaubert's novelistic moves, one reflected in the larger decorum of a book that insists on casting its heterogeneous (Bakhtin might say heteroglossic) components in the appropriate formal mode and consequently revising our perception of familiar conventions. This touch best characterizes his revisionist treatment of what had previously been the *decorum* of the novel, a poetics to which writers of farce, comedy, romance, and melodrama conscientiously adhered. After all, even the great novels of the past were self-limiting. Cast in a given subgenre, they tended to maintain a set emotional, tonal, and topical range. Flaubert's move may not startle us today, but in its time, though no one noticed, it was more outrageous than the subject matter that dictated it. Indeed, modal mixing, by highlighting precisely the conventions that were being subverted, may have contributed as much to the court's attempt at censorship as did the explicit violations of moral codes. We may also argue that it put greater demands on the writer's ingenuity than any other aspect of his project, since, though ultimately more exposed and surreptitiously more unsettling, it appears to contribute more to unity than to the dissolution of the global narrative structure.

The point is not so much that Flaubert was there first, or that, even now, the formal contribution of the nineteenth century to modernist innovation remains largely unappreciated. Much the same thing can still be said about Joyce's contribution to high modernism. Rather the point is that, with hindsight and in the light of study, we may begin to see not only how certain basic devices work today in their more blatant uses but also how, over the years, they have contributed to our pleasure. Accordingly, in my discussion of texts that foreground tactics and sublimate narrative content, I shall assume and assert the constant and essential return of the (formal) repressed as a validating mechanism in the modern. Implicit in this approach is a view of the past as a persistent presence and a view of revolution as a reversal in the sense of "a turn of the wheel." Also implicit is a belief that the antimimetic art of our times conceals a profound mimetic impulse, that the experience it records or simulates may attain another sort of mimesis.

Finally, though the tactics of my book are confrontational, my literary instances are essentially illustrations designed to show how a given device has independently come into its own within a variety of cultures. If, in my analyses of carefully isolated techniques, I have frequently returned to certain writers, it is because their work best illustrates particular applications and shows how interrelated such techniques can be. My procedure is designed to suggest how such devices inform the aesthetic production of our seemingly anarchic period without losing their own plastic potential or being fully digested by the literary system, how they succeed in remaining doggedly modern in our time.

If we bear in mind the existence of the larger tradition that never fails to express itself through even the most rebellious production, a careful analysis of devices whose utility has been discovered more or less independently may disclose the outlines of an ongoing development, or rather, two distinct developments, in an age of change and difference. Twentieth-century modernism has played out its high aesthetic destiny within the tradition exemplified by Flaubert and Mallarmé against a backdrop of an anti-aestheticism that appears to have begun in France, if not with Sade, probably with Lautréamont and Rimbaud. We may trace present-day modernism as well, however, to a trait usually associated with farcical literature, to the fascination with ugliness and disgust rendered respectable by Baudelaire in his urban poetry, by the novels of Flaubert, and by the naturalist novel, to a convention exhibiting a curious ambivalence toward elegance of form and expression.

The anti-aesthetic impulse persists today side by side and even within performances of extraordinary polish and quasi-absolute pretensions, works that shock by destabilizing and rewriting the rules. It has found expression in the ragged industriaphilia and programmatic violence of futurism and vorticism and the carefully manipulated subjective outrage of the expressionists, to say nothing of the radical but

ingenious refusal of dada, and surrealism's frequently masterly appeal
to uncontrolled impulse. Interestingly, we can in each of these instances describe the verbal comportment of members of these schools
in the same language used to describe their plastic performances. Furthermore, in contemporary versions of expressionism, surrealism, and
dada, we find ample illustration of anti-aestheticism linked to a powerful minimalizing impulse that paradoxically purifies the impact and
underscores the extent to which outrage lends itself to control, submit-
ting to decorums of its own creation and contributing to the elaboration of fresh perceptual patterns.

An effort to document the frequently contradictory formal implications of the break with aestheticism, the gradual demise or displacement of the fin de siècle establishment, might recognize three distinct
tendencies with roots in the first decades of this century: first, the
tendency to match ugly subject matter with an an-aesthetic approach
to form; second, the seemingly opposite tendency to give the commonplace, banal, and frequently unacceptable subject matter a pleas-
ing and subtly distanced formulation. Authors belonging to the second
category—figures such as Joyce, Lawrence, Döblin, and Eliot—frequently participate as well in a third and seemingly dominant convention: the delicately nuanced presentation of a highly colored and frequently exotic total human situation. (This mode is best illustrated by
Proust, Woolf, Mann, Musil, and Gide.)[2]

The aesthetic distance characteristic of works manifesting the third
tendency is controlled and characterized by moderation and subtle
distinctions. This "middle distance" establishes a relationship between
reader and text that can be qualified as an engaged detachment. It is
conveyed through the imposition of more or less constant modifications within a carefully limited range, and its optimal result is a satisfying sense of balance and coherence. Such is the Proustian and Wool-
fian distance and that of their followers; it hardly ever calls attention to
its operations and permits the reader to float in a stream devoid of
rocks while attending to a discourse remarkable for its polish and
persuasive in all of its details. Also within the range of middle distance

[2]Viewed from other angles, the pie might be differently divided, as indeed it is in
Allen Thiher's brilliant study *Words in Reflection: Modern Language Theory and Postmodern
Fiction* (Chicago: University of Chicago Press, 1984). I intend to emphasize what I
perceive to be important formal considerations, so I shall downplay questions of subject
matter, philosophy, and ideology.

but constantly threatening to break out are works like Wyndham Lewis's *Tarr*, with its deliberately grating style, hard-edge situations, and jarring irony; Djuna Barnes's *Nightwood*, which treats aberrant behavior with infinite discretion in a style that constitutes in some senses its own subject matter; André Malraux's *La Condition humaine*, which applies the photographer's and the chronicler's instincts to a violent historico-politico fiction; and, of course, Joyce's polyvalent *Ulysses*, in which whimsical-seeming style and structure repeatedly violate the reader's expectations in the service of the sort of excitement that characterizes Barthes's "readerly" text. In *Ulysses*, *longueurs* and intellectual and discursive difficulties test the reader's dedication by denying ready access to the narrative situation (as opposed to the textual one). It could be argued that novels like these are already on the verge of a new kind of distance or at least one that has gone largely unnoticed: a revisionist or "double-distance" that seemingly refuses to perform the essential high modernist function of separating the reader from the world as experience without exacting a commitment to the reality of the textual universe. Hence the topic of my first chapter.

Such textual behavior, by destabilizing the reading process, makes distancing procedures a part of the message. Through "double-distancing," which we might also call antithetical distancing, the arts have evolved willy-nilly an alternative relationship (or a range of such relationships) of reader to art object, one that might finally be seen as complementing rather than negating the high aesthetic tradition (with which it is often openly at odds). In works that resemble in many ways the rough-textured canvases of Dubuffet or Tàpies or the collage sculptures of Rauschenberg, works that play on familiarity and in the process alienate, writers have found ways to employ aspects of daily experience and expressive forms that were formerly excluded from "high" art. They have simultaneously succeeded in objectifying their procedures. Extremes of attraction and repulsion or engagement and indifference have created a fresh aesthetic space in which the per-ceiver/experiencer takes on the difficult role of mediator/shaper. The net effect is that of questioning the status of the novel or narrative as artwork and the artist as producer. Another result is the reaestheticiza-tion of the an-aesthetic work and the cooption of the previously re-jected impulses.

Though only a fragment of a process and far from ubiquitous, the extreme case of double-distancing is central to our understanding of how certain contemporary works function. Obviously, however, like any other mechanism employed in the formation and manipulation of aesthetic significance, double-distancing can be as much a tendency as a trait. That is, there can be more or less strongly acented examples. Since the problematic of distancing is itself very difficult to discuss from a mechanics perspective, my treatment of this topic will concentrate on the clearer, stronger instances.

One of the commoner contexts for the rejection of traditionally mediated distance I have called the "impossible object" (see Chapter 2), a text drawing on a radical revision of narrative or graphic or dramatic verisimilitude. In such works, credibility is deliberately short-circuited, not in the service of another sort of verisimilitude, as in the fairy tale or fantasy, and not as a metaphorical or satiric reflection on reality, but as a manifestation of the artist's freedom from the need to make such statements. A discourse is established that continually and pointedly undercuts itself, producing something like conceptual dust and making the text seem transparently self-sufficient.

At issue is the question, what does it mean to portray, and the awareness that portrayal or portraiture is not only impossible but perhaps undesirable and even tantamount to a betrayal. We may see in this question a further manifestation of the creative agony and self-distrust implicit in the procedures and products of writers as different as Flaubert and Mallarmé, in short of the essential and driving spirit of the last century. Later creators, however, have not been content to set before us their half-successful illusionism or their incommunicable impulse. Instead, by questioning and even denying the value of re-producible reality in an age accustomed to all manner of factitious "truths," they declare the independence of their art from a validity that it cannot hope to convey. Paradoxically but appropriately, they generally do so in terms of an unmatched precision of detail, a literary hyperrealism validated by procedures of self-deflation and distortion.

By establishing tactics whose prime function is denial but whose rhetoric is singularly unobtrusive or accessible, such artists manifest qualities recalling those of the Belgian surrealist Magritte, whose late-flowering surrealism projects a profoundly motivated and largely un-programmed psychoanalytic validity. That is, when certain controls are removed from texts that are generally full of images and pregnant with associations, what reigns is a relatively unmediated personal truth whose keys are less important than its impact on readers attuned by the text to its preoccupations. In an important sense, such texts belong to the genre of the literary dream, for without resorting to the tired image of the dreamer, they bring into play encoded but undecipherable acts and images with an immediacy that can be keyed to the psychic life of both writer and reader.

While rejecting conventional narrative logic without having recourse to the verisimilitude of sustained illusion, texts using impossible objectivity generally accept responsibility for the new freedoms they generate. Obviously, interest must spring from sources other than the "what will happen now" or "how will it end" or "who did what" or "what is that" of normal fictions. It must derive from the logic of improbability, from the well-accentuated and engaging patterns to which the reader goes not only for reassurance but for pleasure, from the inventive use of detail and the manifestations of coherence through change and variation, all of which are qualities that impose fresh demands on the text.

The satisfaction of such demands does not rule out the invention of fresh sources of pleasure deriving from the tension between the new forms and the conventions they deny—tensions sharpened by the fact that such established (if frequently subliterary) forms are available as trace material or even as armatures in the texts bent on deconstructing them. The ruins of the traveler's journal and nineteenth-century science fantasies undergird the novels of Roussel. Pornographic thrillers, detective fictions, spy stories, and mysteries provide Alain Robbe-Grillet with his pretexts. The exotic adventure novel and the quest romance are alive *and* ailing in the comic objects of Harry Mathews. To a greater or lesser degree, all of these writers toy with the procedures of narrative suspense. This toying, however, generally has the spirit more of pastiche than of parody, tending toward an arabesque effect, an embroidery upon a recognizable form with the intent of producing difference. In short, despite the risk they run of confusing or boring their reader or overloading him with readerly responsibilities, impossible objects can and sometimes do have the best of several worlds.

Drawing perhaps on our uneasy relationship to the icons of the everyday, impossible objectivity proposes and subverts clearly delineated objects and situations, to say nothing of a simple story and clear plot line. It features and uses protagonists while eschewing characterization. Because its sensibility is essentially baroque, however, it can become immensely involved, even to the point of placing its structural patterns at risk. As a result, even this, the most conventional of the anticonventions we are discussing, may need to employ what I am calling "nodality," using clustering and repetition to produce accessible patterns. Generally, however, though it too is a reactive procedure, nodality presupposes the suppression or radical diffusion of plot and character and the deemphasis of objects, actions, and situations. In short, as demonstrated by the late work of Joyce, William Gass's novel-in-progress *The Tunnel*, Haroldo de Campos's elegantly crafted prose polyptyche *Galaxias*, Maurice Roche's spatial fictions, and Philippe Sollers's impressionistically voiced near-chronicle *H*, nodality is a feature of the deboned novel, a text that foregrounds language and rhetorical effects while ceaselessly redirecting its energies and calling upon the reader to find and even produce its rationale.

Texts organized by nodality cope with self-imposed deprivation (or a radical liberation from narrative constraints) by elaborating systems of echoes, permutations, interlocking patterns, and overtones to which the reader has immediate recourse in the quest to impose a rhythm of coherence and extract a play of significations. We may of course find nodal procedures in just about any text, reading them as part of the submerged textuality, but closer parallels are to be found in the sort of semiotic patterns discussed by Roman Jacobson or the systems of citations studied by Michael Riffaterre, or in what may be called the register of a writer's total oeuvre (its overriding semiotic and semantic infrasystem).

Such secret structures may be in some measure consciously elaborated, composed, but given their intricacy and the interrelatedness of their particulars, the fact of their labyrinthine presence in every fiber, we may doubt that any writer is fully aware of their extent or consciously in charge of their performance. It is also improbable that any given reader will be able to control all of their ramifications and vibrations. Here we have one of the qualities that sets the modern nodal procedures off from the symbolic or thematic or even motival substructure to which we have become accustomed in our fiction; for the nodal structure foregrounds the complexity recognized by Roland Barthes as covert in Balzac's "Sarrasine." That is, it is a signifying supplement to which the text and its reader go for support, one that is partly mnemonic, partly aesthetic, and partly structural. Unlike the system of Balzac's tale, however, it is more than a contributory aspect of the textual mechanism.

My next point, therefore, is that this partial system supplies the necessary articulation for plotless or relatively plotless structures. I am speaking, of course, of texts governed by nodality, those that ground their larger formal coherence on the availability of echoes of the sort generated by clearly articulated signifying systems embedded in and radiating from a seemingly undifferentiated context. Such systems need not and should not be apprehended in their entirety. Their surplus, after all, contributes to the effect of infinity, the frustrating satisfaction derived from the awareness that there will always be further overtones, other meanings. Given the weight that the nodal aspect carries in seemingly disjunct or amorphous works, however, we need not be surprised that it may have a stronger, more immediate, more reassuring, and in some sense a longer-lasting impact than many other attributes of its host text.

Anti- and nonnarrative novels, works that are predicated on the persistence of narrative traces, become readable by virtue of structures whose basis is motival and thematic, whose impact is rhythmical, and whose projected appearance is highly patterned. The more complex the novel, the richer its content, the more elaborate, necessary, and *visible* its nodal structure becomes. What would the reader of *Finnegans Wake* do were there not, apart from the chapter and book structures, numerous nodal systems (galaxies in de Campos's sense or the components of an infinitely unstable star chart)? It is very helpful to find fragments of the "Tristan and Isolde" myth distributed widely and more or less visibly throughout the *Wake* and coalescing about a clearly stated and centrally located narrative passage. Then again, how readable would one of Robbe-Grillet's recent texts be were it not perceived as a system of interrelated narrative tropes? On a simpler level, how nice it is to have such controls when we read and reread the initially amorphous novels of Beckett in which the minimal but welcome narrative or imagistic detail reinforces our sense of aesthetic control in a conceptual chaos by using repetition that hints at paraphrasable significance without actually delivering it.

The American New Critics first systematically asserted the self-containedness of the poem, its contextuality, and the difficulties of access. Since then, structuralists, following Saussure, have theoretically severed discourse from experience. The tactic treated here under the heading "self-generation," however, signals something other than a confident acceptance of the work's autonomy. Works exhibiting this trait are in fact struggling to be free rather than acknowledging or asserting their independence. These works, at present few in number, seem bent on dramatizing their production, making writing as gesture an important part of their subject matter.

Traditionally, at least three novelistic conventions have drawn upon the writing process for their narrative substance. In the epistolary novel, from Laclos's *Liaisons* to Barth's *Letters*, we participate more or less directly in the production of the text as action through a medium that purports to carry directly the words of an active protagonist, words that include commentary on the circumstances of their writing. Novels completely or partially in diary form, such as Rilke's astonishing *Malte Laurids Brigge* or Gide's *The Counterfeiters*, constitute an even more intimate variant of this convention.

Another category comprises works that elaborate on their own history and even on the practice of their production, from which they draw both themes and interest. Proust's novel may be the outstanding instance, though there are dozens of others. Marcel is writing the book about which he is writing, which is writing him. That is, his engagement with his life is focused by his engagement with the project of the text that he is both producing and rationalizing. The modern tendency to make writing a subject was initiated, if not by Cervantes, at least by Fielding, whose discussions of the genre of *Tom Jones* are the essential countersign to the adventures of his upstart hero. Such novels are self-reflexive, not properly self-generated.

A third category exists, but it is a far more shadowy affair, since, even when writing is one of its main concerns, its defining trait is less laid on than built into the narrative discourse. Included are novels that enact, or better, embody, their production rather than talking about it. Perhaps, though it is also primarily self-reflexive, Sterne's *Tristram Shandy* is the source of this procedure. That is, when Tristram or the text concentrates on telling (itself), when we follow its growth within its texture, we are experiencing an early form of "self-generation." Though not simply or perhaps actually associative in their nature, such texts generally present themselves as the products of an associative process that is transparently available in the very texture of the narrative. As readers, we can trace the *textual* source of the development, simultaneously perceiving and engaging with narrative substance struggling to grow out of its own language.

In a very important sense, this procedure is related to that used by Flaubert when he drew his portrait of a servant girl for *A Simple Heart*. In that work, we are privy to every impulse that shaped not so much the life as the vision of life. The resulting portrait evolves from impressions accumulating to produce an identity with vivid and integral associations. Félicité's life which emerges sequentially from the texture of her experiences, may be equated with her education for a (mock-) saintly death. The most immediate descendant of the procedure is the Joycean portrait, the "curve of an emotion"[3] that informs *A Portrait of the Artist as a Young Man*. Here too, though in a bolder and more complex way, we are given the complete record of a developing consciousness in which experience-generated associations play a major part.

In neither of these cases, nor in others we could mention, are we watching the text grow immediately out of its own texture. Still, the true self-generating procedure may be seen as a logical extension of the need of such works to bear witness to their own narrative substance, an impulse toward self-containedness and detachment. Self-generation implies the derivation of each succeeding fragment of textual substance from the language that precedes it, not from the psyche of the writer, but from the psyche of the text or of the writing protagonist as a textual presence. Though in practice even this more rigorous form of self-generation may have a thematic component, as indeed it does in the famous "letter" of *Finnegans Wake* or the manuscripts produced by the personae of Beckett's *Molloy*, its most imposing component is formal. The internal processes of production constitute in large measure the action of the text.

When we speak of the conceptual and formal self-generation that underlies Raymond Roussel's texts and the self-generative components of their realization, we are alluding less to a successful procedure than to a demanding project. Roussel's attempt to produce a verbal universe is as doomed to failure as Flaubert's "book about nothing" or Mallarmé's universal "Livre." The same may be said, however, though in

---

[3]See Joyce's essay, "A Portrait of the Artist," included in the Viking Critical Library edition of *A Portrait of the Artist as a Young Man*, ed. Chester Anderson (New York: Viking, 1968), pp. 257–66.

a different register, of the texts growing from Beckett's verbal wraiths' experience of language. In contrast, the language of Joyce's *Wake* seems to evolve from its own potential to mean, a fact evidenced not only by the finished work but also by the book's draft history. We may perhaps see such projects in the light of Deleuze's and Guattari's "logic of desire," which from the outset is doomed to fall short of its object because it obliges us to choose between production (or process) and acquisition, or the stilling of process.[4] As if to mimic the logic of desire, such texts produce a sense of production and leave us with not only a textual acquisition but also, and more important, an incomplete procedure: our own self-perpetuating reading conducted in the light of the text's writing and unwriting of itself.

The incomplete, the overfull, and the potential are staples of our literary and artistic era. Perhaps their most pervasive vehicle is the revolutionary device I am calling "Paratactics." Conventional novels and even many that are unconventional have always adhered to hypotactic procedures, stressing proper coordination and subordination, imposing not only regularity, or the illusion of the seamless surface, but also a hierarchical arrangement of materials on all levels of their discourse. Only that gross outsider the farcical novel, in its effort to be more fully itself by mimicking the abrupt gestures of outrage and chaos, has on occasion violated this dominant grammatical decorum. Even in farce, however—even in Rabelais and Sterne—one finds nothing to compare to the radical but superbly controlled micro- and macroparatactics of a Joyce or a Céline, and no age has seen anything like the florid disjunction so obvious in the aesthetic production of our century.

Simply stated, what I am calling paratactics is an extension of a grammatical form that does without subordination and coordination. Relatively rare in the normal discourse in modern European languages, parataxis is not in itself a disjunctive mode. I need only note that the medieval *Chanson de Roland* features grammatical parataxis. Indeed, through its proximity to the form of the list, it could be our most powerful ordering device. On the other hand, since it facilitates the conjunction of radically different materials, it has lent itself to the

---

[4]Gilles Deleuze and Félix Guattari, *L'Anti-Oedipe* (Paris: Editions de Minuit, 1972), p. 32 and passim.

generation of works, frequently in a mock-encyclopedic vein, that develop a logic of confrontational juxtaposition.

In this domain the contribution of James Joyce seems decisive, even though Joyce was not alone in using paratactics as a means of abbreviating and extending his narratives. His works exemplify the new trend, frequently exhibiting vigorous and even brutal parataxis while executing perhaps the most ambitious tightrope walk over the abyss of uncertainty in the history of the arts. For all the ingenuity of Joycean paratactics—the variety of his effects, the powerful prismatic vision, and the control—it is not exhaustive. Indeed, the range of already tried effects is so impressive, and their recent growth has been so prodigious, that I have felt obliged to shape my analysis in terms of a rough chronology, beginning in our century with Gertrude Stein and cubism.

The potential for paratactics has always existed. In the last century, for example, not only the prose narrative of the naturalists but also the prose poetry of the fin de siècle could have lent themselves to some such tactic. It is easy to imagine Rimbaud or Lautréamont or even Beardsley employing formal as well as conceptual disjunction. We may wonder why the frenzy of Sade remained within the bounds of a rigorously hypotactic Enlightenment prose, finding no baroque outlets. Strange to say, even Flaubert, who dared so much, after cautiously inserting paratactics into his comice chapter, chose not to reinforce the divergencies of his encyclopedic masterpiece *Bouvard et Pécuchet* and failed to underscore formally the hectic vision of his St. Anthony. To my knowledge, in the nineteenth century, only Lautréamont's dislocated macrotext, Whitman's catalogues in *Leaves of Grass*, and the more vividly paratactic but neglected masterpieces of Jules Valles approximated and foreshadowed contemporary practice.[5]

Perhaps writers of other extravagant works were wary, as well they should have been, of the dangers posed by parataxis to texts that themselves teetered on the edge. Only in our post-realist/naturalist/symbolist moment has narrative prose as well as poetry, and in

---

[5]Valles was that curious animal a pamphleteer who knew how to apply his hyperbolic methods to a bildungsroman sequence. His *L'Étudiant* (1881) is often radically paratactic in its details and even makes frequent use of the three points Céline claimed to have invented.

conjunction with the plastic arts and music, dared avail itself of reiteration, disjunction, and stylistic discord to accent its rhythms, enliven its textures, and complicate its structure. Only in an age that turns its verbal artifacts into veritable *Gesamtkunstwerke* capable of integrating all manner of modes and metres, to say nothing of subject matter, has paratactics come into its own. Still, perhaps I am putting the cart before the horse. Perhaps the willingness to employ the full range of disjunctive effects and the ability to invent fresh ones facilitated the Gesamtkunstwerk effect characteristic of so much of our art.

In the wake of Joyce, Pound, and Eliot, to say nothing of Jarry, Céline, and J. P. Donleavy, internal change and difference are quite as common today as is the variation from work to work. It is no more unusual to find a writer like Pynchon or Grass producing a big variegated novel replete with verbal shock effects than to find in a given writer's oeuvre a wide range of forms and styles. Because we are still far from exhausting its potential, a fact that may explain its continuing vitality, paratactics remains the most startling and disconcerting mode of contestation. Perhaps, in a century marked by continual and catastrophic disruptions in all domains, a device that enables the artwork on the one hand to mimic and on the other to control chaos, uncertainty, and proliferating knowledge is as reassuring as it is diverting.

These tactics or crypto-conventions cannot exhaust or fully describe twentieth-century or even contemporary practices. Viewed as part of a coherent trend, however, they do reflect the principles underlying a good number of works, and they may even signal the existence of an evolving period style. A close study of their operation will show how various their applications have been and how they conform chameleonlike to a context, functioning in a range of texts much as leitmotifs do in modernist fiction, acquiring different attributes for each appearance but retaining a strong identity. Though the uninspired abuse or overuse of even the most versatile technique will lead to fatigue, it follows that such devices can contribute to the vitality of any number of works without becoming redundant or clichéd, mere hackneyed *astuces*.

The following chapters treat the five tactics as functioning attributes of works whose shapes they help determine, works that in turn delimit the given technique's range of applications and suggest its potential. As suggested earlier, formal devices and narrative tactics are aspects of a culturally determined semiotic system, aspects that draw intertexually upon earlier practice. In each instance, therefore, we shall attempt to establish a lineage extended, modified, or even subverted by recent literary practice.

The impulse that prompts new movements, like new religions, to discover forebears, ridiculous as it sometimes appears, does not totally lack grounds. Even more appropriate, if safer, is the tendency of individual talents to make much of unappreciated figures from the recent past, figures whose tactics they see themselves as continuing but whose practice licenses their "revolt." In a much broader sense, quite beyond the range of impact and influence, contestation revises, subverts, and even reverses older conventions, acquiring its requisite strangeness without obliterating the traces that permit access through our textual habits.

If, on the one hand, new approaches are belated homages to fringe forebears, on the other hand they are radical adjustments of the normative practices that persist as more or less dynamic subtexts. We can show that double-distancing is as much a replique to the conventional middle-distancing of the last century as to the more self-conscious medial distance of high modernism. Clearly, impossible objectivity responds, as do so many of the artistic trends of this century, not only to the extreme canons of realism but also to a seemingly ineradicable illusionism, by inverting the novelistic expectations that must be counted among its subjects. The nodal text is foregrounding and deconstructing the sorts of meaning that more overtly plotted texts use to add conceptual density. Self-generation reveals not so much the writer as the writing of texts that pretend to draw their substance from without and to rely solely on the rules of coherence and logic. Finally, paratactics discloses the conceptual and representational gaps concealed by the rhetorical practices of hypotactic fictions to which they have frequent, if not extensive, recourse. In other terms, devices that strike us as different owe their difference to the fact that they themselves are instinct with and vitalized by that to which they react.

The following chapters have multiple functions: (1) to define as precisely and dynamically as possible traits that are central to a significant body of modern fiction; (2) to outline none too rigidly and from within what may be an emerging "period style" for the late modernist period; (3) to illustrate in texts selected from several literatures and

modes the range of our tactics' applications; (4) to establish their prehistory, placing them within a larger tradition and thus rendering
them more accessible without reducing them to commonplaces; (5) to
shed light through a study of specific tactics and their various functions on works that reward examination. It should go without saying
that the results of this study, which might be regarded as a pro-
legomenon, are exhaustive in terms neither of the uses to which these
devices can be put nor of the tradition nor of the works employing
such tactics. No more than a fraction of the texts to which such devices
contribute can be cited, the more so, since I have chosen to deal with
works drawn from a variety of cultures designed to illustrate a variety
of formal manifestations. It should be even clearer that my choices are
motivated by personal predilections as well as appropriateness and that
all of them are perceived from a self-limiting formal bias.

Still, Chapters 1–5 should help illustrate from a writerly/readerly
perspective significant aspects of the mechanics or operative modes of
the individual text defining itself in terms of its choices and procedures. I believe that this double, or writer/reader, perspective is
essential precisely because modern texts, thanks to their increasingly
self-conscious and self-engaged nature, put much of the creative or re-
creative onus on the reader.

I

Double-Distancing

In his classic essay " 'Psychical Distance' as a Factor in Art and as an Aesthetic Principle," Edward Bullough described distance as the quality through which expression achieves aesthetic validity: "Distancing means the separation of personal affections, whether idea or complex experience, from the concrete personality of the experience."[1] He also coined the terms overdistanced, or melodrama as experienced by the sophisticated, and underdistanced, or melodrama as experienced by the unsophisticated, to describe qualities of the aesthetically inauthentic work. Consciously or not, Bullough himself was responding to the procedures proper to post-Flaubertian modernism. At about the same time the young James Joyce distinguished crudely but effectively between "kinetic" and "static" art: "The feelings excited by improper art are kinetic, desire and loathing. Desire urges us to possess, to go to something; loathing urges us to abandon, to go from something. The aesthetic emotion (I use the general term) is therefore static. The mind is arrested and raised above desire and loathing."[2] Neglecting overdistance, or indifference, Joyce is accurately describing underdistance

[1] First published in 1912 in *British Journal of Psychology* 2, pp. 87–118. Most recently reprinted in *Aesthetics: Lectures and Essays*, ed. Elizabeth M. Wilkinson (Stanford: Stanford University Press, 1957); the quotation appears on p. 127.

[2] James Joyce, *A Portrait of the Artist as a Young Man* (New York: Viking, 1968), p. 205. See also *The Critical Writings of James Joyce*, ed. Ellsworth Mason and Richard Ellmann (New York: Viking, 1959), pp. 143–44.

and is extending as well as clarifying Bullough's strictures. Both positions were fresh and appropriate at the beginning of the century, applicable to a wide range of discourse, and scrupulously orthodox. Now, though still valid for most art forms, they are repeatedly stretched out of shape by what might be called the marginalizing arts.

High modernist fiction (that of Proust, Mann, Woolf, Musil, Malraux, Faulkner, Joyce in the early and middle years, and Barnes), no matter how innovative its features, is characterized by fine-tuned and delicately balanced ironic productions that toy with the "kinetic" but maintain a cautious balance by confining motion to the formal tensions within the artifact and by refusing both definition and the absolute conclusion. True, empathy and even antipathy are available as part of the mix of attitudes that enable the implied reader momentarily to discover himself in the persona's predicament, but for this seeming violation to be viable, the text must impose an extra measure of distance with the aid of irony, humor, symbolism, and allegory. Distance is controlled most frequently through irony, through a device that generates a double (or multiple) vision. With its help, even Joyce's *Portrait* can introduce at certain points something like total empathy. The conclusion of the Christmas dinner sequence and the "pandying" in chapter 1, and the "Bird Girl" incident in chapter 4 come to mind. Even at such moments of maximum involvement, some detail or memory intervenes to dampen and distance, to modify the *given* position. Thus Stephen's hand is struck only twice, while his friend has previously received six blows, and our young "hero" pauses to tie his shoes together before wading into the feared rivulet at a safe distance from the "feary" sea. Closer study reveals much more, and in the larger context of the book, ironic foreshadowings and echoes add a diachronic and rhythmic dimension, showing that distance may be imposed by hindsight. Characterized by a rage for middle-distancing and a refusal, balancing, or undercutting of melodramatic hyperbole, "high-modernist" texts have established a vibrant distance that functions like the aperture of a camera lens, a mechanism capable of accommodating any increase or decrease in the brilliance of the instant.

Middle-distance has a long and honorable history. Modernism can claim only to have modified its operation, rendering it more self-conscious and visible. Such modifications are, however, important. For one thing, they have resulted in the progressive alteration of narrative configurations in works that foreground their ironic effects and undermine conventions of narrative autonomy, works as seemingly traditional as the early novellas of Thomas Mann or the later Henry James. It is equally important that the visual arts have of late forged ahead of narrative in their manipulation of distance, perhaps because distancing procedures are more immediately available to the viewer of advanced painting than they are to the reader of the more complexly articulated narrative forms. We cannot properly perceive difference in painting without adjusting our vision to the painter's rhetorical stance, but it could be argued that a narrative can be appreciated as a suspenseful rendering of behavior even without a corresponding sense of the subtleties of its production and the originality of its conception.

Reacting to the late romantic dictum of art for art's sake, Flaubert was the first to establish, if only in his own mind, the idea that the novel, that stepchild of the arts, required the same attention to its form that had traditionally been accorded the poem. (It can be shown that, as narrative encroached on poetic discourse, poetry, beginning with poets in the thrall of Poe and Baudelaire, became increasingly disciplined and conscious of its powers, even its ability to make use of prose.) Flaubert's attempt to move prose toward the condition of poetry meant more than is suggested by his quest for the mot juste or even by his projected "novel about nothing." The effort meant, for example, that the psychological development of a romantically inclined provincial housewife should be conveyed with immediacy and sympathy but with little or no unmediated empathy. It implied a range of attitudes that excluded but flirted with both indifference and a passionate, quasi-physical attachment.

Flaubert chose to portray a flawed and undistinguished heroine, dispassionately treating her romantic escapades and moral dissolution. For background he provided a wonderfully nuanced comico/farcical treatment of provincial life, establishing the sort of interaction and balance of attitudes that was appropriate to both components in such a way as to guarantee the preservation of the dynamic middle distance we are describing. The enterprise was anything but risk free. Much of his material was painfully commonplace; some of it was dangerously near the stuff of the exemplary tale so dear to writers of theological tracts; some, like the sequence concerning the comice agricole, came perilously close to pure farce. His aim was not to write a caricature, but the stuff of caricature was in his subject matter: adultery and provincial life. His handling of that subject matter might be said to

have veered inevitably and alternatively in several directions, like a
boat driven by shifting winds. His achievement was to keep his
course, falling victim to no one tendency, modulating and integrating
all, using farce against melodrama and comedy against tragedy in the
service of a credible account of human motives and responses in a
context of ignorance and hope, daydream and despair.

Bovary is perhaps the classic realist novel, one that aims at a complex
and integral view of experience, refusing to sacrifice aesthetic integrity
even though it is building its vision out of the spare parts of the
intertextual experience. Its range is astonishing. Homais is a nineteenth-century French provincial version of the Commedia dell'arte
doctor, a man whose existence is the sum of his post-Enlightenment
scientific commonplaces. Emma Bovary, on the other hand, is a latter
day Phèdre/Columbine whose aspirations are the warmed-over glamor
of second-rate romantic fictions and whose life is defined by the tension between aspiration and possibility. If one of them is played for
bitter laughter, the other inspires an ironic and bittersweet sympathy.
The fullness and modesty of both visions with their opposing but
interlocked modal imperatives, extended as they are by the provincial
universe and by Charles's mediocre but engaging human needs, ensure
the preservation of conventional high aesthetic middle distance, that
and the fact that each of these visions is instinct with its opposite—
contaminated, so to speak.

This painfully won control exhibits signs of strain. The fact that the
competing impulses do not become excessive and are never reduced to
the stereotypes that in some sense generate them does not conceal the
potential drive toward extremes of parody and satire, high erotic melodrama and the anatomy, the potential flirtation, in short, with the hot
and cool dimensions of the novel's materials. The novel doubtless owes
its appeal partly to this repeatedly restated tension. Flaubert succeeds
brilliantly in avoiding the maudlin when he produces the distinctly
unpleasant death sequence or when he artfully skirts the reefs of erot-
icism. He is almost lighthearted and usually funny when exposing
distressingly ordinary and potentially dull small town life, and he
manages to make cliché-ridden conversation and transparent hypoc-
risy something more than a relief from Emma's emotional gymnastics.

It is not too much, however, to claim that the seeds have been sown
for a very different treatment of such materials, one that, capitalizing
on the precedent of the Flaubertian balancing act, would restore some

of the charge of the original materials while maintaining the elements of balance. Such a work, written by a hypothetical latter-day Flaubert, might stress the tensions rather than downplay them, deliberately overheating Emma's development as a female Lothario, for example, while maintaining its anatomical distance. The buffoonery implicit in the portrait of the townspeople might be slightly overblown; Homais's catalogues could be extended and perhaps even annotated. If it were tactfully handled, such an anti-Bovary might be something more than a burlesque, laying claim perhaps to aesthetic validity while approaching the condition of double-distancing. I should add that, in the hands of a contemporary Flaubert, plot and characterization would be radically simplified, eliminating much of the rich detail that makes Flaubert's effort so rewarding, relying far more heavily on the implicit intertextual echoes and creating through a layer of tempered irreverence a radically different sort of equilibrium. To achieve such a result, there would be no need to go quite as far as did Duchamps when he painted his mustache on the Mona Lisa, producing for the plastic arts a paradigm of what we have been calling the double-distanced text and prefiguring the treatment of found objects by Robert Rauschenberg and Antoni Tàpies and the reworked photographs of Arnolf Rainer and Antonio Saura.

This modest profanation of Flaubert, the unquestioned progenitor of modernist aesthetic control, may help suggest how consistent and even conservative the new distance is. If it would be wrong to pretend to find in *Bovary* the necessary raw materials for the New Novel, there is some point in discovering foreshadowings of its *chosism* in the late Flaubert, especially *Bouvard et Pécuchet*, where the strain is more evident and the leap less monstrous.

In our quest for texts that are simultaneously over- and underdistanced, works that eschew middle distance, preferring to oscillate boldly between cool intellection and heated engagement, we are drawn perversely but inevitably toward the novels of the Marquis de Sade. Whatever the literary qualities displayed by such works, their importance in setting a formal precedent should not be underestimated. After all, Sade, responding to the demands of his textual mission, found ways to splice scenes of pornographic outrage to lengthy and weighty passages of philosophic discourse and/or dialogue filled with deliberately inflated rhetoric. He even managed to generate interest in his theory while using it to dampen the impact of his sexual circuses.

Typically his novelistic catalogues *involve* readers in the sexual behavior of psychologically inane puppets, using engagingly offensive tactile sexuality to illustrate a perversely post-Enlightenment "philosophy." Like the authors of other current texts, Sade is clearly rereading both the science/philosophy and the popular romantic/pornographic literature of his period, recasting their material in such a way as to engage both submodes in a mutual subversion. Because it sets his work off from the general run of narrative, this minimally mediated interpenetration of attitudinal opposites may strike us as most modern. Moreover, beyond the display of sexual pathology for which he is justly famous, this quality makes him the eighteenth-century writer who, apart from Laurence Sterne, has had the greatest impact on contemporary distancing procedures.

In the wake of Sade, the mid-nineteenth century produced on the one hand Lautréamont's *Les Chants de Maldoror*, with its high camp melodramatic outrage through which shines a heady self-inculpation. On the other, in a less extravagant vein, there was Huysmans's *A Rebours*, which explores the sensual universe of a decadent ex-dandy with the dry/wry thoroughness of a bemused anatomist, and his *Là Bas*, which does something similar for the universe of violent perversity. Then again, there is that magnificent ruin *Salammbô*, the testing ground for so many of Flaubert's more innovative tactics. A torrid archeological epic, *Salammbô* casts the myth of the East as heady sentimental romance instinct with sadistic violence staged operatically against a remarkably cool and distanced historical setting that itself contains some searing satirical commentary on the political, economic, and social mores of the contemporary French. (The choice of a commercial state, Carthage, ruled by merchants jealous of their independence and wealth and defended by mercenaries, can hardly be innocent. On another, less frivolous, level, this novel could represent Flaubert's belated coming to terms with the Terror that scarred the French Revolution.) Before the filmic mayhem of directors like Sam Peckinpah, there was probably nothing in the popular idiom to rival the spectacularly sensuous impact of *Salammbô's* conclusion, in which, with clinical precision, a man is progressively disassembled by a mob. Perhaps only after the work of Freud and the surrealists, Antonin Artaud and Georges Bataille, to say nothing of Céline, Henry Miller, William Burroughs, Alain Robbe-Grillet, and Philippe Sollers, has the antithetical distance imposed by such writing become aesthetically viable.

During the fin de siècle such tactics found less radical practitioners. Alfred Jarry's post-Rimbaldian antitheater uses sadistic puppets to perpetrate Grand Guignol destruction on mindless stereotypes of innocence. His procedures hold enormous significance for subsequent developments; Jarry managed to engage his audience in visceral violence while denying his victims and their clownish tormentors anything more than residual validity. His good milksop of a prince is no more real than his hideous bourgeois torturer, but though cooled by Jarry's tactics and by the prescribed monotone of the undeniably comic mayhem, the audience's relationship to this theatrical vision approaches that of the reader of later double-distanced works. On the other side of the coin, perhaps more civilized if no less adolescent, we may mention Aubrey Beardsley's pornographic masterpiece *Under the Hill* or *Venus and Tannhäuser*, which turns Sade's kinky sexual violence into a decorative and indecorous display of polymorphous perversity. There, too, a grotesquely inappropriate treatment of unacceptable material creates a fresh aesthetic field.

For a variety of reasons, some of them having to do with contemporary morality, none of these earlier instances of double-distancing had much impact on the "official" art (to use a concept dear to Mikhail Bakhtin) of its moment, being eclipsed by work in more congenial modes. It may be that, even today, society has fewer problems with crude pornography and cheap romance than it does with a high art in which such tendencies overtly participate. On the other hand, perhaps because it enables us to face the impossible, the art of assertive denial has assumed the status of a dominant tendency in the advanced art of our postatomic, post-Holocaust apocalyptic age. As might be expected, the work to which I alluded above is now receiving the serious critical attention it merits. All the more reason for recognizing the single most striking formal contribution of the tendency it prefigures.

Since distance is a feature of all the arts and not just narrative discourse, alternative uses can shed some light on the potential and scope of our topic. We can find examples of overheated/overcooled expression in the spiked flat iron of dada and more recently in both abstract expressionism and pop art. Quite beyond its antifunctional-

ity, the iron's spikes attack our sensibilities, adding an emotive component to an otherwise neutral household object. In a no less effective
way, the abstract expressionists underscore their procedures while
denying access to images; yet their paintings engage the viewer in the
accidents and gestures of production and product on an almost visceral
level. Pop art, like dada, toys with social *Dreck*, turning the super-
market, the photo magazine, the comic strip, and the junkyard into
objects for contemplation, proclaiming the apotheosis of the common
even as it isolates, modifies, and disintegrates it. The soap opera of life
becomes strangely unattainable, though never conventionally beautiful, through essentially literary procedures. Objects so trite as to be
devoid of emotional content are subjected to a quasi-farcical manipulation, made to bear witness in their replication, recombination or display to a disruption orderly in its presentation. In contrast, abstract
expressionism is a cousin to melodrama and romance, disembodied
emotion rendered through strokes of color, synecdoches for actions
and sentiments that refuse to be anthropomorphized.

The purest melodrama, the unabashed tearjerker tinkers with audience response, drawing its viewer into the web of experience by
engaging surface sentiments: trite feelings that must ultimately derive
from man's basic urges. This call upon the least subtle response is a
denial of aesthetic distance, a refusal to permit contemplation, and a
surrender to strong and ready feeling. It is also the enemy of thought.
True, when properly modulated, melodrama can enter the realm of
"serious literature." Double-distancing, however, achieves that result
without recourse to modulation, seemingly scorning public assent
while playing fast and loose with public emotions. The double-distanced text exhibits an inverted sophistication but a sophistication
nonetheless, the inevitable reversal of the perceptual field that follows
the extreme development of any method, something akin to the merging of Northrop Frye's ironic mode with his mythic mode. What we
have been witnessing and what we may find less clearly stated in Sade
and his followers is a turn toward the revision of the social myths
treated so disparagingly in Barthes's *Mythologies:* myths that reflect the
dominant ideologies artists tend to disparage in their reproduction.
This duplicitous handling of social matter, combined with equally
broad/sly mistreatments of formal conventions, characterizes contemporary double-distancing.

Despite the apparent primacy of Sade among the precursors of double-distancing, it is possible to employ the technique without being his disciple. Still, it may not be happenstance that some of the clearest examples of this eccentric procedure are found in the work of a novelist for whom Sade is exemplary, though Alain Robbe-Grillet, the writer in question, would rank method over subject matter. The vision of the novel enunciated in *For a New Novel* centers on the rejection of the time-honored illusion of depth. Tantamount to a rejection of the perspectival "old" novel (and the conjuring up of its traces as subtext), this implies a new focus on the textual surface, the elaborate and ostentatious disruption of all the conventions of narrative discourse. It also implies the foregrounding of that which has been sacrificed and a concomitant radicalizing of distance. On the level of subject matter, Robbe-Grillet's project/vision has led to an intense scrutiny of physical surfaces, a refusal to identify narrative language with experience, the apparent rejection of all illusions of profundity, including psychologism and symbolism, and, because such rejections are inevitably dialectic, the foregrounding of mechanisms that were previously occulted.

In novel after novel Robbe-Grillet has moved ever closer to his original goals, finding more efficacious ways to counter illusion. In the early work, the focus on surfaces and the withholding of narrative data did not really impede the diagetic movement of plot development or even obliterate a psychological dimension that became mysterious rather than inoperative. It was the novels of his middle period, such works as *Maison de rendezvous* and *Projet pour une révolution à New York*, that finally did away with chronicity, a coherent diagetic development, and the last vestiges of characterization. As a result, they constitute one of the clearest instances of modern double-distancing.

We can follow the "action" of *The Voyeur* practically minute by minute even if we cannot account for the lost time at the moment when the murder is committed. As Bruce Morrissette has shown, even while identifying the text as the true voyeur, we may intuit the psychopathology of Mathias.[3] In *Projet*, character is nebulous or clichéd and "place" is indeterminate: a New York of nightmare and popular superstition mingled with the specifics of a Paris landscape. At no point are

[3]Bruce Morrissette, *The Novels of Robbe-Grillet* (Ithaca: Cornell University Press, 1975), pp. 102–3 and passim.

we certain that the perspective and details are accurate. A flux of self-generating (associative) language engages us as much in its own signifying procedures as in the development of any of its several interacting but mutually contradictory actions. We are teased into alertness, repeatedly called to order, obliged to repress and revise habits of perception that have become almost irrepressible.

To the degree that it succeeds, as it does to a very large degree, this text approaches a sort of absolute dual and an-aesthetic distance, one that denies the reader access to a "real" world, instituting an experience of convention (myth) as convention pure and simple, as product. It insists, for example, on modes of masking that serve structural and stylistic as well as simply thematic ends. On the one hand there is the running evocation of plastic masks and their wearers, of masks metamorphosed into faces and vice versa; on the other hand there is the deliberate dehumanizing of seemingly human situations by means of outrageously explicit use of trite devices drawn from popular literature. Repeatedly, we are denied access to the proffered experience, obliged to recover our balance after having bent too far in the direction of a particular version of the "truth."

An important aspect of the distancing process is "voicing," or the establishment of a discursive range that enables the text to convey appropriate attitudes. In some texts, voicing is adjusted to encourage the reader to experience the textual voice as a presence by means, say, of a predominantly familiar or informal discourse. Examples include Dostoievski's *Brothers Karamazov*, Forster's *Howards End*, Maurice Roche's *Codex*, Vonnegut's *Slaughterhouse-Five*, and Barthelme's *Snow White*. In these works, voicing constitutes a range of gestures and resembles the use of the spoken word in theater. Though we do not directly hear the written text, we do sound it in our minds and in effect hear its inflections. In contrast, Robbe-Grillet, a former *ingénieur agronome* who still carries his credentials with him wherever he goes, writes in a style that is deliberately colorless, somewhat approximating the "denotative" prose of scientific discourse. (It is worth noting that both Jarry and Beckett instruct their actors to avoid expressive vocal gestures.)

As a conscious choice, this tactic may constitute the major gesture of the Robbe-Grillet text. Still, the fact of his static dedication to precision, "objectivity," or even passivity generates a wide range of attitudes. It is one thing to describe dispassionately a mechanical device or an architectural detail. It is something else to treat in that way a human body in conventionally enticing or agonizing poses, or a moment of seemingly unbearable suspence. Such tactics are designed to create maximum distance from the narrative predicament, to flatten the text much as Fernand Léger insisted upon the flatness of the walls on which he painted his decorative visions of humanoids in space. An encounter with the text as an aesthetic procedure, or even as an object capable of arousing feeling, is apparently obviated. We might say that an absolute distance (or overdistance) is generated in relation to materials that demand a total visceral engagement (or underdistance).[4] Robbe-Grillet is, or seems to be, flying in the face of Bullough, who posits an overdistanced response from the sophisticated viewer of melodrama rather than a seemingly irrational combination of over- and underdistancing in the same reader to the same phenomenon. As we shall see, thanks largely to his voicing procedures, he has turned Bullough's reader into one who can participate in an embarrassment of melodramatic (or mythic) clichés while wholeheartedly and with humor rejecting them.

Voice is not everything, of course. Another source of excess distance is Robbe-Grillet's decision to turn narrative montage and associational linkage against the flow of the story line, his subversion of plot and verisimilitude. At every turn, this text frustrates the implied reader's desire to see an action completed and to control the associative flux. The latter begins on the very first page when a view of the mock-wood paint on the front door of a house suggests to the narrative eye/I a bound nude whose condition, by the very force of its depiction, draws the image, the narrator, and the reader into a magic space subject in its turn to arbitrary dissolution. We enter a universe of willed but never completely accepted frustration, characterized by a pattern of coitus interruptus that makes commitment to the action both necessary and, in any conventional sense, impossible, a pattern that engages us in a maze of forbidden pleasures and unacceptable risks.

In addition, we have, first, the deliberate and calculated neglect of

---

[4]Ironically, this narrative stance is very nearly a precise inversion of the tactic of Sade, whose discourse is often excessively florid at such moments, effectively undercutting (but in some sense increasing) its conventional impact. See, for example, the wonderfully inappropriate discursive procedures of *Justine*, in which innocence protests too much and common rogues justify their lust in the language of philosophers.

character, a mannequinization along the lines of pop culture stereotypes, the insistence on glaringly programmed behavior. Second,
there is the undermining of the significance of an "objective" or starkly
objectified world and a graphically described action. The renowned
chosisme of the new novel, by returning things to their thingness, refusing to assign meaning or readings through coherence of development
or statement, at once assaults and frees the reader accustomed to as-
sessing meanings.

All of these techniques and others conspire to justify the epithet "icy
playboy" used by a British critic to describe the author as stand-in for
his text. And there is no denying that the Robbe-Grillet text is a cool
medium. Even the existence of what we may describe as a willed
failure of distance (or underdistance) fails to alter that quality.

The antithetical distancing effect is already evident in the evocation
of the erotic "object" with which *Project for a Revolution in New York*
begins:

> The wood around the window is coated with a brownish varnish in
> which thin lines of a lighter color, lines which are the imitation of imagi-
> nary veins running through another substance considered more deco-
> rative, constitute parallel networks or networks of only slightly divergent
> curves outlining darker knots, round or oval or even triangular, a group
> of changing signs in which I have discerned human figures for a long
> time: a young woman lying on her left side and facing me, apparently
> naked since her nipples and pubic hair are discernible; her legs are bent,
> the left one more than the right, its knee pointing forward, on the floor;
> the right foot therefore crosses over the left one, the ankles are evidently
> bound together, just as the wrists are bound behind her back as usual, it
> would seem, for both arms disappear from view behind the upper part of
> the body: the left arm below the elbow and the right one just above it.[5]

Robbe-Grillet treats with equally meticulous care the sensuous surface
of the artificial wood pattern painted on a typical French apartment
door and the fully imagined frontal nudity of a bound girl. The first,
which clearly inspires and justifies the second, is among the most
unappealing surfaces available to the Parisian. The second is blatantly
erotic and will become more so. The contrast between painted sin-

[5] Alain Robbe-Grillet, *Project for a Revolution in New York*, trans. Richard Howard
(New York: Grove, 1972), pp. 1–2.

uosity and the contorted human figure is muted by its tonality and by our awareness that the overactive imagination of the narrator produced the latter. As the sequence progresses, however, the assurance of the narrator, his ability to sustain the nude-in-distress image, will combine with reader expectations to reinforce a sensuality that will in its turn be muted by the transparent use of a melodramatic commonplace. This is only the first instance of an erotic cliché. There will be many more, building toward a sado-masochistic climax with the torture of a mannequin and mingling with other sorts of conventional distress, a range of fully articulated and broadly undercut myths.

By way of contrast here is a slightly more individualized trope: the nymphet "Laura," who flits through a variety of "Alice" roles and undergoes all manner of threats while remaining perilously intact and frantically innocent:

Made threatening perhaps by the raised arm, the extent of the movement, the muffled impact of the fist against the wood in the sudden darkness, the half-glimpsed image has alarmed the young woman, who utters a faint moan. She then hears, on the thick carpeting which covers the entire floor of the room, the heavy footsteps coming closer to her bed. She tries to scream, but a firm warm hand presses against her mouth, while she feels the sensation of a crushing mass which slides toward her and soon overwhelms her altogether.[6]

Though each of these passages belongs to the convention of sadomasochistic pornography, the second incorporates elements of suspense fiction, turning the sensual assault into an affront to the reader, who is engaged, in this instance, with the victim. Equally significant, both passages share in the development of a magic space that turns languaged experience into what we shall be calling an impossible object—impossible both textually, in terms of the internal logic of the discourse, and physically, in terms of the experience purportedly delineated. Thanks to this deliberate and multiple perversion of narrative procedures, we are able to read what in another context would be received by sophisticated readers as a ridiculous and sterile imitation of mass-produced literature. Instead of the embarrassed smile or grimace at an overworked convention, we may smile at our own capitulation to and rejection of manipulation as display. In any case, the impact is

6Ibid., p. 9.

immediate and reflexive, even though (and perhaps because) the stimulus is recognized as part of a game structure. If anything, the effect is enhanced by the cool delivery that disarms those who would automatically reject any heightened rendering. The absolute positive (over)distance established repeatedly for the text as development licenses the absolute negative (under)distance of the melodramatic contexts. Furthermore, disgust is in this case as empathetic a response as enjoyment (see Joyce's desire and loathing).

The text has set up two conflicting tactics, the one designed to stifle reader participation by closing off the traditional means of access to the action, the other designed to involve the reader on the level of stimulus-response in a seemingly endless and only mechanically related series of high-intensity sensual events. We may stress the quality of the event as opposed to the development, but we should also note that the micro-events by their sheer number give the novel its particular coloration. Even though humor is often obviously used to release the tension created by the exposure to naked (in both senses) stimuli, the stimulus remains, like its trace in the reader's consciousness, determining his response to the text as a whole. The text has resorted to the mythology of sex and intrigue within a context antagonistic in terms of its handling of novelistic materials.

This conjunction of the cliché and its antidote creates the effect of double-distancing, but our two poles are in practice far less separate than the raw phenomenon of their statement would suggest. Though the cool treatment is designed to eliminate emotional, to say nothing of aesthetic, considerations, the text arouses expectations proper to the novel and hence to its own missing dimensions. The reader is engaged, despite reiterated rejections of novelistic time/space considerations, in the process of adjusting time and space to the demands of, say, the Balzac novel. Thus the absolute positive distance is modified by habit, becoming instead of a fixed relationship, a palpitation toward the opposite pole. In the place of the savant modulation of realistic fiction, the lens adjustment effect that ceaselessly modifies distance, making such modification a source of interest, we experience in *Project for a Revolution in New York* an involuntary mental adjustment, a tension that pulls us toward the absent signifiers as toward an imagined (or amputated) experience.[7]

---

[7]For a clear and convincing statement of a similar view of the mechanics of Robbe-Grillet's text, see Susan Suleiman, "Reading Robbe-Grillet: Sadism and *Projet pour une révolution à New York,*" *Romanic Review* 68 (1977), 43–62.

At the other end of the spectrum, the melodramatic distance induced by the use of myths is modified by the objectivization of event that renders the experience brittle and unconvincing. It is also modified, cooled, by the sheer extravagance of its statement, by the surplus of the obvious, by the too deliberate adherence to cliché, by the outrageous call to habit, and finally by our text-conditioned awareness of strategies of deception. (The reader quickly learns that desires are never truly fulfilled and that even fears are short-circuited.) Here too, drawing upon the traditional and not just the gothic or the pornographic novelistic frame of reference, the text oscillates toward the center. Together, the two extremes create a double motion best diagrammed as shown below.

	overdistance	middle distance	underdistance
enforced	←		→
actual	←	→	← →

The forced marriage of two antagonistic *an*aesthetic procedures results in a measured and coherent flux of distance that coopts conventional middle distance. The ironic tension between cool disengagement and overheated commitment generates an evanescent but quite firmly mediated middle-distanced effect. The latter is apparently the product less of the textual presentation than of the reader's ordering impulse, the need to accommodate both the presented and the overwritten (subtextual) attitudinal dialectics. Since this operation occurs largely on ground excluded from the text, the locus of that distance (its real context) may appear to be within the reading process, and its perception is in fact largely the product of what one might call "reading work."

It should be self-evident that the precise nature of double-distancing will vary from work to work and that texts can provide more or less extreme instances of the procedure, but in each case the coexistence of under- and overdistanced stimuli will be a central contributing factor. That is, a dialectic of excess is necessary and not simply a testing of the boundaries of a given textual decorum. This condition may be said to exist when the focus is less on the largely eliminated middle range of engagement than on the fringes from which the middle may derive its energy.

When Samuel Beckett decided to write for the stage, he adapted to that medium the methods of a prose writer in open revolt against conventional narrative. We might make a case for his use of double-distancing in the trilogy *Molloy, Malone Dies*, and *The Unnamable*, noting that he uses materials and a method radically different from those employed by Robbe-Grillet to cool and heat his medium. It suits my purposes better, however, to demonstrate the cross-media potential of this strategy by studying his manipulation of stage conventions.

Beckett's work is generally characterized by a stripping, refocusing, and stretching of the conventions of his media. His theater has come a long way from the minimal dramatic statements of *Godot*, a play about waiting that uses waiting as its major action (providing a commentary on the nature of suspense) and frustration as its major effect, and *Endgame*, a play about waste and isolation that takes place in a metaphorical skull. These are admittedly anti-dramatic dramas, texts that use the stage as a pretext for action that undermines the possibility of acts. Like Beckett's novels, these dramas seem to be indulging in a species of parthenogenesis; a systematic aimlessness gives birth to the accidents of its own production. Thus the idea of waste that inspires the setting and unseen landscape of *Endgame* also generates the image of parents handily housed in ashcans. Theatricality becomes a careful abuse of space that, ultimately, as in this case, includes the space of the audience, unmoving by definition but moved through its commitment to an intensely personal vision.

The later plays extend the process toward its limits. In *Play* the three jugged human characters in postmortal pain are joined by a light that functions as animator of their action. Consequently, there are two very distinct actions. In the first and more obvious, the tale of a sordid little love triangle leading to an uninspired domestic tragedy is told piecemeal by the talking heads, corpses whose mutterings continue in an unfocused babble when they are not singled out for attention by the focusing light. Such a tale would be monotonous were it told only once, hardly worth a paragraph in the human interest columns of the daily newspaper—the stuff, in short, of soap opera. The second action is that of the light, which, by focusing on each of the three in seemingly random order, controls their discourse. This aspect is evident from the start, though the audience, unsettled by the circumstance and intrigued by the procedures, may not be aware of it. Halfway through the narration, however, the personae begin individually addressing the light, cursing it for forcing them to speak.

Three versions of the same simple tale, coaxed out of three unwilling corpses by an insistent light (conscience, habit, God, the devil, and so forth) might seem disturbing enough, but after the action has been completed, we experience it all over again verbatim. This third action, a sign that the repetitions will never stop, makes the drama more Dantesque and, for the viewer, more desperately personal.

Distancing under these circumstances is particularly complex. The faces are virtually undifferentiated, the voices monotonous, the circumstance recounted trivial enough to bring tears of laughter. The main drama is in the rhetoric of presentation, the chief actor being the brutally impersonal light coming from the audience's direction and inculpating the viewer in the process of extracting what might qualify as crude gossip, giving the third degree while perversely satisfying the confessional urge of the jugged bodies. The theatrical convention is boldly distorted when the traditional means of enabling the perception of action, the lighting, becomes the source of all action, when action is indeed confined to precisely the movement audiences are not supposed to notice, when the light becomes associated with the glance of the viewer and when the darkened space of the theater, which guarantees the viewer his anonymity as voyeur, is implicitly violated.

On the surface, Beckett's theatrical procedures clear the stage of theatrical conventions that would underdistance. The directing light is not consciously directed by us and does not seem even to represent our needs. The static bodies, ashen in their ashen jugs, undifferentiated and incapable of expressive modulation are will-less puppets, mindless toys. The absence of physical action seems to rule out human sympathy. The basic gestures are those of the invisible demiurge, the imposing shaper of this experience in which we are somehow trapped. Yet though emitted by humanoid but infrahuman voices or beings, the narrative of weakness, anger, despair, and loss heats the atmosphere and engages us against the grain on more than one level.

It is a forceful statement of human banality, of course, so banal as to include us all in its net as potential actors. But the extreme of empathy comes only after the light is identified as a power by the speakers, after they become identified as victims of the force that victimizes us as it does them. Empathy is intensified, or rather, the potential for empathy is intensified when the second round begins and we sense the horror of this perpetual repetition, the hellish vision that Beckett has imaged. I say "the potential for empathy," since both extremes of distance are under the circumstances centered more emphatically than they are in Robbe-Grillet. The double-distance is neutralized by the topography of the theater and the biology of theatrical experience. The text's refusal to observe the norms (technical and literary) upon which our perception depends and to which it ceaselessly refers makes sustained absolute distancing impossible. The audience is bound to participate in both extremes, oscillating beyond sympathy and empathy only to find the focus centering on the existential nucleus constituted by the viewing presence. This is a play about viewing as much as about things viewed.

Already so clear in *Play*, Beckett's procedures become practically transparent in *Not I*. Here the principal action is performed by a pair of disembodied lips spotlighted center stage, whose movement, as Beckett once suggested, may be more important than their words. Still, the words, a painful babble designed to reject the one word that would announce a personal existence, can no more be overlooked than can the circumstance of their being directed by a female voice to a theater audience. Once again every effort is made to flatten the circumstance, to distance it, to milk it of its human content. Words are spoken rapidly by a monotonous and characterless voice to a semivisible interlocutor who is seemingly only an aspect of the eyeless speaker's psychic makeup, but various gestures trap the viewer by their poignancy: the speed of the enunciation, the avoidance (punctuated by pauses) of the first-person singular, the isolation of the lips, and the viewer's consequent isolation in relation to them. All of this leads toward identification of the not-I with the viewing I, a disturbing absence of distance modified by the equally disturbing imposition of maximum distance, enforced by the refusal of individualization, the denial of the theatrical conventions and the destruction not only of action but of space. Claustrophobia is induced and avoidance of enclosure is sought. The viewer is trapped in his seat, attempting to break the code of the discourse that ensnares, by virtue of its signifying breaks, the absence.

Like the novelistic conventions aborted by Robbe-Grillet, the stage with its manipulation of time and space has played a part in Beckett's minimalizing formulations, as has the theater, with its enforced intimacy. To find a cinematic correlative, we must turn to Michael Snow's film *Wavelength*. Like Beckett's tyrannical spotlight, Snow's camera inching toward a photo on the wall is a relentless force, matched only by the slowly augmenting hum or whine that gives the film its name. The basic device is painfully simple. Camera moving toward its goal and sound augmenting become protagonists engaging the viewer in their activities on the reflexive level. Film, traditionally capable of so much more, becomes in this context a true medium, underscoring the absence of "true" action, focusing our attention on minimal signifying instances: the whine, flashes of red light, cars and trucks passing outside the windows that flank the narrow strip of wall to which the photo is affixed, irregularities in the film, sprocket holes, and unmotivated shifts from night to day and back.

As if to emphasize this violation of accepted cinematic decorum, the film deliberately transgresses its own decorum, introducing, for example, gratuitous and badly acted sequences with live characters. A man enters and falls center scene, a girl enters and telephones a friend to announce the presence of a by-now-invisible corpse in the room. The effect is less to increase suspense than to relieve it, breaking intense monotony by introducing elements of texture that help distance the viewer by permitting participation in the stuff of the more purely filmic event. Thus, paradoxically, in this interminable-seeming film, distance is increased by the use of incident, the mocking exploitation and perversion of the accepted codes of cinema. Ultimately, the viewer reads a text that is virtually nonverbal. That is, the procedures by which the text is perceived are strikingly similar in kind to those by which a book is read, a scanning of signs on a printed surface (the screen), signs that signify but convey nothing significant.

Ordinarily, this procedure would turn the text into an object perceived, hence aesthetically distanced, an object that one might or might not enjoy perceiving. In fact, the objective quality of the film, focusing as it does on *un*interesting and *un*engrossing effects as well as on a featureless wall, sterilizes the film as text and moves it beyond the aesthetic, turning it into a statement about making films. The overdistance is accordingly excessive, making extraordinary demands on the viewer's patience, stamina, and goodwill.

The same may be said in the opposing sense of the underdistance in *Wavelength*. That is, the two suspense-inducing dimensions become virtually unbearable, engaging the viewer's nerves through the implementation of anticonventionally visible and audible motion, the inevitable development that will be more significant as process than anything its finale could possibly reveal. (The ultimate revelation, incidentally, is of a seascape looking toward the shore and a measured diminution of the by-then-intense and almost unbearable pitch.) These empathetic elements are clearly assaults on the senses rather than pleasurable experiences. The paradox should be underscored: empathy-antipathy on the aesthetic scale. We have long known that the extremely ugly is by no means aesthetically unpleasing. In this case, however, the cineast has done his best to bypass the aesthetic, producing empathy ironically with the very instruments of our torture, the moving camera and the increasing wave length. That is, we engage in these processes as we are engaged by them.

Why, then, given the extremely meager appeal of the performance, do we sit through and remain impressed and even moved by this film? Once again, we derive our pleasure from the procedures of our own minds as they reaestheticize the deaestheticized text, performing on it operations dictated by it but seemingly against its grain. In this sense the effect or dynamic of double-distancing accounts for much of the appeal of the work and even for its memorability (partly a function of the visual saturation process over a period of time). By virtue of a refusal of aesthetic interest, of objects or patterns capable of eliciting a pleasurable response, this text, like those of Robbe-Grillet and Beckett but to a different degree and in a radically different way, imposes on the viewer the task of apprehending the absent patterns and shapes. Not that the viewer reconstitutes an image or a pattern, but rather, a trace is experienced, in terms of the presented and in relation to the omitted, which draws us toward the aesthetic, a component held in abeyance.

The works we have been discussing provide us with clear instances of double- or antithetical distancing, extending in radical ways an underground convention. Without claiming to have delineated a constant in late modernist art, I would suggest that, in many other texts, the conventional distancing of early and high modernism is either not attempted or is consciously violated. What such works lack in subtle and modulated distancing effects they often make up for in procedures that are bold, innovative, and otherwise complexly engaging.

This development was already foreshadowed by Joyce, who, without completely forsaking his ideal of a "static" work of art vibrating internally toward a balanced distance, radically altered the terms of his later works' appeal. Thus, in *Ulysses*, the obscenity of the "Penelope" monologue[8] can be contrasted to the calculated coolness of the rhetorical play in "Oxen of the Sun" and the forced encyclopedic objectivity of "Ithaca." The latter chapters demand equally extreme modes of compensatory activity and meticulous preparation within the text and the mind of the reader intent on recovering the lost human dimensions of the narrative. Even before he begins the radical experiments that characterize the second half of his novel, Joyce introduces all manner of extreme literary behavior, testing the aesthetic responses and tolerance of his readers. Such formal impediments create the effect of extreme overdistancing by announcing the presence of an enigmatic overseeing, meddling, or "arranging" impulse external to the narrative development, a source of apparent "static."[9] On the other hand, there are moments when the reader is engaged by the poignancy of the protagonists' situation in a manner that can best be described as lyrical and immediate. In neither instance should this be seen as true double-distancing, since the modulation is as imperious as are the liberties taken with form and content, to say nothing of emotions.

Joyce went further in *Finnegans Wake*. There the overarching pun-filled rhetoric accommodates virtually any subject matter and appeals directly to the psyche in a language that rejects empathy but demands the most personal sort of engagement through participation. The content screened and revealed by language elicits at once a commitment to the text as process and an almost perversely scholarly detachment. The same may be said of the interaction of the many modes, rhythms, and subgenres featured in this extremely varied and kaleidoscopic text.

Though clearly in advance of most of his contemporaries, Joyce had

---

[8]Whatever the morality of printing the excessively private erotic/pornographic letters Joyce wrote his wife, Nora, during his visit to Ireland in 1909, we must thank Richard Ellmann for supplying the texts that mark Joyce's preparation for writing the fully articulated sexual statement that is *Ulysses*. Once we have passed the shock of their frontal masturbatory dimension, we may see in them a fine exploration of the full range of erotic modalities, from the crudest obscenity to the blandest and most sentimental erotic effusion. It is particularly striking that Joyce was able to exhibit this range in a single letter. In fact, the letters lack only the ironic distance necessary to turn them into literature. On the other hand, they constitute one pole of the double-distancing procedure to which Joyce pointed but never fully acceded. See *The Selected Letters of James Joyce*, ed. Richard Ellmann (New York: Viking, 1975), pp. 157–96.

[9]The term "arranging" has become controversial since I first introduced it in 1970, but it has not been replaced by a more descriptive one. See David Hayman, *Ulysses: The Mechanics of Meaning*, rev. ed. (Madison: University of Wisconsin Press, 1982), pp. 88–104, 122–25.

company in all of the arts, in Schoenberg and Webern, in the cubists and futurists, in Pound, Céline, Roussel, and Stein, and so on. All of these and others launched attacks on institutionalized subject matter and styles, insisting on quality and understanding conventions, calling attention to product and procedure while demanding and eventually achieving a remarkable degree of participatory viewing.

More recently, other writers have followed suit, exploring different but contiguous avenues, innovating an unprecedented array of styles and special effects, revising the concept of the subject, mastering literary outrage and tact. One of them is Arno Schmidt, whose post-Wakean novels include *Zettels Traum*, a text presented as a mammoth typescript-in-progress, the record of a free-wheeling seminar on the scatological underpinnings of the prim pages of Edgar Allan Poe. In *Compact*, as in his more recent texts, Maurice Roche has produced a novel whose morbid but pervasive (and frequently interstitial) humor is tensed against an extraordinary range of occulted allusions and obtrusive typographical play. William Gass's *Willie Masters' Lonesome Wife* features a burlesque script in the worst possible literary taste pockmarked by footnotes and set within the monologue of a versatile "female" voice that is subjected to a vigorously inventive panoply of typographical and other visual effects.[10] Such verbivocovisual fantasies can be supplemented by more strictly verbal and superficially more orthodox narratives, works as different from each other as the short fictions of Borges and the novels of Flann O'Brien, especially *At Swim-Two-Birds*. Finally, certain novels by Philippe Sollers, offer a particularly challenging modification of antithetical distance.

Sollers's *H* is superficially an unpunctuated rush of words capable of incorporating all manner of moods, rhythms, subject matter, dialogue, and even passages of description designed to tickle reader awareness and try reader patience. Despite the author's claim to have written this highly charged work spontaneously and even under the influence of hashish, this is a carefully articulated novel, stressing those aspects of conventional narration that are most apt to be lost behind the opacities of tale telling. As a result, the reader is denied access to a development but is profoundly engaged by the particulars of a neobaroque perfor-

---

[10]It is worth noting that Gass continues to mine this vein in *The Tunnel*, chapters from which have appeared in various little magazines.

mance,[11] made accomplice to the formation of evanescent mini-incidents and the elaboration of an encyclopedic range of associations and allusions.

Analysis would show that Sollers's practice, like that of other writers engaged in fleshing out the gains of the New Novel, locates his work on the borderline of double-distance. By means of a subtle interweaving of semantically and semiotically (or gesturally) over/underdistanced components, he has mitigated and complicated the problem of judging distance as a factor in aesthetic experience. The result is a difficult and subtle doubling of the dialectic. Not only is there a persistent and primary tension between the polar extremes, but there is a secondary tension, between double-distancing and a species of middle distancing, resulting in part from the experience of smaller and more disjunct units and in part from the actual use of modernist distancing procedures within specific units. Such a development is natural when we move from Spartan formulations like those of Robbe-Grillet, Beckett, and Snow (to whose contributions we might add the music of Philip Glass and the spectacles of Robert Wilson) toward freer and more lavish rhetorical display. In *H*, the mere fact of repeated choices, incessant juxtapositions, and even superpositions produces a pervasive aesthetic patina, as does the introduction of subtler and more numerous intertexts. If this sort of distancing forces our categories by altering the force vectors, it does so while restating the conditions for double-distancing which it helps to broaden and enrich.

Distance is a quality that adheres to all texts as a subliminal constituent. That is, it belongs to a family of active but occulted codes all of which contribute to the shape of the text and its perception. Along with such features as decorum (that of the individual text, as opposed to that of a given convention), attitude, rhythm, and gesture, distancing contributes silently to the dynamic of emission and perception in ways that defy critical exposition. The subliminal system constitutes perhaps the greatest mystery and challenge facing the critic today: how to deal descriptively as well as theoretically with the nature and

---

[11]Sollers has increasingly viewed his novels as performances to be delivered in his own voice, a fact that adds significantly to the gestural underpinnings of the printed word. The whole of the first volume of *Paradis* has been not only recorded but broadcast over the radio.

functions of what Julia Kristeva might call the total semiotic substance.[12] Such presemantic signing is most immediately available in
texts that insist upon its presence, and that is precisely what double-
distancing does for distancing procedures, providing a voice for a
mechanism that is by definition voiceless. Even the naive reader will
recognize the tensed relationship between aesthetic extremes imposed
by our principal examples, which, by reaching unabashedly beyond
the opposing poles of aesthetic viability, makes distance a highly visible component and enables us to perceive the text as action.

There is an additional factor, however. By exposing and violating
the limits of middle distancing, such texts revise those limits for what
will follow. Even as it propels us toward the absent center, the double-
distanced text deliberately situates itself on the fringes, repeatedly,
seemingly endlessly, drawing the reader toward a double exile from
art and from its contrary, from both the popular or mass discourse that
gives it so much of its energy and from the deadening but revitalizable
conventions of the academy. Born of the tradition of marginality
(Sade, Flaubert, Lautréamont),[13] double-distancing seems to bring
into being an aesthetic or aestheticizing urge that simultaneously centers the margin and destabilizes the center. In the process it produces
what might be called a mimesis of the margin. That is, by focusing
attention on its decentering procedures, it turns the work into a frame
that, in addition to constituting a setting for absence, becomes a source
of interest in its own right.

The procedure manifests itself differently in each work, but we may
see a disruptive dynamic of assertion/denial in Robbe-Grillet, whose
well-stated cliché becomes an object for contemplation once it has been
destabilized. A somewhat more graphic immediacy is evident in a
Michael Snow film, where the aesthetic ground becomes at once the
dramatized reproductive activity and the hospitable but antagonistic
awareness of the viewer. The process is deepened and complicated by
Beckett, who perhaps more than any other modern writer has established, thematically as well as formally, the centrality of the excluded.
Rather than frame the utterance, such texts utter the frame.

[12]More than any other critic, Kristeva has pointed us toward this domain of silent
signaling and toward the essence of textuality. See her *Semiotiki: Recherches pour une
semanalyse* (Paris: Seuil, 1969), pp. 27–112.
[13]See Philippe Muray, "Le Siècle de Céline," *L'Infini* 8 (1984) 31 and passim.

2

Impossible Objectivity

Perhaps we owe what might be called the realist interlude to the English eighteenth century, to Defoe and others who doubtless felt the tug of puritan straitlacing, to the utilitarian urge toward moralization and documentation. Or perhaps we owe it to the English and French reaction to the Spanish antiromance or picaresque novel. At any rate, it was by a sleight of hand that perspective entered the realm of fiction. As a result, fiction became a counterfeit; the lie became an excuse, validating a form that is at base an elaborate subterfuge, a free play of lies. At the risk of making a baroque argument even less tidy, we might return to roots, recognizing the probability that the true and original source of fiction was supposed fact and even demonstrable fact, that documentation (of events as of ancestry) and rationalization (of phenomena as of behavior) may have provided the earliest instances of narrative discourse. It would follow that only the loss of belief and lapse of memory turned such narratives into what we have learned to call fiction: texts that we need not believe, that we should not believe, that we enjoy because they simultaneously permit and disallow credence, being "neither true nor false,"[1] because they frame and limit our responses much as do our public festivities. Even after the realist interlude, it is well to underscore, as has Robert Alter,[2] the predomi-

[1]See Robert Champigny's neglected but remarkable essay *Le Genre romanesque* (Monte-Carlo: Editions Regain, 1963), pp. 147ff.

[2]Robert Alter, *Partial Magic: The Novel as a Self-Conscious Genre* (Berkeley: University of California Press, 1975), pp. 97–98 and passim.

nance of open illusion in Western fiction, the easily documented insistence on artifice that peaked in seventeenth-century France with the invention of the *roman*, the burlesque, and the *conte des fées*, dominated romantic and symbolist fictions, and found echoes even in the work of Balzac, Dostoievski, and Dickens. The avowal of illusion, however, is nothing alongside its display and subversion as practiced by what I am calling "impossible objects," manifestly *anti*realistic fictions that owe their existence to the triumph of referential verisimilitude as the dominant convention.[3]

Nicholas Mosley coined the term in a novel called precisely *Impossible Object*,[4] which depicts in a series of vignettes a group of characters whose roles and contexts shift, generating contradictory identities and a convention of reader disorientation. Readers of impossible object texts quickly become aware that they have entered an unabashedly artificial realm predicated on the reliability of most fictional discourse. Using a device that might better be called a tactic and that can be applied to parts as well as to wholes, a growing number of writers systematically represent experiences that more or less systematically annul themselves in the process of their presentation. Thus in the opening sentence of his "The Library of Babel," Borges's persona declares with wit and precision that the "universe (which others call the Library) is composed of an indefinite and perhaps infinite number of hexagonal galleries with vast air shafts between, surrounded by very low railings."[5] This narrative, laced with circumstantial details drawn from Western history and civilization and bolstered by the allegorical freight of its title, is less a programmatic effort to undo realism than a structure emerging from and nourished by a dead realistic tradition and shaped by its own central metaphor.

---

[3]To cite further complications, the novel's rediscovery of illusion follows at some distance the rejection of realism by painting in the face of the mastery of such effects by photography (though there were doubtless other underlying causes). It also follows the rediscovery by painting of its particular means and larger conventions. Furthermore, it finds its own roots in Flaubert's theory and practice, especially the practice in his postrealist work. It is reinforced of course by the rediscovery of the neglected work of other writers of fiction (e.g., Sterne, Villiers, Lautréamont). What matters, however, is not so much the hidden or suppressed history as our habits of not-seeing that are being subverted by the revision of fictional method begun late in the last century.

[4]Nicholas Mosley, *Impossible Object: A Novel* (London: Hodder & Stoughton, 1968).

[5]Jorge Luis Borges, *Labyrinths: Selected Stories and Other Writings*, ed. Donald A. Yates and Charles E. Irby (New York: New Directions, 1962), p. 51.

Despite its apparent freshness, there are precedents for this tactic, beginning with Homer's delightful display of that vitalized artifact the shield of Achilles, itself a clear metaphor for his own accomplishment. The "Feast of Trimalchio" in Petronius's *Satyricon* consists of a progression of improbabilities whose outrageousness enhances the reader's pleasure and underscores the writer's skills. Such a context makes doubt, if not disbelief, as important as credence, but then the context is farcical. Not surprisingly, the major precursors of this tradition have been satirical/farcical/encyclopedic, what Mikhail Bakhtin calls "carnivalesque":[6] *Gargantua and Pantagruel, Tristram Shandy, Gulliver's Travels, Candide,* the Alice books of Lewis Carroll, and the later chapters of *Ulysses.* These texts, even when they engage us in their action, delight us with their play, their self-annulments, their witty reflections on the eternally human, their undersidedness. Though they are self-conscious artifacts, however, as readers we are privy less to their procedures than to the liberties they take with our commitment. As predecessors of today's impossible object text, they share space with a flourishing tradition of mixed theatrical forms that dates from at least the sixteenth century, leading in our times to the self-conscious cinematography of Busby Berkeley, Buñuel, Godard, Fellini, and any number of illusionists for whom illusion is less a goal than a procedure. The fascination with artifice is essentially and timelessly baroque, belonging to the realm of fancy more than to that of Coleridgean imagination.[7] More than a manifest and parodic reaction to realism, impossible objectivity is a rediscovery of the illusionistic, ornamental, and gratuitous powers of language, an attempt to refocus the prerogatives of fiction and the textual nature of the printed word in a skeptical century.

Situated somewhere between Lewis Carroll and Vladimir Nabokov but radically different from both, Raymond Roussel is the true father of a convention that has become remarkably versatile. A wealthy French eccentric, Roussel lived his art to the point of orchestrating his suicide and issuing posthumously the much-studied *How I Wrote Certain of My Books,* in which, like the ultimate conjurer, he reveals the

[6]Mikhail Bakhtin, *The World of Rabelais,* trans. Hélène Iswolsky (Cambridge, Mass.: MIT Press, 1971).

[7]This is to be taken not as an evaluative statement but only as an attempt to balance the books of the arts, to recognize an essential component for what it is, the hallmark of a periodic mind-set.

extent to which his books are self-generative.[8] Still, even Roussel had significant predecessors whom he subtly and powerfully, if not mischievously, modified. We find in his work traces of Poe's tales of ratiocination along with echoes of Mary Shelley's *Frankenstein* and E. T. A. Hoffmann's "The Sandman."

A more immediate model is Villiers de L'Isle Adam's neglected masterwork *L'Eve future*, itself derived explicitly from Poe, Wagner, and Hoffmann.[9] Accommodating himself to the industrial age, Villiers produced in *L'Eve* a late nineteenth-century (mock) romantic Gothic spin-off set in Menlo Park, New Jersey. The novel tells how a wealthy young man who has been disappointed in love receives as a replacement fetish a mechanical maiden designed and built by that modern Merlin Thomas Alva Edison. The details of the impossible gadget's construction and operation constitute the major interest of this allegorical melodrama, whose narrative content is so slight as to be vaguely ludicrous.[10]

With these precedents in mind, we will see that Roussel made his own peculiarly postindustrial, postromantic, and postsymbolist contribution to narrative form.[11] His second novel, *Locus Solus* (1914), is set in a Boschian garden of delights controlled by a latter-day Edison. The mystery, suspense, plot, allegory, and characterization that supported the predecessor narratives, however, are minimized in this spare forerunner of the science-fictionist's *Popular Mechanics*. It also lacks the romantic high seriousness of other possible forerunners such as Jules Verne and H. G. Wells. Here the novelist's special effects, his gadgetry, provide interest and even a kind of suspense. We are treated to a sequence of cleverly mounted scientific-spectacular displays, each of which is meticulously described before being explained with equal precision. It is as if a magician were to explain each of his tricks

---

[8]See, especially, Michel Foucault, *Raymond Roussel* (Paris: Gallimard, 1963), pp. 20–40 and passim.

[9]Villiers cites these figures as providing patterns for his ideal woman. Villiers de L'Isle Adam, *Oeuvres complètes*, vol. 1: *L'Eve future* (Paris: Mercure de France, 1922), p. 127.

[10]Both Villiers and Roussel owe something to Huysmans's *A rebours*, with its serial account of the production of a paradise through artifice.

[11]I am referring to his direct formal contribution and not at this time to his belatedly significant use of aleatory generation. I am also playing down his after-the-fact surrealist associations, but it is significant that three literary movements claimed him after his contemporaries rejected his work.

immediately after performing it or as if the spectators at a sixteenth-century masque (or modern space epic) were to witness the spectacular effects of the staging and then go behind the scenes to see how those effects were achieved.

There is a crucial difference, however: Roussel's explanations are ultimately and predictably as gratuitous as his "inventions." He does not derive suspense from the sort of verbal sleight of hand others use to plaster over the gaps in their narrative's surface and to generate interest in the development of plot and character, nor does he justify his special effects by building them into a spectacle or, like Poe and Villiers, incorporating them in an elaborate fictional development. He has moved beyond even Huysmans to foreground their production, beyond the gothic to foreground the explanations. As a result, the emphasis falls on the text itself, which generates what are patently inexplicable and antireal verbal shapes. This last trait distinguishes Roussel and establishes him as a significant and exemplary figure.[12]

How does he do it? In *Locus Solus*, in slow motion, with almost painful precision, in virtually unaccentuated prose, he presents, first, the phenomenal but whimsical inventions of Professor Canterel. Then, with equal precision, he gives us the professor's explanation of them. In each instance, if the invention is bizarre or mystifying, the explanation is unenlightening or even absurd. One example is the mosaic-laying machine that uses for tesserae variously discolored human teeth that have been extracted by a magnetic process invented by that French Thomas Edison:

> Shortly afterwards a flash of light darted from the lens, which had abruptly made a quarter-turn by pivoting on the axis of its horizontal diameter and was now perpendicularly intersecting the oblique, descending path of the light pencil emitted by the mirror pointing south. As a result of this manoeuvre the rays passed through the special glass and became powerfully concentrated on the whole area of the yellow sub-

[12]Jean Ricardou speaks of Roussel's use of "scriptural mutation," which he illustrates with the writer's description of a modern shield of Achilles, the label on a bottle of mineral water: "an effect of hyper-realism (one describes a scene more carefully than the image can sustain) provokes an effect of anti-realism (the life-like effect that results eclipses what we know to be the image itself)" ("Le nouveau roman est-il Rousselien?" *L'Arc* 68, 65–67, my translation). See also Alain Robbe-Grillet's discussion "Enigma and Transparency in Raymond Roussel," in *For a New Novel: Essays on Fiction*, trans. Richard Howard (New York: Grove, 1965).

stance spread out on the circular tray beneath the aerostat; a few of the delicate lower threads of the netting striped this suddenly glistening expanse with imperceptible shadows. As an effect of the intense heat thus generated, the ocre material must have released a light gas which entered the balloon through its bell-mouthed opening, for the envelope gradually began to swell. The upward force was soon great enough to lift the whole apparatus, which leapt gently into the air—while the lens made another quarter turn in the same direction and darkened the yellow mixture by ceasing to concentrate the sun's rays upon it.[13]

We follow each calibrated movement of this Rube Goldberg machine in a description worthy of the *Encyclopédie* of d'Alembert and Diderot, a passage that calls to mind both Kafka's treatment of the infernal machine in "In the Penal Colony" and Beckett's rendering of detail in *Fizzles*. Still, unlike Kafka and Beckett, who turn their skills to metaphysical or quasi-metaphysical ends, Roussel uses his pseudoscientific impulses to no apparent end other than amusement and bafflement and the consequent engagement of the reader's imaginative faculties. His forte, like that of the New Novelists, is the matter-of-fact description of technical detail, a discourse proper to the scientific paper, one that is relatively free of metaphor and devoid of affective language, if not of affective imagery. The reader's mind and sense of whimsy collaborate in a project that would become wearisome were it not for the richness of the writer's imagination, his frequent self-subversions, his deliberate use of a wry intertextuality, and the access afforded to his curious sensibility.

Only when the descriptive material abuts human situations demanding nontechnical explanations does Roussel resort to narratives of events, giving them in each instance a charteristic twist. The third major exhibit in the professor's waxworks is a giant cage of glass containing a number of tableaux morts/vivants, scenes from a variety of lives thrown together in random sequence. After "witnessing" the "acts" and finding out that they are designed to illustrate two inventions—one for reanimating corpses, the other for keeping their tissues cool—we are given seriatim the background for each scene. These narratives prove to be as random and inconsequent as the tableaux, each of which was furnished with a number of enigmatic de-

[13]Raymond Roussel, *Locus Solus*, trans. Rupert Copeland Cuningham (Berkeley: University of California Press, 1970), p. 29.

tails. The latter are now explained away with comical precision. We may recall the fanatic ordering of events in the Japanese classic film *The Seven Samurai*, where the feats and fate of each hero must be accounted for separately and in sequence, but then, conventional narrative has always been constrained to justify its details. Characteristically, without falling into gratuitous self-deflation, Roussel makes his details fit into a crazy quilt of forced relationships that leaves us bemused while revealing the action as purely verbal. The more detailed the explanation, the more obvious the stratagem that produced it, and the further we are from reality. No wonder the surrealists claimed Roussel. Even when we learn how he generated his texts from minimal rearrangements of letters in a sentence, we must recognize that the results reveal a curiously twisted genius, a brilliance and control born of a remarkable inner freedom.

To illustrate this procedure we need only cite from the convoluted and circumstantial account of the suicide of François-Charles Cortier. Here Roussel describes the behavior of the beloved daughter of François-Charles's father, François-Jules, just before she is burned to death by the fire in the hearth:

> Lydia was anxious not to be a source of distraction, so she sat down on the floor behind the large, littered table on which her father was leaning his elbows, so that he was then unable to see her.
>
> As she played quietly with her doll she thought of the snow, and was moved to pity by the coldness of the porcelain face against her fingers. Quickly she laid the barrister doll on its back before the hearth where a great fire was blazing, just as though it were a human-being frozen with the cold. But the heat soon melted the glue on the two glass eyes, which dropped almost simultaneously to the back of its head.
>
> In vexation the child seized the doll again, and held it up to her eyes to examine the effects of the accident at close range. The barrister was then silhouetted against the wall fitted with the black shelves; and all at once Lydia was involuntarily struck by the relationship, between the death's-heads on display and the pink artificial face, which was established by the emptiness of the eye-sockets common to both.[14]

We note the details on the one hand and the unwarranted assumptions concerning the child's motivation on the other. Throughout the nar-

[14]Ibid., p. 165.

rative we are never allowed to forget the need to decipher an encoded image. As we progress, the arbitrary quality of this account becomes inescapable, as does the woodenness of the discourse, its freight of clichés. Even in this classical melodramatic situation, the prose is transparent (except when, for effect, the rhetoric is slightly off). The impact is that of *de*realization. Furthermore, the passage reeks of conventional gothic tricks. With its burden of skulls, phrenology, child death, and later, Lolita-love, it brings to mind Poe's preoccupations. Simultaneously, by flattening its prose, it annuls the expectations aroused by such preoccupations. In effect, this elaborate reconstruction or rationalization generates illusions designed to obliterate themselves. Even the frequent use of melodramatic tropes (like those in Robbe-Grillet) serves as much to dampen as to heighten the verisimilitude. For the context undercuts the melodrama, as does the mechanical filling of the squares, the deliberate discovery of functions, the absurd particularity, the relentless, contrived baroquery. Hoffmann and Villiers may stand behind this text, but their materials are turned to radically fresh ends in a novel that reduces narrative in many cases to the status of the list by using techniques so transparent that they highlight their very seams. Note, for example, that the disparate tableaux vivants in the glass cage are accounted for in narrative vignettes preceded by numbers. The vignette in question is number 8.

Roussel himself may have seen self-generation as his prime procedure, and certainly the mechanical decoding process is suggestive, but the true informing principle is antirealism and *dis*illusionism. Thus in the first half of what for me is his best work, *Impressions d'Afrique*, we have a minutely evocative sequence of vaudeville skits and sideshow turns, a perverse *ballet de cour* given in honor of a victorious African tyrant. Presented in random sequence, the acts are engrossing less because we want to see larger plot mysteries resolved than because we delight in the surprises occasioned by the consistent improbability of the details. Michel Butor has characterized Flaubert's strategy in *Bouvard et Pécuchet* as that of the parade master, or rather he has suggested that the reader is engaged by the elaboration of a chain of incidents whose variousness makes up for the absence of plot and character interest.[15] We might say the same for Roussel's meticulous and malicious elaboration of impossible circumstances that include an

---

[15]In a paper delivered at the University of Iowa in 1969.

instrument controlled by the action of a worm, another by a marvelous metal that "submitted to various temperatures, changed its volume, proportionately, according to a scale which could be measured from one to ten,"[16] a midget whose head is the length of his body, a loom that weaves elaborate patterns automatically, pastilles that produce in a river precise realistic pictures, a plant in which strange scenes are seen with the aid of a bright light, and so on.

Improbability as a function of change is clearly the main lure, since there is literally no plot, even though mystery is introduced to elicit interest and even though we may speak of subplots or mini-events. Still, Roussel presents his invariably irrational and even absurd proceedings in a rational manner, supplying brief explanations, implicitly promising others. As a result, we do not have the easy out of the willing suspension of disbelief when we find it impossible to justify mechanisms that we can visualize with however much difficulty. Furthermore, the negation is not accomplished simply by comparing the textual vision with some version of sensed or experienced reality. Validity is tested and found wanting in terms of the text itself. Impossibility is conveyed as a pure given rather than as what is possible in some other realm.

If, as readers, we fail to question the vaudeville acts or the logic of their ordering, the second half of *Impressions d'Afrique* will do so for us. It does so long after we have abandoned our own imaginative reconstructions and rationalizations, relaxing into the position of acquiescing spectators to a bewildering and delightful array of discontinuous events. It is almost shocking to see this nonnovel suddenly turn into a conventional-seeming narrative in which everything is in its place and the process of placement and resolution is relentless. In fact, however, the second half is sequential only to the degree that it ties together systematically and in the order of presentation the loose ends of the first half. Like *Locus Solus*, it does so with a logic that defies all reason and quickly subverts the convention that it pretends to sustain. The subversion gains its power precisely from the eliminated norms of narrative discourse. It is the subverted (or sublimated) that valorizes the subversion, making Roussel's text accessible, reassuring the reader with a transparent subterfuge.

---

[16]Raymond Roussel, *Impressions of Africa*, trans. Lindy Foord and Rayner Heppenstall (Berkeley: University of California Press, 1967), p. 41.

Even if it were possible, any true unraveling of the absurdities of part one would lead to a banality: the solved puzzle, the closed system of rational discourse, the illusion of control and coherence, and the consequent failure of fiction as artifice. Instead, we have the ultimate and preeminently satisfying logical absurdity, the text that point for point discredits its own account. Ostensibly, we learn who everyone is and what function the celebration served. We also go behind the scenes to learn how each trick was conceived and accomplished. Rather than clear up the mysteries, however, the explanations reconfirm the impossibility of the trick, adding in each case further levels of improbability. A sequence of tableaux vivants (not so much impossible in their presentation as impenetrable in their organization) is explained by a laborious narrative that, with obviously forced logic, accounts for all the details at the expense of all reason. In the process it produces a narrative that rivals the outrageously coincidence-ridden plots of the seventeenth-century romances, seemingly parodying them and their potboiling progeny but actually giving them a new respectability. We have been treated to a fantastical (though not fantastic) baroque confection in the guise of a narrative sequence, a confection that plays upon our stubborn ingrained habit of accepting anything that has been dipped in a syrup of fiction.

This mismanagement of logical verisimilitude, like that of Sterne, is a tour de force. The reader's habits of perception are turned against themselves to reveal the writer's methods of deception. Fiction's false perspectives turn into the wall of speckled white that is the page. At the root is the undoing of illusion, but the tactics are designed to incorporate in the text the conventions it is systematically bent on dishonoring, the same conventions upon which its validity ultimately hangs. How could we appreciate Roussel, to say nothing of Beckett and Robbe-Grillet, if we no longer succumbed to the narrative temptation?

We must now pause to address a potential contradiction. The crux of impossible objectivity is its exploitation of the techniques of verisimilitude and rational discourse to undermine belief. The destabilization of illusion is a tactic, however, perhaps *the* tactic, of traditional satire and allegory, both of which use transparent or permeable narrative in order to point beyond and through their surface toward the underlying message. Similarly, verisimilitude is the precondition for both representational ("realistic") and fantastic literature. In Roussel's work the goals of the essentially metaphoric satire and allegory and those of the essentially metanymic representational and fantastic modes are subverted, together with the expectations that these modes raise in the reader properly attuned to their conventions.

This absence (of which traces inevitably remain) makes Roussel's enterprise startlingly original and pure. He resisted the pull of these competing conventions, drawn allegedly by his guiding mechanism, his conundrums. All of the strategies I have described perhaps derive logically from that original tactic, yet it is not the originating procedure but what that procedure facilitated that generates our interest. Consciously or not, in deciding to play his verbal games, Roussel introduced a highly personal aesthetic component, widening the field of choices and substituting subconscious logic for logical validity. We may without exaggeration compare his tactics to those of Rorschach. His nonsense lines are a variation on the inkblot. Consequently and inevitably, his solutions will have psychoanalytic implications. Roussel's peculiar choices are made almost subliminally available to a reader preoccupied with fitting together the pieces of mystery and solution. The freedom from convention derived from his method seems to have locked the outwardly cool Roussel into his own psyche. Much the same thing can be said of his disciple Alain Robbe-Grillet. It would appear that the lifting of certain restraints automatically results in the introduction of an element of compulsive choice. Surrealism has entered our argument by the back door, deprived of its explicit program. By a process of self-denial, the author reveals both himself and the reader engrossed in unraveling that self.[17]

In Roussel, illusion points directly to itself and through itself, not to the world, as would satire or allegory, but to the twin processes of generation and apprehension and the hidden or sublimated allegory of the mind. The ultimate impossible object is the reader's text, the

---

[17]One of his most perceptive readers, Michel Leiris, has said that Roussel "rediscovered," when he innovated his creative method, a central "pattern of the human mind; the formation of myths starting with words. That is (as though he had decided to illustrate Max Müller's theory that myths were born out of a sort of 'disease of language'), transposition of what was in fact a simple fact of language into a dramatic action" (cited in *How I Wrote Certain of My Books*, trans. Trevor Winkfield [New York: Sun, 1977], p. 53). This reading takes us a step closer to surrealism, but it also suggests why Roussel's curious constructs have exercised so strong a fascination on so many diverse talents. We may see similar effects, derived from procedures rather than from word games, in the works of Alain Robbe-Grillet and Harry Mathews.

reading process by which we are enmeshed in the text's procedures and which enables us to take our pleasure. At this point our reading may make contact with the writer's rationalization of chance verbal configurations in the service of an irrational goal, but all such games are after all implicit in the text and need no keys to expose their outlines. We know as we read that the decorum of the novel dictates the misapplication of conventional properties. We are aware, for example, that, though narrative resolution is achieved on all levels, its essence is in each instance falsified. In receiving the expected rewards, we contribute to the making/unmaking of desire. An adequate resolution in this case is one that fails to convince or rather resolves in terms of a built-in unresolvability, one that gives no more than the appearance of resolution, completing a pattern of presentation, of action leading to counteraction. The absence of conventional irony becomes all the more significant as a result. Roussel is not attacking or complicating meaning, nor is he parodying an outworn form, though both avenues are clearly available to him. If he is laughing, his laughter is closely contained. What we have, therefore, is a new narrative formulation that we read as much for its suppressions, or *ratures*, as for its entertainment value.

The mastery of improbability can take many forms, and nothing could seem more different from Roussel's elaborate self-concealment (or self-revelation by indirection) than Kafka's painful and open self-scrutiny. Yet the texts of the two writers share qualities pertaining to impossible objectivity: a pellucid style, meticulous delimitation of situations, a seemingly unadorned narrative, controlled internal contradictions, and wit (so wry and dry that generations of readers overlooked it). Essential, too, but more pronounced in Kafka is the dreamlike perspective that makes it at once possible and impossible to visualize the "court" and the "castle," to say nothing of the magic world of "America." The latter trait makes our engagement qualitatively other, for it can oblige us, despite all its contradictions and absurdities, to accept, for example, the phantasmal judicial system that permeates a "real" city and exacts retribution for unstated crimes from more or less willing, if not demonstrably guilty, citizens.

What moves Kafka's novels is the powerful, if unspecified and unspecifiable, allegorical component, the floating irony, and the poignant simplicity that separate him decisively from Roussel and diminish in importance the qualities we have ascribed to impossible objectivity. In terms of their implied though never stated or fixed metaphysics, these texts tend to validate rather than destabilize even the oddest of their images. Where Roussel avoids attributing significance to any one particular, focusing on the mimetic procedures and irrational development and hence on the textual process, Kafka develops in each book and story a single incredible detail, relentlessly probing its implications, announcing within the text its improbable exposure to a credible and paradoxically validating quotidian reality. While Roussel's images tend to evaporate, leaving only a dim glow capable of stimulating later associations, ceding their space to that which follows, Kafka's method inscribes the image indelibly on the reader's consciousness. The Castle's reiterated unreality, registered but discounted by the awareness that we share with the protagonist, underscores various intensely personal allegorical readings, taking on a special sort of validity, a truth to experience and a seriousness lacking in or banished from Roussel's Africa. No matter how tenuous their links to experience, Kafka's objects become ever more possible as the narratives affirm the characters' dependence on the situation's logical ramifications, as the reader discovers in him/herself an increasing engagement in unresolvable but engrossing circumstances. Ultimately, these images are far less subversive than those of Roussel. Still, in both writers we experience a failure of conventional logic, an unblinking absurdity that holds our attention but does not invite full acceptance or pretend to be verifiable.

In the light of these similarities and differences, perhaps we may speak of Kafka and Roussel as standing at opposite ends of a spectrum on a line stretching from imagination to fancy but stopping short of absolute or fixed allegory on the one hand and fantasy on the other. At the same time, we may conceive of impossible objectivity as a convention that accommodates both poles, being defined by the exclusion of accessible allegory and satire, the fantastic, and the realistic. Perhaps we can diagram it in terms of the limits shown in the figure below. Since impossible objectivity is essentially reactive, a denial of accepted modes, it is bound to contain traces of the tendencies it rejects. It will also stand as an open invitation to the appropriative impulse of critics, lending itself to readings that conform to custom, reactive readings that it tends to destabilize. Thus critics of Beckett and Kafka have frequently read these authors as allegorists or satirists. Critics of Robbe-Grillet have strained to discover plot, psychology, and representation. Despite his disclaimer, Roussel encouraged a surrealist reading bordering on fantasy. All such readings are responses to traps

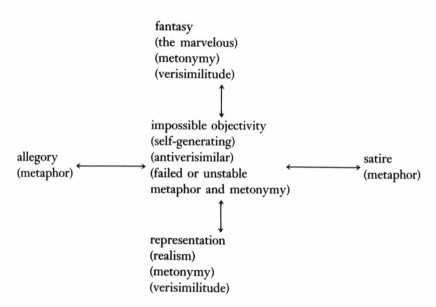

fantasy
(the marvelous)
(metonymy)
(verisimilitude)

impossible objectivity
(self-generating)
allegory   (antiverisimilar)   satire
(metaphor)   (failed or unstable   (metaphor)
                                  metaphor and metonymy)

representation
(realism)
(metonymy)
(verisimilitude)

laid consciously or not by the texts, evidence of procedures that seem to demand recuperation. They are doubtless symptoms of a malaise experienced by the critic as reader, a malaise that could be better accounted for by a study of reactions in relation to stimuli. For impossible objectivity functions to destabilize literary illusion, disclosing the function of reading and, as a result, reorienting the reader and bringing about a reevaluation of textuality. (It is significant that Roussel stands behind both the New Novel and the radical inquisition of poststructuralism, with its attendant narrative forms.)

I suggest that, in all impossible objectivity texts, the dominant formal thrust as toward continuity or elevation, that is, toward a rhythmic and/or an attitudinal range that tends to underscore credibility and to enlist the reader's sympathy. To rectify that thrust, or rather to generate fruitful imbalance within a frequently rigid mimesis of order, these texts introduce disorder and irreverence in the form of unsettling detail, irrational shifts in focus, unexpected and disturbing juxtapositions, and the general refusal of verisimilitude. The effect is to undermine an established order, but the texts go further, since they elaborate an order that is palpably unstable. Just as we find in the description of the Rousselian gadget ample evidence that it would not work in the real world, the truths presented in any of the impossible objectivity segments of the texts we will be considering are undercut by the details of their presentation. Without necessarily becoming fantastic or supernatural, objects fade imperceptibly into other objects and suffer curious distortions. As we watch, they take on strange attributes, despite the extraordinary clarity of the prose. Identities blur and dissolve, or sudden shifts render the commonplace strange, but the tone remains matter-of-fact, the discourse logical, and the rhetoric precise, even when it is florid. The baroquery is less in the ornament than in the fluidity of outline, the trompe l'oeil or trompe l'oreille that delight in destroying the very illusions they produce, the magic space to which clarity adds confusion.

The qualities we have been describing are in large measure exemplified by the novels of Harry Mathews, which openly exhibit traces of the aesthetic of Roussel while moving progressively away from the strict adherence to Rousselian impossibility. It is no accident that Mathews founded, along with other members of the New York School, a review called *Locus Solus* or that he makes frequent allusions to Roussel in his three novels. The first of these, *The Conversions* (1966), seems initially to be a pastiche but quickly turns into an homage (rather like Godard's tribute to Céline in *Pierrot le Fou*). It opens, however, on an almost unmistakable note, with the description of an enigmatic adze. The possession of that ceremonial implement and the consequent possession of the fabulous Fod fortune motivates the central protagonist's quest for the answer to the riddle of the adze's incised imagery. (One thinks inevitably of certain of Pynchon's tropes.) The following passage from the second chapter, "Preparations," illustrates the tone of this deliberate fiction and exhibits the acknowledged debt:

> Tonight's game, he said, will be a race. The contestants are Bea and Is, whom you all know, and—this gentleman. The prize will be an antique adze.
> Servants entered to draw back the curtains at one side of the drawing-room, then to open the sliding panels of glass that formed the wall behind. We overlooked a greenhouse, whose fragrant heat rose quickly about us, but which we could see little of: it was unlighted except for three parallel bands, about two yards long, that were sunk in its floor near us. These shone dull green.
> That is the course, said Mr. Wayl. The bands, which are covered with a thin layer of salt slime, are lighted from below so that you can follow the race.
> The contestants will be represented by these. He held out his opened

cigarette case: in it lay small sticks of tobacco-colored stuff with a tuft of
tangled white thread at the end of each.
    Worms called zephyrs. They are dried out but alive; moisture will
quicken them. On the course, which is wet, they will find in front of
them a trail of their habitual food (tiny pharaohs) that will lead them to
the finish.
    As for the human contestants, they will do more than watch. Each
must accompany his worm's advance with an ascending major scale, to
be played on one of these instruments; as you doubtless know, they are
named serpents.[18]

These lines precede a description of the race, whose curious rules and
incredible details glow from the start with an arcane half light that is
missing from Roussel's frontal approach to a universe worthy of the
Belgian surrealist Magritte. We note, however, that, Mathews's account, like Roussel's, is rigorously precise, colored by an understated
wit, and set in a never-never world of the imagination to which we
need give no adherence.
    Though all three of Mathews's novels refer to real places and histor-
ical (or possibly historical) events, the associations with these places are
never credible, and the temporality is always skewed. Furthermore,
though Mathews's plots are more complexly articulated than Roussel's,
they too are modeled after recognizable stereotypes that they wittily
distort. It is as though false or deceptive actions were taking place
against familiar but equally deceptive backcloths in the theater of the
mind. The actors in these dramas are closer to functions than people,
even though the two quirky treasure-hunting correspondents of *The
Sinking of Odradek Stadium* are superficially more "rounded."
    All of the books are filled with *set* pieces, chapters built around a bit
of remarkable stage machinery, a miracle element that, without being
precisely magical, leaves one delightfully disoriented. There is a race
in *Tlooth* that is every bit as grotesque and improbable as the one in *The
Conversions*. "Science fiction," some would say. If so, it is science
fiction without faith in the powers of science. Thus the hero of the
adventure story *Tlooth* introduces himself as a member of an imaginary
sect called Imperfect Baptists and a prisoner in a Siberian camp. A
dentist with a suppurating "syphilitic" hand, he travels toward free-

[18]Harry Mathews, *The Conversions*, in *The Sinking of Odradek Stadium and Other Novels*
(New York: Harper & Row, 1975), pp. 7–8.

dom and his cure through a landscape full of perverse imaginings. At one point, having reached Venice, he is commissioned to write a pornographic movie that, in true impossible objectivity fashion, invades the text we read. The script, which is rejected,[19] brings to mind (and explodes) some of Robbe-Grillet's trendier tricks:

> Two hours later: a dozen new abstractions litter the floor. The girl is dressing; Claude is at the telephone. Hanging up, he opens a door marked *Dott. Claudio Morora.* Through it we follow him into a small office.
>
> Claude puts a leather bag on the desk by the office window and starts filling it with wooden crosses, which he takes from an adjacent medicine cabinet. The feet of the crosses are pointed, like stakes.
>
> The view shifts to a glass case in a corner of the office. A stenciled sign has been nailed to its top: *Anal & Vaginal Insertions.* As the camera moves in close-up along the shelves, it distinguishes a few of the exhibited objects:
>
> a crushed pingpong ball A
> a golf ball V
> an English bicycle saddle V
> a stethoscope A
> the Willendorf Venus in replica V
> a roll of 10,000-lire bills A
> a policeman's night stick V
> a fifth of Wachenheimer Oberstnest '52 A
> a brass bath faucet V
> an electric toothbrush V
> a pumice stone A
> cucumbers, eggplants, mangoes V (now withered)
> cutting abruptly to the convent lawn. Nuns walk slowly about, singly or in pairs, against a view of fields.
>
> We wandered among gangs of chattering males.
> 'What do you think of the new fad? I mean their pants.'
> Several dapper men wore richly embroidered trouserflies.[20]

A study of Mathews's novels suggests that he is dedicated, first, to the elaboration of plots whose verisimilitude is constantly being under-

---

[19]There are moments when Mathews's novels resemble those of another experimentalist, Jerome Charyn.

[20]Mathews, *Tlooth*, in *The Sinking of Odradek Stadium and Other Novels*, pp. 298–99.

mined; second, to the destabilization of repeatedly reasserted clichés; and third, to the generation of unlikely situations and whimsically dubious details in contexts characterized by tongue-in-cheek magic. Unlike Roussel, he deals in conventional suspense, complicating, continuing, even completing coherent actions. By repeatedly giving the lie to narrative particulars, he satisfies both our urge to read a good yarn and our desire, as sophisticated readers, not to be taken in. Furthermore, he lets us enjoy seeing ourselves as clever in terms of his crazed mirror held up to conventions and even specific models (the recognition factor is strong) even as he points up the meaninglessness of such facile wit. Finally, like Roussel, he reveals himself most clearly in his choice of unconventional and whimsical images and behavior.

Mathews's co-disciple, Robbe-Grillet, not only acknowledges his debt to Roussel[21] but also praises two related figures, Lewis Carroll and Vladimir Nabokov, claiming, for example, to have drawn his nubile girls after Alice and Lolita.[22] He too programatically eschews plot, suspense (except in his sub-sequences or vignettes, where it is shortcircuited), and character development, especially in his later work. His sequences are frequently reminiscent of Roussel's in that something is amiss in their presentation, a quality that suggests links with surrealism.[23] What is most striking is his insistence, first, on stillness in motion or rather the quality of the snapshot or animated still life, and second, on the fluidity of his images and their development. That is, his scenes tend to be posed, deliberately artificial, and unsettling because they freeze actions into unnatural, strained, and trite positions that are activated by our expectations. Motion against the grain of stillness is the hallmark of both his fiction and his films (beginning with *Last Year in Marienbad*, for which he wrote the script). A favorite ploy in *Project for a Revolution in New York* is the exchange of a wax mannequin for an agonizing girl, a procedure that equivocally

---

[21]See Robbe-Grillet, "Enigmas and Transparency in Raymond Roussel," pp. 79–87.
[22]David Hayman, "An Interview with Alain Robbe-Grillet," in *Interviews with Contemporary Writers*, 2d ser., 1972–82, ed. L. S. Dembo (Madison: University of Wisconsin Press, 1983), p. 155 (reprinted from *Contemporary Literature* 16 [Summer, 1975], 280).
[23]Without subscribing to the tenets of surrealism, Robbe-Grillet has been able to accommodate some of their *trouvailles*. For example he has made ample use of the visual techniques of both Delvaux and Magritte in constructing his stop-action and slow-motion vignettes. Delvaux along with the pop artist Rauschenberg and the stylish photographer David Hamilton served as one of the sources of inspiration for Robbe-Grillet's book *Topography of a Phantom City* (New York: Grove, 1977).

short-circuits the sadistic impulse. (It should be noted, however, that the word and hence the concept "mannequin" elicit a pun on the living and the artificial model.) This tactic is consistent with, though hardly imitative of, Roussel, but it is poles apart from Mathews, whose vignettes are artificial but active, outrageously and yet subtly strange, frankly antirealistic rather than realistically posed. The corollary attribute of the still/moving image in Robbe-Grillet's fiction is its fluidity or *glissage* (slippage), a trait alien to Roussel but not to Mathews. In passage after passage we find one set image or action floating associatively into another, both having been clearly delineated with Rousselian precision and deliberate attention to detail. However quirky the action, for all his tendency to deanimate his theater, to mannequinize his personae, Robbe-Grillet's impossible resides more in juxtapositions and interpenetrations than in the situations themselves. Despite certain *trouvailles*, he seldom shines through his inventive powers. His effects, unlike those of other practitioners, startle less than they manipulate. Among them, the most effective may be the calculated lie: that is, the contradiction in a later passage of something that has earlier been carefully elaborated.

Faced with something radically different from the conventional untrustworthy narrative in which the source of our information is a characterized persona, the reader is left to puzzle over the status of the voice and the nature of truth in relation to the evolving image. Is it a matter of simple misapprehension, in which case the new, corrected vision generates its own rationale—or has the narrative deliberately misled us? The question is never answered, but the effect is clear.

A further characteristic of the Robbe-Grillet texts is the heavy reliance on description and the manner in which it conveys/freezes action. Very seldom is a complex action developed. Instead, we witness a sequence of stills or semistills between which things occur. Typically, a descriptive passage will be used to convey an obvious convention/sequence designed to point up, not the viability of the treatment and the verisimilitude of the event, but its formulaic nature. Thus, "The Hidden Room," a story in the collection *Snapshots*, evokes in grim detail a scene in the manner of the symbolist painter Gustave Moreau. It is essentially, therefore, an exercise in the delineation of an aura: "gothic" decadence. Without specifying that its object is a painting, the narrative discloses a sensual surface, explores its violent message, implies significant motion, all in such a way as to violate the conventions both of painting and of narrative point of view. Comprising a series of "cinematic" frames, the story opens with the description of a red stain whose dimensions it inspects in such a way that the stain seems to expand to cover and reveal a lovely breast, that of a young victim chained to an altar/table. From there we move (our eyes) out into the room, establishing the context as an underground chamber or vault. The scene is gradually modified by the apparent reversal of temporality, the appearance of a vanished murderer, the stop-action reenactment of the event, and so on. In short, we are repeatedly disoriented by the introduction of distortions and contradictions, though the latter are never excessive. Only in the last lines does the locus of the action become inescapably a canvas and by extension the overactive imagination of the viewer/narrator. By this time both canvas and text have attained the status of impossible objects in which we have experienced subtly shifting perspectives opening onto improbable but hardly fantastic horizons. Throughout, the viewing reader is obliged to scurry mentally in search of an adequate point of view, to rationalize the shifts, and ultimately to admit failure, delighting in both search and admission. In short, we have been actively engaged in the text's double-distancing.

The later Robbe-Grillet (novelist and cineast) pushes these procedures further. Unexpected change quickly becomes a convention, as does the nonsequitur. Scene shifts associatively produce the effect at once of self-generation and of a modified parataxis. Thus in *Project for a Revolution*, a window full of carefully described plastic masks generates a world of "characters" who use such masks to disguise themselves as others, thus subverting narrative control as well as "real" identity even though the cool textual discourse continues without skipping a beat. What we have previously accepted is now thrown in doubt. Though the several popular subtexts remain in place as models, the spy-narrative, the sado-masochistic romance, and the urban guerrilla conventions function here as patterns of difference, and the divergences are available as meaning to even the most casual reader. In the same novel, the action witnessed on a television screen is extended by events in the world of the witness. In addition, the text frequently conjoins disparate actions and locales to create hybrid sequences for which a new logic must be discovered.

Discrepancies lubricate Robbe-Grillet's impossible machines, facilitating our savoring of the outlandish and frequently perverse situations and smiling where we might otherwise wince. The obvious use of clashing or complementary conventions, of which I have mentioned only three, facilitates disbelief while underscoring the fact that it is usually easier to suspend disbelief within a coherently organized and well-managed fictional context than it is to disbelieve. The writer bent on subverting and ventilating traditional practice must be able to re-affirm improbability in ways sufficiently various to engage readers in procedures that could easily become tedious. This implies the continual making and unmaking of suspense and the use of a new sort of tact to compensate for the subversion of conventional suspense, interest, coherence, and resolution, rewards that have been systematically withheld. Such tact is a function of timing and manipulation: timing of what appear to be cinematic cuts in a special montage effect, one resembling the postsurrealist splicing of Robbe-Grillet's later films and the introduction into his pop subtexts of what Ricardou characterizes as hyperrealism,[24] a trait we have already seen in Roussel's descriptions, where it is applied to objects, not people.

The texts treated this far have tended to fall along what might be called the Roussel-Carroll axis. That is, though both Mathews and Robbe-Grillet introduce satiric and allegorical overtones, and though each, by his choice of image and situation, has evolved a very personal idiom, the dominant thrust of their fictions is toward play and fancy (between "realism" and "fantasy") rather than meaning and message. This is in many ways a strength. Allegory and satire, if foregrounded, would detract from the revolutionary form and conventionalize these books. There are, however, writers whose books oscillate between Roussel and Kafka on a "metaphoric" axis, drawing their strength not so much from allegory/satire as from the contradictions inherent in joining those tactics with radical undecidability.

Since Borges is a giant among such writers, the contrast between his procedures and those of Robbe-Grillet is instructive. Borges's acknowledged masters include not only Kafka but Kipling, a writer famous for the clarity of his prose, his "plain talk" manner.[25] Kipling, however, is not only followed but savantly mauled by this Argentine writer proud of his fraction of English blood. Thus while Robbe-

---

[24]See above, note 13.
[25]Emir Rodriguez-Monegal notes that Borges "has followed some obvious models: Agatha Christie's *The Murder of Roger Ackroyd* (1926) for the surprise ending . . . ; Chesterton and Kipling for the invention of circumstantial details and vivid visual images; and von Sternberg's movies for the cutting and editing, which is sharp, lean, taut" (*Jorge Luis Borges: A Literary Biography* [New York: Dutton, 1978], p. 254).

Grillet produces supermimetic but antinarrative texts tending toward paratactics, Borges seems bent on forcing nonnarrative substance, the stuff of bibliography, scientific research, philology, and the essay into molds that are unquestionably narrative and rigorously hypotactic. His parables point, however wryly and ambiguously, toward an allegorical and/or satirical message.

As titles like *Labyrinths* and *Dream Tigers* suggest, however, both impossibility and insolubility are central to Borges. "The Library of Babel," like Kafka's "The Burrow," uses a most unlikely point of view, that of a librarian who, never having left the confines of an allegorical structure, a latter-day Tower of Babel, can in good faith insist on the universality of his experience. He is, by definition, an arch chauvinist fighting a desperate battle against disillusionment. As readers, we are inside a mind, inside an enclosure, inside a universe mysteriously infected by the refrains of a history that is recognizably ours. On the face of it, the librarian cannot be allowed to imagine that which cannot be contained within his universe/library; yet the library cannot be understood except in relation to the external, to the reader's own universe and his/her awareness of it. Borges plays with this and other impossibilities. Indeed, the pleasure derived from this tale must come in large measure from our sense that none of the levels of narrative awareness is recuperable, from our conscientious attempts to naturalize the strangeness. We must smile at the awareness that no solution is forthcoming or possible while habit urges us to read toward a thoroughly ambiguous conclusion.

The allegorical/satirical implications are, like everything else in this paradoxical tale, in flux. Aware of the biblical analogy, we may read the tale as an attack on nationalism or rather on a world subdivided against humanity. Still, such a reading must be set against conflicting interpretations: for example, an attack on internationalism or the pretensions of libraries to inclusiveness. Throughout, we are held by the learned whimsy of this tale, its use of our knowledge to undercut its own pretensions or those of the librarian with whose despair we may be in sympathy. In this sense, it could be a heady spoof of knowledge as an end or a commentary on containedness and order as desirable and attainable goals. Finally, it may well reflect the author's own position as a librarian and his near-total blindness.

There is another aspect: the personal history of the librarian and the anguish that grows out of his self-assurance. For this is the story of a survivor asking ultimate questions amid the ruins of a culture, the last priest of a dying religion, a doomed individual. Yet the pathos of his position is constantly undercut by the details of his narration, the contradictions shining through the texture of his presentation. Perhaps the whole problem of attitude is summed up by the concluding footnote, which seems to expose the narrative as an elaborate hypothesis rather than a personal drama and introduces a solitary woman into this perversely male environment:

> Letizia Álvarez de Toledo has observed that this vast Library is useless: rigorously speaking, *a single volume* would be sufficient, a volume of ordinary format, printed in nine or ten point type, containing an infinite number of infinitely thin leaves. (In the early seventeenth century, Cavalieri said that all solid bodies are the superimposition of an infinite number of planes.) The handling of this silky vade mecum would not be convenient: each apparent page would unfold into other analogous ones; the inconceivable middle page would have no reverse.[26]

Granting that the vision that dominates this tale undermines any attempt to *realize* or naturalize it, we note that at every stage in the narrative's development we are alerted to the persistence of mimetic conventions. That is, we are never free to relax into fantasy and enjoy fantastic verisimilitude even in the sense advanced by Tzvetan Todorov. The narrative always and inevitably returns to our own condition and to our own history.

A major preoccupation of the Borgesian narrative is precisely the generation of non- or extrafantastic situations that, while hardly credible, are anchored in the everyday dimension or, at least, in the historical. An example would be the encyclopedic lucubration in "Tlön, Uqbar, Orbis Tertius." There a world imagined by scholars and enshrined in a rare volume in a format identical with that of a well-known encyclopedia seems to be substantiated by a series of ambiguous occurrences of which the appearance of a coin of nonterrestrial weight is the most striking. In effect, the story has swallowed its tail by validating a fantasy that, when confirmed, invalidates the narrative that contains it. Another story, "Funes the Memorious" posits a man whose "photographic" memory results in an incredible mental clutter

[26]Borges, *Labyrinths*, p. 58.

and constitutes in his mind a universe parallel to the one described in "The Library of Babel." Like the other creators of impossible objects, Borges relies heavily on established literary patterns. His books are full of references to detective fiction, spy stories, adventure fiction. He too treats of time-honored themes and conventions with appropriate iconoclasm, and though he uses narrative devices more obviously than the other writers I have discussed, Borges's narratives tend to dispel suspense rather than to develop it. That is, like Roussel, he works against his givens though (more than Roussel) within the conventions he has chosen to mistreat. His detective stories hark back to Poe's ratiocinations but at the same time point up their own gratuitous encyclopedism. His discovery of an unknown world in "Tlön" is evoked in bookish terms alien to adventure narratives. "The Garden of the Forked Paths," with its O'Henry ending and elaborate casuistry, is less a suspense narrative than a cleverly worked-out acrostic or conundrum. Furthermore, like Robbe-Grillet and Roussel, he seems to have only one voice, and that one has limited tonal variation. As a result, our eyes are directed *through* the mode of presentation to the essential strangeness of the presented, from there to forms against which the text reacts.

We turn to Borges for invention in much the same way we turn to Roussel, even though the invention is not gadgetry—or rather even though the story is the ultimate gadget. The real appeal, however, derives from the allegorical temptation, the sense that something lies just beyond our ken in his tales, that there is the possibility of meaning but not the need for elucidation, that the difficult vision justifies a serious reading of what is after all frequently an elaborate and witty spoof, that we can be amused by what reads as often as not like a serious and learned essay on some arcane subject. Ultimately, Borges is writing about writing or about the processes, if not the products, of the mind. In Borges we discover ourselves reading Borges. Without passing judgment on this process or on what generates it, I would suggest that the implied narcissism is also tonic. That is, the reader by playing the game discovers a flaw in the reading self. The project of Sterne has been reinterpreted.

If, like Borges, John Barth makes of his minimal situation in "Night Sea Journey" (the voyage of a sperm cell to the ovum) a carrier for the specifics of human history, he also works out the logic of that situation (unfortunately leaving this reader with a sense of labored cleverness).[27] A first-person voice, unaware of its function and goal, recounts in the present tense its blind quest. Mankind is satirized and its history allegorized, but the focus is less on the message than on the mode of its delivery. As if to compensate for the didactic quality, the texture and rhythm are cleverly modulated. That is, the clear and direct delivery of unbelievable detail (characteristic of impossible objectivity) is replaced by a readily solved puzzle and a baroque surface.

In contrast, a remarkable Swiftian allegory of selfishness and fanaticism plays curiously on the *theme* of impossibility in Robert Coover's "The Brother."[28] Although the boat built in the middle of the midwestern farmland seems absurd, we are soon aware that the biblical parallel is fully applicable, and this modern ark becomes the key to the allegory and hence poignantly possible. Coover's refusal to introduce his Noah except through the doomed brother's first-person narrative and his insistence on the family situation of the brother and on his charitable behavior lead to the ultimate but hardly crucial impossibility. How can the drowned brother have transmitted this tale? To whom are his comments directed? Here again, a possible solution breaks out of the limits of impossible objectivity in a more than metaphorical way. The reader is isolated on the last hilltop along with the brother, waiting with him for the rising tide of a rain that tradition and religion have assigned to God's wrath. Highlighted here is not our doubt, as in other, more obvious examples of the convention, but the rational component of the text and our powers of acceptance. Thus, though Borges's stories might have inspired Coover to invert the biblical myth, the emphasis here is on meaning and interpretation rather than on the text as process and the impossible freight it can carry.

Julio Cortazar's story "Axolotl" is a brilliant adaptation of certain Borgesian procedures. An I-persona describes his/its transformation into an amphibian, opening with this startling statement: "There was a time when I thought a great deal about the axolotls. I went to see them in the aquarium at the Jardin des Plantes and stayed for hours watching them, observing their immobility, their faint movements. Now I

---

[27]In John Barth, *Lost in the Funhouse: Fiction for print, tape, live voice* (New York: Doubleday, 1968).
[28]In Robert Coover, *Pricksongs and Descants* (New York: Plume Books, 1969).

am an axolotl."[29] We go from there to a proof of the change, a step-by-step account of self-hypnosis that may also be, must also be, cannot also be, an actual physiological transformation. The human being on the outside of the glass case housing the clustered salamanderlike creatures moves by stages recorded in, if not justified by, interjections in the voice of the confined presence. In the end he declares the completion of a process of inhatching or personality transferal that leaves the human body outside and perhaps empty without accounting for the production of the text we have read. One obvious consequence is that the text itself is also an impossible object, produced by a voice that cannot be heard, though it has by some fluke been recorded on the page before us. This is a long way from Roussel, with his emotion-free accounts of spectacle/acts rather than dramatic actions, his superobjective rendering of nonexperience or of flattened melodramatic clichés. The pathos and humor are less important, however, than the rejection of credibility and the text's insistence on self-consumption

The practice we have been studying implies the ab-use of the very body of literature upon which it depends for sustenance; yet that same practice frequently sustains a refocusing and refining of literary means. Because Robbe-Grillet uses pornography, mystery fiction, and pulp romance as his narrative cement, he seems to be saying that, if these are unacceptable and inappropriate vehicles, they remain valid as reflections of social perversions and needs. In choosing the library as a universal metaphor and scholarship as a vehicle, Borges is in a sense reacting against them, if not condemning them, as carriers of culture while glorying in his commitment to them. Both writers are liberating fiction from the fictive and the real through a process that can best be seen as cannibalistic. They are *not*, however, "what they eat."

Impossible objectivity regarded as an isolable literary operation may well be a literary alchemy capable of turning base metals into gold, or again, it may be another, the latest, method of refreshing outworn modes, a way to revalidate and personalize story. I would suggest that it is also a tactic that revitalizes and revises the baroque tradition of magic space, a convention that insists upon its power to generate illusions rather than upon the validity of the illusions per se. Like the baroque artifact, it can and frequently does have a hidden social agen-

[29]In Julio Cortazar, *The End of the Game and Other Stories* (New York: Random House, 1977), p. 3.

da. The production of magical effects is after all a power function, a celebration of control over words and, through them, the space they convey. Such a procedure is far from innocent in that it uses language to dispel the power frequently exploited by users of words to manipulate responses. On the other hand, by repeatedly reasserting (and then denying) its own capacity to induce illusion, it reasserts the force of fiction or myth as a social tool.

Roussel's proto-surrealist use of languaged objects or word-things made up of improbable conjunctions produces a stark personal statement composed of masks. That is, the author, by means of his "aleatory" procedures, or rather by means of his deliberate attempts to rationalize or order chance items into a narrative structure, produces a text that could be an accurate profile of his own troubled spirit. Extending and blending procedures used by his exemplary predecessors, refusing to treat the page as three-dimensional space except in his vignettes and descriptions, he produces an elaborately doubled vision, at once literary and antiliterary. Dispelling illusion, evoking allusion, and invoking and mocking conventional responses, his texts are as near to the regal toys of the sixteenth and seventeenth centuries as literature can take us. They are in fact verbal pageants, ceremonies designed to promote and obliterate life, putting signs in its place, obliging the reader to recognize the sort of self-loss surreptitiously elicited by fictions of all sorts. Roussel (and by extension the reader) plays at death and rehearses suicide by exercising absolute power over life, a power that resides in artfully manipulated signs, in the ultimate cynicism of repeatedly asserting what is repeatedly denied. There is, consequently, danger in the reader's participation, though that danger will not be readily available. In revealing the literary artifact, Roussel undermines artifice, defuses the daydream, and purges to some degree the need for convenient lies. With his writing, story and illusion die.

Each in his own way, Mathews and Robbe-Grillet testify to that death and celebrate it. Mathews finds convenient and engaging plot molds in which to cast his heterogeneous subject matter, produces devilish mechanical contrivances capable of echoing the crotchets of the age but dedicated to the craft of elaborating verbal surfaces convincing in their manipulative potential. That is, his novels, far more than those of Roussel and Robbe-Grillet, elicit suspense and pleasure, giving the adventure novel a new lease on life. Though humor is a constant in most of these texts, Mathews's wit is easier, less equivocal, more engaging, frequently dovetailing with the absurdity of his situations so that impossible objectivity becomes a locus as well as a pretext for laughter.

Though Robbe-Grillet prides himself on the quality of his (superdry) wit, the outstanding quality of his books is their patterning or orchestration. Once aware of the basic procedures by which half-animate things turn into other things, melting their identities, the reader is engaged by the rhythm of repetition and change, by the way a topos reappears with a difference as it follows its narrative trajectory, impinged upon en route by other topoi in a somewhat more accessible rendering of the Joycean kaleidoscope.[30] Far more than the texts of either Roussel or Mathews, Robbe-Grillet's are the ultimate impossible objects in a universe of nonfunctional relationships and infinitely plastic forms, a universe of masked identities reminiscent of the extravaganzas of the Belgian painter James Ensor. The result is appropriately dreamlike but in the cool, distanced way that characterizes the work of Paul Devaux, another Belgian, whose work inspired parts of *Topography of a Phantom City*. Robbe-Grillet appears to be committed to the unreality of even the most trivial languaged experience, the randomness of the daily, and the rationalization through calibrated forms of chance encounters. One senses that his is a universe of found objects (à la Rauschenberg), designed to mediate between fear and desire.

Borges raises different specters. The verbal universe in his short narratives is more reminiscent of Kafka in its single-mindedness. Like Cortazar, Coover, and Barth, he is in each instance elaborating the narrative potential of a simple improbability. To this degree his reader is more rigorously and conventionally engaged by narrative. Development, being exclusively and straightforwardly diachronic, becomes paradoxically more, not less, absurd and impossible, less spectacular, deceptively allegorical. The metaphor wells up toward the universal before subsiding into the learned footnote, leaving an aftertaste of library ink and blotting paper. More than any of the other writers, Borges is writing into books out of words. By positing a universe of signs resigning themselves to the absence of signification, his method permits him to elope with aspects of the world, converting them into language, imprisoning them on the page from which there is no refer-

---

[30]Joyce uses the term "collideorscape" to describe his dream universe. See *Finnegans Wake* (New York: Viking, 1939), p. 143.

ential out. Belief, even in the system of narrative discourse, is continually and deliberately undermined precisely by and within the assertive mode of the narration.

Just how malleable and oblique impossible objectivity can be is illustrated by William Gass's *Willie Masters' Lonesome Wife*, a polymorphic concrete-narrative/presentation replete in typographical and other visual effects. That "novel" can stand in for a whole range of extravagance. There is a family resemblance between it and Arno Schmidt's typographical extravaganza *Zettles Traum*, a dream of pages, deriving from *A Midsummer Night's* (or Bottom's) *Dream* as seen through the crazed glass of Joyce's *Wake* in relation to Poe Freudanalyzed; Maurice Roche's visual novels with their clever avoidance of character, plot, situation, and apparent coherence and their foregrounded typographical, pictorial, and spatial effects; and the fractured intertextual romance of Julián Ríos's *Larva*, in which characters share the stage with a comic strip carnival of literary and cultural allusions. Such texts are properly viewed as post-Wakean manifestations in which so many devices are developed that the play of impossibility falls out of focus, being reduced to the status of a given that has been digested by the universalizing vision capable of incorporating any and all difference.

Gass's book resembles a powerful and seemingly indiscriminate intertextual machine that uses proliferating graphemes to rewrite Molly Bloom for our time in an overpunctuated, mock-confessional mode. In contradistinction to Joyce's show-stopping woman, this *Weib* is denied an identity, a surround. Her monologue is a thing in itself. Consequently, her voice, together with the situation suggested by her choice of topics, is just as poignant and pungent whether we read her as the disembodied muse (a female "unnamable"), as the neglected suburban housewife, or as a projection of male fancy. The choice of techniques, the mix of styles, and the wildly obscene subject matter are just as funny. We find the impossible component in a visual extravagance used to buttress the verbal excess of the text but also in the ambiguities surrounding the identity of the voice. Not only is this "persona" no simple discontented housewife whiling away the dreary hours with elaborate fantasies like the inset and footnoted burlesque skit. She/he/it seems to have no settled identity outside the language that frames it/him/her. The text, while dealing with all manner of kinky sexuality, is full of inappropriately elevated references. Its generating presence, a version of the Joycean arranging presence, though explicitly identified with the speaker, cavalierly controls a wealth of typographical and other visual effects: photographs, notes, asterisks, stains, and typefaces. In short, the textual events and, by extension, the narrative itself defy appeals to possibility and engage the reader directly in the substance and potential of the page.

Perhaps Gass's comic text can pass for a manifestation of a (complex and indeterminate) presence experiencing and expressing credible anxiety, (self-)loathing, and rage. In this sense it is closer to Beckett and Kafka than to the cool and distanced near-allegories of Borges or the technically splendid fanciful lucubrations of Nabokov. Such affinities are less important, however, than Gass's highly original method of drawing strength from the constant reassertion of fundamentally indeterminate and irrecoverable versions of reality. In such texts the dynamic philosophical potential of textual impossiblity is best perceived, appearing as a manifestation of the most elemental aspects of presentation.

Without recourse to transparent farce, or the carnivalesque, but still, like the Rabelais evoked by Renaissance scholar Terence Cave in his extremely useful description of the "fallen text," this family of convention-violating fictions may be indulging in "deviation, evasion, the blocking of the reader's desire for coherence" in order to assert their "'authenticity' and the proliferation of [their] significance."[31] Perhaps, in a period when any nonironic statement is suspect but fiction is still readily accepted as fact, the impulse to derealize is tonic. For some, it can serve as an assertion through refusal, one that enables writing to "go on," focusing the text as a mode of "living." For others, it provides a stage for the reenactment of other discourses, borrowed flames, so to speak, that donate their residual vitality to the self-denying text. When such narratives succeed, they do so in good measure by taking what they refuse to give, drawing from the reader that to which they allude and which they subvert in the way of, inter alia, narrative convention and objective reality.

[31]Terence Cave, *The Cornucopian Text* (Oxford: Oxford University Press, 1979), pp. 100–101.

3

Nodality, or Plot Displaced

It seems obvious that an increasing number of books advertising themselves as novels refuse to tell tales. To the extent that such books retain vestiges of plot and narrative discourse, both are attenuated and/or sublimated. Questions of plot, character, setting, and point of view, if not of narrative tension, are displaced by the question of organization, and *that* is most often *nodal*. Such texts are frequently informed by systems of interrelated passages (scenes, images, visions, treatments of topics, and so forth) that do not contribute to a coherent and generalized narrative development but rather break the narrative surface, standing out against or being readily isolable before blending into the verbal context. The passages in question can best be regarded as nodes or clusters of signifiers in "open works."[1]

In their nature and function, fictional nodes will vary from text to text, but generally a major node is a complex, foregrounded moment capable of subdivision and subject to expansion. Typically a fully developed node will find enriching echoes in other parts of the book. While such echoes need resolve nothing on the level of plot or argument, they gradually contribute to the formation of nodal systems. Nodes tend to be fundamental statements of the textual predicament; so we may expect aspects of a given nodal system to overlap with those

[1]See Umberto Eco's discussion in "La poétique de l'oeuvre ouverte" in *L'Oeuvre ouverte* (Paris: Seuil, 1965), pp. 15–36.

of others, contributing to networks that gradually reveal their significance and simultaneously give the reader a sense of the text's articulation, its essential structure. The latter, while displacing linear discourse by complementing other structuring systems, ultimately
reassures by imposing, through a device we may call rhyming or
significant redundancy, a more profound, though generally vibrant,
order. Thus a text that defies conventions will evolve its own articulation and will reveal unexpected but palpable coherence.

Since nodality is most obvious in "difficult," "hermetic," and "revolutionary" texts, structures that tend to be sui generis, it is subject to
radically distinct applications. There are traces of it in writers as
different as Guillermo Cabrera Infante, Juan Goytisolo, Samuel Beckett, and Alain Robbe-Grillet. It informs Virginia Woolf's *The Waves*,
Philippe Sollers's *H*, and Maurice Roche's *Compact*. From both a
historical and a formal perspective, however, our best example may be
Joyce's enormous and amorphous-seeming conundrum, *Finnegans
Wake*.[2]

Evidence from Joyce's letters and in the manuscripts suggests that,
from the start—that is, even before the elaboration of the pun-filled
night language—the *Wake* was to be organized around a group of
seminal minicontexts. These received their initial and clearest formulation in a series of narrative vignettes dealing with different aspects
of the Irish condition, character, and history. By extension they dealt
with the generalized human condition through history. Written for the
most part before he began working on his chapters, these brief parodic
interludes constitute the germ of the book's preliminary *and* final organization. They are interrelated, however, mainly by their broad pas-
tiche/parody tactic and their Irish subject matter. In fact, Joyce took
pains to set most of them off one from the other, ultimately placing
them strategically at the beginning, middle and end of his book, thus
making gentle mock of Aristotle.

Though by no means the only prime nodes in the completed work,
these pastiches are sufficiently foregrounded to constitute significant
points of reference for a study of the Wakean nodal macrosystem and
of nodal structures in general. Typically, they are brief, well-defined

---

[2]What follows is a brief, updated, and refocused summary of my argument in
"Nodality and the Infra-Structure of *Finnegans Wake*," *James Joyce Quarterly* 16 (Fall
1978-Winter 1979), 135–50.

units, each with a consistent focus and rhetoric and a logical narrative line to which isolable motifs and refrains contribute. Their narrative content invites elaboration and suggests associations, but such elaboration is never accomplished in the immediate context or in anything resembling a plotted line. Instead, strategically located within the larger chapter structure, other noncontiguous passages extend and complicate the basic sketch in a manner reminiscent of the development of a musical theme.[3]

An example of the procedure would be the parodic treatment of the seduction scene from Wagner's *Tristan and Isolde*, the second passage written in 1923 for the embryonic *Wake*. This sketch now falls at the center of the book (Book II, chapter 4). It introduces not only the lovers but the aging Mark, evoking the themes of guilty love and betrayal, of youth taking the place of age, of the connection between the Gaelic nations, of the poet versus the athlete, of voyeurism, and so on. A typical secondary node is the somewhat less transparent treatment of the lovers' tryst in the palace garden, a voyeuristic passage using sexual geography to focus the betrayal theme while introducing the message/writing/letter motifs (Book III chapter 4). Arrangements and proportions will vary, but in this case the major node is buttressed by three such secondary nodes falling near the beginning, middle, and end of the book, with the central item a good distance from the seduction passage. There is also a tertiary level, consisting of briefer, less obvious, but far more numerous allusions placed strategically throughout the book. Finally, a fourth level of extremely short and quite oblique allusions is woven into just about every part of the verbal fabric.[4] Since each succeeding level is at once less marked and more broadly based, we may see the typical nodal system as hierarchized in the shape of a triangle.

Beyond the nodal microsystem centered around a single textual moment, there is the macrosystem, which would include a number of

[3]See the position developed by Clive Hart in the second half of *Structure and Motif in "Finnegans Wake"* (Evanston, Ill.: Northwestern University Press, 1962). His system roughly reverses my emphasis, moving from the fragment toward the cluster but emphasizing the randomness of the latter rather than the sort of system I claim underlay Joyce's procedures from the very start.

[4]The reader interested in a full or at least compendious listing of the allusions to Tristan and Isolde should consult both Adaline Glasheen's account in her *Third Census of Finnegans Wake* (Berkeley: University of California Press, 1977) and my attempt at a fuller thematic listing in *A Wake Newslitter*, n.s. 11 (1965), 3–14.

parallel or otherwise interrelated nodal systems generated by passages in analogous forms. The six[5] sketches written early in 1923 combine in such a system to present with considerable clarity and concision the basic symbols and essential myth of the *Wake:* the story of the rise, fall, and resurrection of the hero and the celebration of his family as generative of the known world and its history. The system of reinforcing passages that join these various moments becomes immensely complex as allusions develop, proliferate, and interrelate to form a structural grid, or better, an internalized three-dimensional scaffolding, part of an infrastructure that is virtually unrecuperable but equally inescapable and dynamic.

Given Joyce's fascination with systems and the fact that the more rules he broke, the more he felt obliged to make, we may be sure that this is only the tip of the *Wake*'s infrastructure. In fact, there are all manner of nodal systems, both micro and macro.[6] The latter include a group of three exchanges in dialogue form, located respectively in chapter I.1 ("Jute and Mutt," on pp. 16–18), chapter II.3 ("Butt and Taff," on pp. 338–355), and Book IV ("Mutta and Juva," on pp. 609–10). Here too we find the beginning/middle/end distribution, but this time we cannot give each passage equal weight. Whereas the first and last deal respectively and briefly with prehistory and the origins of Irish Christianity, the long and extremely elaborate central dialogue with its stage directions and scenic interludes or intermezzi treats an historical moment, the Crimean War. To this clearly major node the others are secondary. It reenacts the death of the archetypal father and leader (in this instance the wild goose Russian General ambushed by a wild goose British tommy). Beyond this schematic two-level develop-

---

[5]Seven, if we include the "Mamalujo," or "Four Old Men" passage, which was combined with the "Tristan" to make up chapter 2.4. It is tempting, however, to regard that extended and fluid historical pastiche as the first chapter written for the *Wake* and the setting for the "Tristan" skit.

[6]In "Nodality and the Infra-Structure of *Finnegans Wake*," I have made a tentative list of eight nodal categories for the *Wake*. These are (1) the early sketches; (2) passages devoted to character exposition; (3) symmetrical passages like the fables; (4) expositions of major themes; (5) developments of aspects of the landscape; (6) allusive parallels that are literary, historical, and religious; (7) key rhythms and rhythmic clusters; and (8) foreign-language word clusters (p. 148). In this, perhaps the most complex nodally organized text to date, there are of course other categories, and there is also an immense amount of overlapping and intermingling. The only text approximating the *Wake*'s use of this technique is Pound's *Cantos*, about which I shall have more to say in connection with paratactics.

ment we may expect to find the system developing in the usual manner.

There is an adjunct to this system of dialogues which while it focuses on the theme of succession or generation, is more obviously an expression of the classic brother battle between the Cain and Abel twins Joyce calls Shem the pen (the artist or speaker of the Word) and Shaun the post (the publicist or propagator of the Word). Here the prime node is the elaborate geometric parable of sexuality from chapter II.2 published separately as "The Muddest Thick That Ever Was Heard Dump" (pp. 293–306). The "Muddest Thick" is a set piece in the voice of Shem around which one of the *Wake*'s longest chapters was eventually built. Falling near the center of the book, it is preceded and followed on a secondary level by two precisely parallel parables after Aesop told by Shaun in I.6 ("The Mookse and the Gripes," pp. 152–59) and III.1 ("The Ondt and the Gracehoper," pp. 414–19). Here again the passages are equilibrated and clearly set off from their surroundings. This system is more complicated than the previous one, however, since each of its elements has generated a full-blown system of its own even though the fables function as secondary nodes to Shem's demonstration. Furthermore, in terms of their placement, these two groups of nodal passages mesh suggestively to form a larger macrosystem for which the following is a crude preliminary diagram.

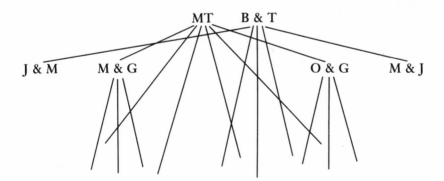

Such a diagram cannot begin to approximate the relationship being established by these two systems, which will inevitably and repeatedly intersect at lower levels.

A map or model of the *Wake*'s complete nodal system, if one were possible, would show smaller systems branching off from the larger ones at different levels, resembling a monstrous genealogical chart. It would reflect the growth of the text from its own particulars and would reinforce our awareness or intuitions of that autogenesis.[7] The project of the *Wake*, one that occasioned an unprecedented proliferation of topics in a wide variety of styles and forms, was to hold a polished and faceted mirror up to the totality of human experience, to give the impression, that is, of an all-inclusive and dynamic verbal universe, a re-creation. Under the circumstances, the mere idea of a conventionally plotted narrative is absurd and the elaboration of the sort of conceptual framework we have been discussing, inevitable. Though there is a clear chapter structure and though we may note a variety of developments within each chapter and in the book as a whole, we turn for reassurance to the systems of repetitions, and they finally make possible our reading. By virtue of their insistent presence, they beg to be analyzed for their ideational content, a demand that in turn imposes form on the text as a total formulation.

At this point, we must pause; for it goes without saying that much, if not all, of the fiction written since the seventeenth century and much that was produced earlier relies heavily on repetition to make its points and often to bring out underlying themes. Thus we find in novel after novel systems of images, actions, or characters functioning as carriers of meaning beyond their obvious contributions to the exigencies of narrative. Such motifs are brought to our attention not only by means of repetition but also by some jarring element in the context, some ungrammaticality. Thus an analysis of Joyce's *Portrait* for its use of imagery derived from the Daedalus and Icarus myth discloses not only a family of topoi but a careful distribution and underscoring of their appearances, together with a tendency to group them so as to suggest a development.[8] A study of the imagery in Flaubert's *Sentimental Educa-tion* reveals among other things a consistent use of flowing or watery images to convey the aimlessness of the age. In short, some sort of nodal underpinning is available even in more conventional texts.

What, then, is so remarkable about the fact that so many recent and contemporary novels are organized nodally? Precisely because they are deprived of the usual narrative focus, which can in other texts carry

---

[7]For a fuller discussion of this topic, see Chapter 4.
[8]See David Hayman, "Daedalian Imagery in *A Portrait of the Artist as a Young Man*," in *Hereditas*, ed. Frederic Will (Austin: University of Texas Press, 1964), pp. 31–54.

the occulted systems of symbolic significance, these novels seem on the one hand hostile to the idea of such a structure and on the other curiously hospitable. That is, they seem to present an opaque surface before they reveal satisfying relationships, unstillable but palpable patternings or internal rhythms—materials that, if noted in more conventional settings, would be left for a later rereading are attended to during the first reading as prime means of organizing the reader's response. This statement is true even if we are not fully aware of the significance to be assigned to them or of the extent and nature of the patterns we have experienced. Thus texts informed by nodality are singular because they reverse the reading procedure, featuring, as do all "transparent bodies," attributes that other texts systematically occult.

It seems unlikely that such procedures have no antecedents, and indeed we can point to a far more open and evident nodality in the *Essays* of Montaigne (and the writings of essayists and diarists in general). There the themes and preoccupations of a life give form and coherence and rhythm to disjunction. Threading their way through the volume are not only major motifs but also minor ones, shaping themselves into nodes and nodal systems in much the same way that they do in *Finnegans Wake* but with the difference that their logic and necessity are immediately grasped. There is nothing particularly surprising in this or in the fact that poetry and poetic cycles often function in a similar fashion (an extreme instance is Pound's *Cantos*) or that the strategy is available in symphonic music. It is normal to experience the musical, even on a primary level, as a web of relationships. We approach such texts, however, with expectations different from those elicited by narrative, fictional or not.

We might say that, with the diminution of narrative interest and action in novels written at the end of the nineteenth century, the movement toward a dominant nodal structure was virtually inevitable. In the quasi-lyrical fictions of Gabriele d'Annunzio, in Joyce's *Portrait*, and in the prose of Rainer Maria Rilke, it is the musical/lyrical expectations that are satisfied (and, in d'Annunzio's case, sometimes glutted).

Rilke's startling *Notebooks of Malte Laurids Brigge*, perhaps the supreme symbolist narrative, is an extreme case, being readable mainly in terms of its sharply etched nodal configurations. The subtly articulated thematic scaffolding of this novel is generated entirely by the interrelated themes of death, love, and identity. Each of these finds its principal statement through narrative vignettes that accumulate to constitute a nodal system similar in its nature to a development but distributed throughout Malte's wide-ranging diary entries within the permanent present of his developing self-awareness. Thus death—the death that Malte claims inhabits us throughout our lives—is staged early on as the monumental dying of his grandfather, Chancellor Brigge,[9] but it has been established earlier in graphic treatments of Paris hospitals, and it returns repeatedly under a variety of guises in less expansive passages that dovetail with other, related systems. Among these, the most impressive may be the mask/face/identity system that is first emphatically stated in the powerful description of the inner wall of a demolished (dead) building: "One saw its inner side. One saw at the different stories the walls of rooms to which paper still clung, and here and there the join of floor or ceiling. Beside these room-walls there still remained, along the whole length of the wall, a dirty-white area, and through this crept in unspeakably disgusting motions, worm-soft and as if digesting, the open, rust-spotted channel of the water-closet pipe."[10] This passage constitutes one of the twin posts of the system. It finds its replique in the extended treatment of historical identities, particularly that of the last great duke of Burgundy, Charles the Bold. Like the building, Charles has lost, to wolves and ice in the wake of the battle of Nancy, a face that has served to mask his inner turmoil.[11] These major nodes, unforgettable epiphanous moments, so radically different in their nature, are buttressed by others of equal or lesser magnitude: a child's traumatic loss of self to a costume, the vision of a poor woman in an attitude of despair, and so on. The novel ends with a lyrically reconceived version of the Prodigal Son, a figure for Malte who rejects love for loving, perversely, to gain control of his own identity and of his death. In short, a narrative without a clearly delineated plot is coordinated by quasi-symphonic motival developments organized by the reading mind into sequences and patterns of considerable vitality.

Complicated as it is by subthemes and overtones, the nodal procedure outlined above is perhaps natural to the lyric sensibility, one

[9]Rainer Maria Rilke, *The Notebooks of Malte Laurids Brigge*, trans. M. D. Herter Norton (New York: Putnam, 1958), pp. 17–23.
[10]Ibid., p. 47.
[11]Ibid., pp. 162–69.

accustomed to acts of avoidance. It is not surprising, therefore, that we find further examples in novels with distinct lyrical qualities, such as Proust's *Remembrance of Things Past*, Woolf's *The Waves*, Lezamo Lima's *Paradizo*, and Djuna Barnes's *Nightwood*. In such novels, narrative, though present and occasionally foregrounded, is generally subordinated to the delineation of mood and reaction. Character is usually filtered through metaphor-rich language, and nuanced metaphor acquires some of the qualities of action. Though in each instance the tactic is tailored to the needs of the novel, we might say that generic imperatives operative here enable us to accept nodal presentation as right and natural within the confines of an early modernism enthralled by the expressive and decorative potential of poetic discourse.

This statement is less true for a growing number of works in which the lyrical impulse has been sublimated or deliberately coarsened, from Pound's *Cantos* and Joyce's *Wake* to positively aberrant novels like Céline's explosive monologue of despair and rage, *Féerie*, Juan Goytisolo's hallucinatory *Count Julian*, Witold Gombrowicz's catalogue-ridden *Cosmos*, and Philippe Sollers's chronicle of post–May 1968, *H*. Differing as radically as they do, these novels display an exemplary range of adaptations of a device that the authors did not know they were using.

In *Finnegans Wake* and *The Cantos*, nodality might be said to account for the entire surface of the text, its wordness. Elsewhere, nodal strategies make possible a semblance of action and even a species of interstitial narrative development. Such is already the case in *Malte*, where the emphasis is on highly mediated themes rendered in a heightened language rich in metaphoric potential. Some novels, however, turn to nodal structuration as a way of articulating varieties of alternative plots. Thus one might say that the narrative content of *Count Julian* is almost more ample than allusive, a tapestry of events. Goytisolo's central subversion, one that William Burroughs carries even further, is in his decision to use a day in the life of his protagonist as a traveling frame (one subject to recall) for a foregrounded hallucinatory existence. The result is a confusion between the present of the I-narrator, an embittered exile from Franco's Spain, and his waking dream of adhesion to the reanimated historico-mythical count who betrayed Spain to the conquering Moors. As a result of this strategy, the reader is obliged to join forces with a speaker capable, on the one hand, of merging with the Islamic horde and, on the other, of becoming the Count's victim/lover, Alvarito, the innocent representative of Spanish boyhood. That is, the protagonist "punishes" himself and Spain in the person of his own childhood and heritage. Goytisolo has found nodally based ways to make such interpenetrations and paradoxes available to us, generating a new sort of simultaneity by superimposing temporal events, bringing into play through the written record all aspects of the (Spanish) historical and cultural experience.

Count Julian opens with a deceptively clear delineation of time and place. It is morning in Tangiers, and we follow the exile on his daily rounds, picking up and hoarding impressions. This overture is designed, as are those of *A Portrait of the Artist, Sentimental Education, Anna Karenina*, and even *Women in Love*, to provide us with an image bank for the later pages. But whereas in more traditional texts the images are integrated, woven into the narrative fabric from which they must later be recovered, *Count Julian* quickly turns the details of its morning into the substance of an antinarrative development. Unlike the *Wake*, which uses its opening chapter to introduce ideas seriatim and diffuses historical time and geographic space, generalizing the few specifics it provides, Goytisolo's opening insists on presenting minute and seemingly useless details in the manner of Joyce's "Calypso" chapter in *Ulysses* or the opening pages of Robbe-Grillet's *Le Voyeur*.

Mingled with such details are hints of an uncanny, neosurrealistic, mock-Gothic development: the protagonist's visit to the library with a cargo of dead insects to be crushed between the pages of Spanish classics, his narrative distortions verging on hallucinations, his repeated allusions to the "first pipe of kef."[12] Once planted and strung together within the account of the stroll through Tangiers, the motifs are subjected to distortion, twisted to fit the nightmare dream of "donjuanesque plans for invasion: a grandiose act of treason, the collapse of entire centuries: the cruel army of Tariq, the destruction of Spain."[13]

If these motifs are drawn from the real world, that world provides no frame for their organization and digestion. Meaning must be generated not from observation but from hallucinations based, like those in Joyce's "Circe," on images that have had time to ripen and interact as components of a mental compost.

---

[12]Juan Goytisolo, *Count Julian*, trans. Helen R. Lane (New York: Viking, 1974), p. 30.

[13]Ibid., p. 39.

What emerges is neither a credible account of the exile's day nor a development of the individual psyche of a frustrated dreamer. Through his tenuous and highly charged second-person, present-tense narrative, an allegory of the Spanish psyche drawing upon his daydreams (or dope-induced visions), our embittered persona weaves about his experience a cocoon of significance from which a beautiful Spanish future fails to emerge. It is the shape of that allegory that interests us, its fundamental antinarrativity, its nodality.

Toward the end of his overture, the narrator discovers in his real context the seeds of fairy tale and myth and the rationale for his labyrinthine discourse in the prospect of

> losing yourself in the maze of the Medina: tracing with your footsteps as you walk (rather than dropping little pebbles or crumbs to make your way back) a complicated pattern that no one (not even you yourself) will ever be able to interpret: finally splitting yourself in two to tail yourself better, as though you were another person: a guardian angel, a jealous lover, a private eye: knowing that the labyrinth lies within: that you are the labyrinth: the famous minotaur, the edible martyr: at once executioner and victim.[14]

If this curious statement underscores and rationalizes the fantastic in *Count Julian*, it also illustrates the freshness of Goytisolo's use of nodality. Emphasizing the labyrinthine pattern, parenthetically mocking it, he hands control over to us, his readers. We too are both Theseus and Minotaur, charged with reading and generating the signs that will extricate us from the verbo-historical trap and ensnare us in it. In effect, we all become Spaniards living in the shadow of our convoluted history, engaged by the levels of our Moorish, Hebraic, and Hispanic identity. Toward the end of the novel, when we discover the monster, are exposed to him, and become his victim, we inevitably discover as well our radically split and unstable sympathies.

The interlocking passages that constitute the novel's nodal structure are ideally suited to accomplish this entrapment or at least to make it viable. Through them and out of our awareness of repeated details to which we cling for support and look for direction, an elaborate web is constructed. The procedure is a risky one, for by boldly stating his

[14]Ibid., p. 40.

central metaphor and later by providing us with the list of "posthumous and unwitting" collaborators, Goytisolo seems to test the seriousness of his own enterprise in ways that even the farcical mode of *Finnegans Wake* does not. In pointing up its principal of organization and supplying its roots, the book also underscores its textual substance, which may be identified with that of the reader, who has, by virtue of this distancing procedure, ample opportunity to escape from the temptations and terrors but who, unlike Carroll's Alice, does not declare the whole thing to be a house of cards.

What, then, is the nature of the fragile and deceptive nodal web that we, together with our Ariadne/Theseus/minotaur, weave and follow? Typically each thread begins with a casual reference, echoed later in a developed description that itself tends to generate fresh nodal motifs. Thus after we note references to homosexuals and homosexual love on pp. 19 and 32, we find on p. 41 a passage introducing the entrapment/seduction theme along with an elaborate penis/serpent motif:

> middle-class Arabs in djellabas and slippers, Jewish craftsmen, delivery boys, fishermen, tourists: and now and again a restless Nordic type who sticks his head into the dark shadows of one cafe after another for a quick look around, fluttering like a butterfly from one terrace to the next with a fleeting, telltale wiggle of his ass: a siren on the lookout for tail, an elegant serpent with a deadly sting: the arty type, with dark circles under his eyes and thick silky eyelashes. . . . a Livingstone for whom Africa holds no secrets: a pilgrim and a frequent visitor, perhaps, of those homely but very convenient little facilities that Lenin generously dreamed of lining in solid gold: once world revolution had triumphed and man had been freed of his petty selfishness.[15]

Thus the text serves clear notice of the homosexual-seduction nodal development that derives from the repeated references to the young Nordic, a presence that shapes the narrative moment. The dominant motif, however, is clearly alloyed by allusions contributing to other nodal systems: subsidiary motifs such as the grotto/toilet complex, the theme of innocence and corruption, the Jew/Arab/Spaniard conjunction, and the theme of the boy/girl or androgeny.

[15]Ibid., pp. 41–42.

The grotto/toilet allusion is clarified in the following passage, which concretizes the central theme by describing graffiti:

> with your mind still reeling from the shock you push the little door open and enter the shadowy corridor, lit only by a dim, niggardly skylight: a few yards from the nearly pitchblack grotto intended for the relief of ordinary, elementary physiological needs: not lined with gold: prerevolutionary, practically invisible, though there is a certain sign pointing to its existence: the suspect damp trail trickling down the entire length of the corridor that has peeled the paint off the filthy walls covered with graffiti: penises with wings, round male spheres, a whole phallic artillery: fortresses that have suddenly surrendered, warm, hospitable tabernacles: accompanied by the inevitable polyglot glosses: cries of anguish or of passionate desire emitted by wretched, suffering human beings in the solitude of the act, resembling curious messages in bottles entrusted to the capricious flow of the tides.[16]

What emerges, along with the amplification and activation through lust of the homosexual love motif, is a latent association of the otherwise feminine grotto (see pp. 18 and 32) with the (male) anus. In addition we find the evocation of oozing/disgust that is elsewhere associated with the Spanish landscape (p. 24). As the passage evolves, further heterosexual imagery is introduced.

In a more conventional novel, such images and events would contribute to a conflict and to resolution on the level of narrative. Joyce upset that tendency in *Ulysses* when, taking experience from the lucid day, he reshuffled it and recombined it to form the hallucinated fresco of the subconscious that is "Circe." Goytisolo, consciously or not, goes beyond *Ulysses* to make the principal action of his book the exposure of the intracranial labyrinth. In the process he puts severe limitations on the amount of daytime, or "rational," experience he presents. He has also moved in the direction of Céline's *Féerie* by inserting foreshadowings of the hallucinated state into the seemingly normative sequence, turning his early pages into something resembling a collage cityscape capable of combining any number of disparate elements. True, it is a motivated collage, all of whose elements can be located in some "real" space, but their conjunction leaves us with a sense of the anomalous.

[16]Ibid., pp. 45–46.

This juxtaposition of images, frequently under the aegis of a dominant motif, typifies Goytisolo's brand of nodality.

We could easily trace the homosexual system through the book, noting various levels, as we did for Joyce. In the process we would discover that Goytisolo does not have Joyce's mania for balance and that his novel does not demand the relatively rigid categories needed to give stability to the Wakean flux of words. Furthermore, given its carefully limited subjective universe, Goytisolo's novelistic vision is less dependent for its coherence on a fully elaborated, if virtually unfathomable, nodal infrastructure. Still, like Joyce, he makes his best-developed and hence most obvious moments function as prime nodes or secondary nodal points and tends to distribute them throughout the book where they overshadow the more conventional instances of narrative resolution.

In this text, nothing is resolved on the level of objective experience. Approaches to resolution occur only within the internal and nodal labyrinth.[17] Climaxes (many of which are sexual) are achieved not so much as a result of conventional causality as of the logic of wish fulfillment or dream, a whimsical recombination of themes and details to attain a new and hallucinatory truth. Thus a major node for the grotto system is the monstrous Boschian visit to the genital cave, Spain's virginal cavity, a bit of sexual geography presented as an attraction to the busload of American tourists first introduced in Tangiers. The passage culminates in a bloody orgy as the Arabs attack with their serpents and the tourists penetrate "the vulva and the hymen, the vagina and the / uterus, the ovaries and the Fallopian tubes / the meandering subterranean galleries of an empty cave / the Cunt, the Cunt, the Cunt!"[18] The image of the serpent is fully developed in the book's final section, which culminates in the rape of Spanish youth by the lurking conqueror.

Goytisolo's use of nodality may best be seen in the light of his use of (a muted) paratactics. Together these two devices control and shape the narrative, contributing heavily to its contemporary aura. A concatenation of juxtaposed particulars in seemingly random order, or rather in the random order of the urban experience, constitutes the

---

[17]For a parallel we should probably go to a drug-epic like William Burroughs's *Naked Lunch.*

[18]Goytisolo, *Count Julian,* p. 147.

main thread of the narrative proper, an action that often reads like a travelogue and leads only to the end of another unsatisfactory day. Onto this sequence of random particulars the author skillfully grafts an equally discontinuous structure of interlocking nodal systems. The latter constitutes the dominant vision, cannibalizing the objective narrative and vitalizing its substance.

From the start the nodal structure of *Count Julian* is a product of *glissage* or infiltration, a distortion of the givens. Yet only in terms of that procedure can anything be said to occur in a text where the transparent daydream usurps the opaque narrative functions. But that daydream, since it is manifestly disjunct and arbitrary in its relationship to what surrounds it, highlights nodality by setting off its components. Furthermore, as in *Finnegans Wake*, it is within the nodal framework that we find the most coherent narrative sequences (as opposed to descriptive passages), the dramatic and absurd situations that rivet our attention. Finally, the "story" of the day makes possible and motivates the nodal systems, with their imposition of fancy on the "real," but the nodal structure justifies the book by elaborating upon the fear/guilt/desire syndrome that in Goytisolo's view characterizes the Spanish psyche not only under Franco but in the centuries since the expulsion or sublimation of Moors and Jews.

What may be most original about *Count Julian*'s method is the process by which infiltration is accomplished, a procedure we may contrast to that used by Joyce in preparing the reader for "Circe." In the latter, the "real," as opposed to the "psychic" or "subconscious" experience, is not subjected to gross distortions, even though the narrative procedures systematically and progressively alter the reader's view of the objective world. In a manner reminiscent of Malcolm Lowry's use of hallucinations in *Under the Volcano*, the protagonist of *Count Julian* is, almost from the start, a prey to his imagination and desire, experiencing (in his/our second person identity) increasingly vivid hallucinations.[19] Unlike Lowry's drunken protagonist, however, *Count Julian*'s "you" generally has a rational basis for his baroque improvements on experience. In the following passage, we have no difficulty moving through the metaphor from weaver to spider to spiderweaver. The

[19]One of the more startling innovations of this novel is the continuous use of the word "you," which implicates the reader (and all of Spain) in the activities of the narrative persona.

imaginative process by which the nodal structure is validated is as
simple as it is subtle and disturbing:

> and the place has the peaceful air of craftsmen working silently and
> diligently: little apprentices holding the loom upright in the middle of the
> street, master weavers tirelessly threading the shuttle back and forth in
> their tiny little shops, like patient, busy arachnida: terrestrial arthopods,
> with chitinous shells, rather undeveloped cephalothoraxes, and huge,
> bulging abdomens: two spiracles and six nipplelike processes with min-
> ute orifices which extrude the threads for the trap: carefully and swiftly
> weaving a treacherous web: dry silk for the center and the radiuses,
> sticky wet silk for the spiral: never moving from their secret hiding places
> at the edge, but immediately aware of what is happening all along the
> web, thanks to a slender supersensitive warning-thread: the moment the
> apprentices touch the loom they are caught fast and their every effort to
> free themselves is useless: the weaver. . . . delicately inserts his poi-
> sonous chelicerae in his little victim's body, injects his own digestive
> juices into it, dissolving the softest parts of it and slowly sucking them
> out.[20]

By the novel's end the spider/weaver and his apprentice/victim,
themselves products of the narrator's insect-trapping preoccupations,
are metamorphosed into the rapist/invader and little Alvarito. The
web of the spider, like the labyrinth of the Medina/text, is yet another
link in the chain of allusions drawn from life to explain the narrator's
activity, his/our relationship to the narrative/experience of the book.
The little boy, shaped from the cumulative images of boyhood, including that of the protagonist himself, steps out of experience, myth, and
fairy tale, a Red Riding Hood of Spanish innocence to be sacrificed to
the corrective lust of the rejected conqueror. With its immense and
ambiguously charming serpent/penis, that climactic passage reacti-
vates frozen imagery trapped in the narrative web and multiplied by
our experience of it. In the process it resolves the dream into a nightmare that is only a dream, turning the text into the sum of its nodal
parts. The obsessions of the exile have found uses for all of the intermingling nodal threads that, without becoming precisely a story, wind
like strands of plot through the account of a day in Tangiers. Thus
Count Julian achieves the status of a totally solipsistic and hence self-

---

[20]Goytisolo, *Count Julian*, pp. 50–51.

consuming vision, a unity contributing to the integrating potential of its parts, the knots of the web magnified by the unquenchable thirst for vengence and self-absorption of the exile.

Because it is fluid and open enough to accommodate and order almost any kind of subject matter treated in just about any imaginable manner, nodality can give the aura of narrative promise to the most disarticulated discourse. That is, a context superficially devoid of development can achieve organization, interest, and even a modicum of suspense through repetition and clustering, as Céline demonstrated in *Féerie pour une autre fois I* and as Beckett confirmed in *The Unnamable*. True, *Féerie*, Céline's least read and least appreciated novel, remains untranslated even in the midst of the Céline boom; and in fact, there are plenty of good formal and substantial reasons for that neglect. After all, the book is formally his most adventurous, being roughly two-thirds diatribe and one-third farcical exemplum, an unhospitable mix at best. What is more, the diatribe, laced though it is with explosive vignettes and mini-actions, is given over to the uncompromising whine/scream/shout of an ex-collaborator in a cell on the death row of a Danish prison. The comic number, featuring an exemplary grotesque, the lascivious but legless sculptor Jules, is less a tale than an elaborate bit of metaphorical stereotyping. The whole is framed in a harsh, uncompromising, associatively organized paratactic discourse. In short, this text gives the reader no quarter. Indeed, it goes so far as to inculpate him/her in the war criminality attributed to the narrating Dr. Destouches.

We have seen a variant of this sort of narrative behavior in *Count Julian*, where the prosaic reality of the Tangiers day provides a narrative frame for the dominant nodal discourse of the vengeful exile. There too, a tactical reversal occurs, and a narrative that occults its skeletal symbolic matrix is upstaged by a motival network or weave that in effect *becomes* the very substance of the disturbed speaker's discourse. I would suggest that, doubtless in response to emotional imperatives, in *Féerie*, Céline took the form of the novel very close to the brink of catastrophe by casting his book in two uncompromisingly austere and antithetical discursive modes. Since Céline's nodal procedures are not unusual in their detail, my point can be made by a brief summary of his approach, focusing on the opening monologue/lament/harangue.

Féerie opens in medias res on a scene that soon becomes the armature of the novel: the visit to the collaborationist Dr. Destouches in his Montmartre apartment by the wife and son of a World War I buddy and ex-friend. The time, one of the few that is specified in this fluid discourse, is just before the German defeat, and Céline/Destouches has been rendered paranoid by threats of vengeance from as far off as London. Accordingly the visit raises the specter of his execution/assassination and brings into play helter-skelter the history not only of his friendship but also of his wartime and prewar behavior. What has begun ostensibly as a narrative sequence quickly turns into a nodal point, the anchor or prime node of a system to which the text obsessively returns, deepening its context without ever resolving the original action. While elaborating on the moment, the situation, and its background, the speaker manages to introduce a battery of topics, each of which will at some point be focused and cursorily developed, and perhaps exploded, in true Célinian fashion: World War I and his heroism, his medical practice and career, his career as a writer, this book and its reader/purchaser/publisher, his situation as a hated collaborator, his confinement in a Danish cell, his attachment to beautiful women and especially to ballet dancers and the dance, his cat (Bébert), maladies afflicting him in prison, and the visits from an embassy official eager to have him return to France and stand trial. All of this and more is indiscriminately poured onto the page and into the ears of a reader teased by dark humor, irony, self-pity, anger, tenderness, black visions, and a curious kind of suspense.

Ultimately this novel seems, like Céline's prewar anti-Semitic pamphlets, to have an agenda rather than a plot or even a thesis. If the avowed purpose of *Bagatelles pour un massacre* was to urge the destruction of the Jews, however, *Féerie* is closer to achieving what may have been the pamphlet's hidden agenda: the bodying forth of the relative but essential blamelessness of its paranoid author/speaker in a climate of generalized blame and guilt, within a hostile world that worships at the altar of immoral clowns like Jules. That is, goaded by fear and hatred, the writer has found the language to dispel, however temporarily, his private demons.

Between the lines, as so often happens in nodal texts, we feel the traces not only of the narrative impulse so carefully blocked by the method but also of a fully articulated plot: an account of how Céline reached this impasse and how he has fared as a prisoner exiled, incarcerated, and under threat of death. This presentation, while refusing diachrony, establishes an emotive and performative context, employing verbal and motival energy and rhetorical climaxes. Like Joyce's "Circe" chapter and Goytisolo's *Count Julian*, and indeed like much of Céline's other work, *Féerie*'s action is essentially conveyed as hallucinatory reaction. Not surprisingly, though only on reinspection, we find that even the vestigial narrative of the opening is for the most part hallucinated. Even the brilliant harlequinade starring Jules is an expanded hallucination, featuring a figure drawn from the universe of the Commedia, *and* an initiatory node in its own right. Ultimately, the elaborate portrait of the artist as public enemy resolves its system in the hallucinatory account given in *Normance* or *Féerie II* of the "bombardment" of Montmartre.

Lest it be assumed that this text is dreary, graceless, punishing, or unrewarding, I should emphasize that the nodes, hallucinatory or not, are cast in a variety of registers. Tenderness and joy are generated by meditations on cats and dancers even if the next moment will evoke the hatred of the tormentor, the scorn of the enemy, the downright fear and despair of the prisoner, and the spleen of the unrepentant collaborator. As in most successful nodal texts, the range of topics and treatments, the variety of moods and modes, and the effect of constant change and difference encourage our participation. The repetition with a difference establishes the rhythmic beat of our reading and gives shape to a globalizing discourse.

Profoundly chameleonic, though universally nonnarrative, the nodal novel can and does take on the colorations of narrative discourse, miming in some measure all of its procedures more or less transparently, though against the grain. It also facilitates, as we see in all our examples and in its lineage, maximalism, globalism, and encyclopedism, achieved by means of a broad approach to experience and a lavish use of variegated detail. This is not a necessary trait, however, and the mimesis of narrative development need not always be dreamlike or hallucinatory. As a study of the Polish novelist Witold Gombrowicz's remarkable pseudo-tale *Cosmos* shows, it can also rationalize absurdity and approximate plot within a minimalized discourse, one that carefully subverts its own mock-encyclopedism along with its narrative pretensions.

As we have seen, both *Féerie* and *Count Julian* generate their nodes by means of metaphor and association, tending to render the commonplace grotesque, imposing the nightmare on the fabric of daily experience by a process of savant distortion, creating bizarre hybrids by blending materials presented objectively elsewhere. In *Cosmos,* where the absurd, the comic, and the uncanny dominate, the reader participates in curiously muted hallucinations stimulated by a severely limited range of unpromising and even trivial material that is given no clear symbolic status, a minimalist encyclopedia.

As in *Count Julian,* the attenuated narrative structure of *Cosmos* is doubled by an explicit nodal structure. Unlike the explosive *Féerie,* this is an unpromising tale told by a student purportedly studying for an exam: how he and a chance acquaintance take lodgings in a country boardinghouse, where they become obsessed with a random assortment of phenomena and eventually participate in an ill-starred outing. If the basic plot is straightforward, chronological, almost embarrassingly simple, the superimposed imaginative structure, which at first decorates but ultimately dominates, is far more intricate. We are engaged by the furious cataloguing mania that consumes a narrator bent on turning fancy into experience.

The stages in the development of this catalogue are marked by the nodal moments introducing each item. Unlike the nodes in Joyce, Céline, and Goytisolo, however, these items are violently rather than organically linked by a speaker impelled to solve the manufactured mystery to which they become the random "clues." The items are so heterogeneous that the absurdity of their conjunction is evident even to the boredom-crazed persona. Thanks to his state of mind alone, their joining becomes as inevitable as it is entertaining, as disturbing and potentially dangerous for all concerned (including the reader/interlocutor). The problem is how to justify each component of the slowly accumulated list.

Each time they are confronted with something that strikes them as anomalous in their surroundings, our protagonists inflate the circumstance, giving it a potential but unspecified significance. In short, they endow it with mystery. As the details accumulate, each takes its place in the litany out of which the narrator strives to make sense. (Thus is the conventional mystery formula turned on its head.) Eventually, the narrator's mania drives him to commit a gratuitous act and, later still, to the verge of committing a pointless murder. In the meantime, perhaps as a result of the suggestive power of the repeated hanging motif, a suicide (apparently) takes place. The silent husband of the landlord's attractive daughter hangs himself during a family outing in the country. Totally imaginary systems have invaded the real world, or so it seems, since the narrator's word is not unimpeachable.

Convention sanctions the use of coincidence, the accumulation of significant detail and, to paraphrase Freud: the return of the novelistic repressed. It is a time-honored novelistic rule that heightened detail is bound to signify on some level. This statement is less true in farcical narrative, however, where disorder is essential, and *Cosmos*, featuring bumbling and disruptive clowns in a field of grotesques, using a form irreverently mauled by inconsequence, could be read as a farce. Gombrowicz does not give us that easy out; for he makes his protagonist sufficiently credible and the circumstances weighty enough to oblige us, at the very least, to consider the possibility that a hung sparrow, a crack in the plaster of a ceiling, a dangling splinter of wood, a deformed mouth, a girl's hand, and a score of other details may eventually coalesce into a meaningful plot.

Furthermore, though the narrator repeatedly expresses his doubts, he is the one ultimately taken in by the system he has elaborated. In contrast, the reader is in the position of the incredulous observer wondering where fancy will take us next, whether these unlikely heroes can indeed put life into obsessively observed details. In the end, this is accomplished by a combination of absurd events and bald trickery on the part of the narrator, who manipulates reality to fit his obsession. We watch a novel being made by an inverted process, one that repeatedly shows us the novelist's hand. The power of this text resides partly in the upsetting of reader expectations, partly in the success of the nodal structure. For the nodal structure to work, however, the nodes themselves must be developed with a care recalling that of Proust, though in a style reminiscent of Beckett.

The decisive moment falls at the beginning of the novel, when the dusty travelers searching for their country accommodations come upon the sparrow:

He plunged deeper into the thicket, where there were shady nooks and corners under the mingling branches of hazel trees and pines. I gazed into the maze of leaves and branches, dappled light, dense vegetation, gaps and recesses and windings and slopes and yawning chasms and heaven knows what else besides that advanced on us and receded, forced

us aside and yielded to us, jostled us and made way for us. . . . Lost and
dripping with sweat, I felt the bare black earth under my feet. But there
among the branches was something peculiar and strange, though at first I
could not make out exactly what it was. My companion had seen it and
was staring at it too.

"It's a sparrow."

"Good heavens alive."

Yes, it was a sparrow. A sparrow hanging from a bit of a wire. It had
been hanged. Its little head was bent and its mouth wide open. It was
hanging by a bit of wire attached to a branch of a tree.

Extraordinary. A hanged bird. A hanged sparrow. This shrieking
eccentricity indicated that a human hand had penetrated this fastness.
Who on earth could have done such a thing and why?[21]

The tone of this passage is absurdly melodramatic; the details are
inflated; a thicket quickly becomes a dense forest, if not a Disneyland
jungle with "yawning chasms and heaven knows what else." The
speaker's rhetoric is marked by redundancy and clichés, and the explanations offered for both the circumstance and the men's reactions are
not satisfying. On the other hand, details are presented in a limpid but
heightened prose to produce a combination of mainly accurate description and inaccurate elaboration. We should also note that, in contrast
to the nodal moments in *Count Julian*, the nodes of *Cosmos* do not differ
markedly in style or pitch from their context, nor is there a tendency
toward nodal glissage or even interaction. In this Gombrowicz is closer
to the novelistic tradition he is subverting.

The hanged bird generates other nodal moments as the action develops. There is the discovery of a hanging splinter in the back garden
wall and the death of the cat, which the narrator, on impulse, hangs.
Finally, there is the suicide of Lena's husband, which only the narrator
seems to have noticed. Together, they form one of the principal axes of
the plot, but by their nature, and because they are never adequately
explained or connected (except by the artificial thread of the nodal
system overtly controlled by the speaker), they subvert the logic of the
realistic plot and have as much significance and insignificance as the
book's closing sentence: "Today we had chicken and rice for lunch."
Thus they are at once arbitrary and essential—arbitrary because one
feels and is encouraged to feel that almost any image would serve as

[21]Witold Gombrowicz, *Cosmos*, trans. Eric Mosbacher (New York: Grove, 1978), p.
10.

well and essential because they have been incorporated in a macrosystem that rationalizes and depends upon a variety of other, similar details.

Chance is the principle that seems to determine significance in this context, but the protagonist's state of mind determines both our response and the expanding nodal structure. Therefore the latter may be seen as contributing to the repeatedly subverted illusion of plot as well as to the portrayal of character within a context *upon which*, in this case, a nodal scaffolding has been superimposed. Once established in our minds as in that of the protagonist/narrator, first by emphatic presentation and then largely by repetition and elaboration, the secondary context becomes part of our personal imaginative framework. By accumulating the puzzle pieces as just that and not as integral parts of an ongoing action, we are led to a resolution that is accomplished less by tying pieces together than by forcing them to find objective contexts and forcing us to participate viscerally in that process. Thus after an intermittent but prolonged preoccupation with mouths, what could be more appropriate for the speaking/vocal narrator than the act of placing his fingers first in the mouth of a hanged man and then in that of a hitchhiking priest? Though we are free to ascribe meaning to these events, it is not so much significance as the search for ways to validate the fundamentally ridiculous but ultimately unsettling nodal systems that constitutes the narrative end.

The wonder of this novel derives from its capacity, promoted by the narrator's intervention in the action, to join the narrative proper to the nodal structure while maintaining the distinction, a capacity evident in a very different way in Goytisolo's book. More important, it can do this without either pretending to symbolic or allegoric meaning or falling into insignificance. In principle *Cosmos* could be collapsed into a mound of jumbled letters after our reading, reduced to something as bland as "chicken and rice for lunch." That it does not, that we are haunted by it, may be ascribed in large measure to the nodal structure.

If all of Philippe Sollers's mature novels, beginning with *Drame*, are in some sense nodal, it is much to his credit that each is structured differently both from its predecessors and from possible sources.[22] As

[22]Sollers's more recent "realistic" fictions, *Femmes* (1982) and *Portrait du joueur* (1984), could be perceived as having another sort of nodal structure, one that is complicated by the introduction of plot and character, a fact that demands elaborate rationalization for which there is no space here.

the most radical of his completed novels, *H* is a particularly challenging and rewarding text for study from our point of view. While omitting the usual initiatory jacket copy and thus refusing to make its procedures explicit, *H* testifies to an exceptionally elaborate structure that has thus far been ignored. Sollers provides a possible key when he describes the mandalalike geometric figure (shown below) that adorns the book's front cover to Giordano Bruno: "Figura Intellectus . . . Articuli centrum et sexaginta adversus huius tempestatis mathematicus atque philosophos."[23] Possibly a system of six topics, each

developing from some central point and repeated six times, dictates the shape of this subtle and various text. Sollers's project may well be perceived as a system of juxtaposed vignettes and/or divagations, themselves divisible into six issues, each of which is derived from a central impulse: say, autobiography, language, sexuality, psychoanalysis, history, Marxism. In practice such topics presented in a variety of voices, styles, rhythms, and modes combine to produce what has proved to be a most disturbing text for the general run of readers and critics.

At first glance, *H* is very much like an encyclopedia whose entries are unlabeled and out of sequence. It is remarkable both for the richness of its rhythms, styles, subject matter, and themes and for the unsettling glissage effect that tends, aided by the lack of punctuation, to abolish frontiers without doing away with differences, an effect in startling contrast to those of Robbe-Grillet. Repeatedly the reader experiences the loss of context and feels obliged to re-adapt. The im-

[23]Philippe Sollers, *H* (Paris: Seuil, 1973), back cover.

pact is at times dreamlike. Still, as we float, or are tossed, from context to context, from image cluster to image cluster, and from voice to voice, there are moments of recognition, significant echoes, and occasionally we fall upon a clearly defined narrative passage, a conversation, or a bit of coherent exposition—a solid object in a generally fluid development. A second reading reveals much more of this sort of presence and order, together with a substantial but virtually subliminal narrative development. Above all, this is a process book that takes on dimensions in the course of repeated readings, as reading and text tend increasingly to coincide.

We might further qualify *H* as a novel from which the narrative has been removed. In it we find the traits proper to the sublimated basic design of the traditional novel, but they are foregrounded and organized in accordance with a different sort of logic. Ultimately, it is Sollers's particular version of nodal structuration that facilitates our reading, constituting both a source of interest and a very special kind of punctuation. Under its influence we tend to group together units dealing with a given subject, passages that are scattered in a seemingly random order throughout the text. The sum of these units defines both a nodal development and a significant elaboration on a theme, though such elaboration would be weak indeed were it seen in isolation.

What transpierces the surface of *H* is the record of a historical moment mirrored in the mind in flux of an engaged/detached protagonist who is single, receptive, and singularly observant to the point of bearing witness to his age. The stimulus for this book was the Paris of May 1968, the climate it engendered, and its disillusioning aftermath. Yet Sollers seems to have set out to do more than simply chronicle the events of that moment of intense hope on the Left. Instead, he chose to establish an array of highly characteristic voices and a cluster of topics to which he could repeatedly return as the book progressed, finally coalescing, in the manner of the Poundian ideogram, into a dynamic self-portrait of the period between 1968 and 1972. A speaker (Sollers?), who seems to be describing this text as a cantata, gives us the best account of its basic procedure: "j'oppose au monologue intérieur le polylogue extérieur."[24] The tactic is to speak each cell of this

---

[24]Ibid., p. 42. Julia Kristeva chose this striking term (with its echoes of Bakhtinian "dialogism") as a title for her fine essay on *H*. See her "The Novel as Polylogue" in *Desire in Language* (New York: Columbia University Press, 1980), pp. 172–73 and passim. See also Roland Barthes, *Sollers écrivain* (Paris: Seuil, 1979), p. 54.

polycellular novel in a typical but unidentified voice. Since these are voices of speech and history rather than reflection, the result is an immediate and protean theatricality. Sollers's theater, however, despite the clarity of its discourses, makes considerable demands on the reader intent on ordering them.

The crucial date is May 1968. We hear voices of the epoch, especially in the opening pages, voices that gradually fade into other contemporary voices as the flow of time carries us into the early 1970s. Beyond that, we have a historical backdrop, a moving one derived from newspaper headlines sardonically presented in a variety of voices. Here, from the end of the book, is a pointed reference to the Yom Kippur war of 1972: ". . . you can't imagine how hot the sinai is on bare feet in the sand how it is today yom kippur kol nidre golda menhir's troops withdraw after having felled what could be 60 to 100 fedayim . . . what's happened to our revolution. . . . ."[25] This intermittent flow of journalistic/popular voices from our retreating past takes the place of what would in other texts be a narrative strand, but in this case its precise nature and its development, mingled as it is with other disparate materials, are hard to fix, as is the attitude it projects. Still, we may locate our citation within a minor nodal strand, one that turns history into a source of continuity and even narrative suspense.

We must speak of nodal strands in *H* rather than nodal systems or hierarchies because items of similar importance are usually generated by a given topic or perspective. The result is clearly more linear, though within one strand we may find allusions (secondary nodes) belonging to another and though the individual elements tend to be linked by association with others to form a unified network that might be regarded as three dimensional. Accordingly, the book's opening pages constitute an aggregate, overture, or minisystem, a cluster of related matter cemented together by repeated references to the topic of the writer's writing experience.

These autobiographical elements are interspersed with nodes from other strands to which they are linked in the totally unpunctuated text by associations or by a disorienting syntactical glissage that masks a basic paratactics. Thus the passage on pp. 9–11 dealing with the author's name and practice is followed by one on the *événements* of 1968. The latter, a fine example of the historical vignette, provides a dynamic overview *through* as much as *in* time:

<hr/>

[25]Sollers, *H*, p. 161, my translation.

. . . a hundred thousand on the square today the police say fifteen there goes their helicopter the party gives the same figure a few more perhaps hostile stupefaction closed mind besides where can this lead the workers haven't budged nothing to do about it you can't keep it up comrades it's deadlocked this won't get you anywhere and yet its happening red flags everywhere flapping in the wind sun they snap it's cooler the buildings are beginning to open up the bourgeois to the balconies cameras to eyes archivists shouts the little one whose been singing into his mike the last hour.[26]

This candidly reported bit of fragmented experience with its dominant voice, interrupted by the remarks of organizers and subject to a float- ing temporality and perspective, illustrates how Sollersian concision borders on the continuous. It is followed by an argument among *copains* and a passage of reflection on the writer's function in *H*. Though growing quite naturally out of a preoccupation with the say- ing of the revolution, the content of these reflections is markedly personal and self-justificatory: ". . . after all you want to write it to do it and write it to take up the volume again you see the adventure novels to bring it over her fold to spread it out bring out new relationships here look i have a mania for climbing live from the tomb i can't really do otherwise its afterward that the troubles begin. . . ."[27]

Though this development is clear and becomes clearer, it is by no means limpid. In order to follow the meandering argument, the reader must assemble and relate the various panels of this immense polyp- tych, pulling together the nodal strands at the same time that he/she strings the nodal beads. Punctuation must be supplied, and breaks in the discourse must be noted so that the new topics can be accommo- dated. Still, the presence of echo passages illustrating the principle of repetition is reassuring, as is the rhythmic component of music, pro- moting a sense of pattern growing out of the problematic: how to write the aftermath of the "revolution" of 1968. For out of that project grew all of the nodal topics, and around Sollers's response are grouped the various strands. In it lies the secret of their interrelationship and the prime source of the book's dynamic unity.

We may ask whether narrative interest, to say nothing of suspense, can survive in a context generated by disparate but meshing systems of significance, but in fact, though *H* is not strictly speaking a narrative,

[26]Ibid., p. 12.
[27]Ibid., p. 13.

plot and narrative interest persist as powerful trace elements. They are manifested not only by the developing wide-screen historical backdrop but also, if less overtly, by Sollers's decision to anchor his text in a specific time and to place his autobiographical persona in its center. On this level all of the nodal strands coalesce, and the reader discovers not only a source of interest but ultimately an engagement in each stage of the text's evolution. Doubtless, that engagement is partly a function of the effort required to *dis*engage the components from their context so that their contribution to the whole may better be understood and so that they may be reintegrated. Like so many other successful nonnarrative texts, however, this *roman* is premised on the reader's being conditioned to perceive narrative development as the given of novels, a powerful thirst for balance and coherence that can be assuaged in this case only by the seeming deconstruction and reconstitution of the text's components. To the latter process nodality contributes the necessary building blocks, but *H* owes much of its considerable aesthetic interest to the process of distinguishing among those elements, aligning them, and appreciating their conflicts and interrelationships.

One must not take Sollers more seriously than he takes himself, and his books are full of self-mockery: ". . . sol sol sol air let him who has ears hear and he who knows how to read should see the meaning deliberately hidden for him . . . you drive them mad with your prophesies parables allegorical in the very heart of a social statement . . ."[28] says a hip Christ returned to hand his mantle to a clownish self-baptized sun-air (Sollers) writer. The joke, however, is sometimes as serious as the assertion. In the following bit of *polylogue extérieur* he projects the image of the great weaver and maker of the world whose project is to write a book like Dante's for our age. The tonality of this passage, so markedly different from that of the earlier autobiography/writing nodes, reflects Sollers's reverence for one of his culture heroes. It also suggests the expressive range of a single nodal line:

. . . o busy invisible weaver stop one word why these endless labors one moment speak but no the shuttle flies the figures emerge floating from the loom from the rolling mill the vats admit not a second's interruption

[28]Ibid., p. 28.

you would say that production wishes more and more to mime perpetual motion to draw near the heart of nature which established us here and we who contemplate the factory are deafened by its humming it is only _ when we distance ourselves that we hear the billions of voices that speak through life envelop death death weaves life I am the image I am the carpet I am the machine and the image of the machine and the machination of the image and its sound . . . I must therefore find a crucible in which to melt myself to the point of being no more than a tiny epitome of bone there you are no no what there is of beauty and of terror in man has never yet been mentioned in books no only one author returned from the land of the dead can tell us that it requires only the one who has passed through the flames. . . .[29]

Appropriately, the overly reverent pose is repeatedly undercut by irony and is finally atomized by what follows on the next page: the advertisement of a pornography merchant, which echoes views typical of two other "heroes," Bataille and Sade, in a graphic enactment of the post-Dantesque Inferno.

We discover by reading *H* as a nodal text certain echoes of Joyce as author of and presence in the *Wake*. The principal or prime node of the *Wake* may be the ALP Letter, which stands not only in the place of the *Word* in the universe but also in the place of the *Wake* itself.[30] In a chapter full of strictures on reading (I.5), we find the following bit of comic jargon addressed irreverently to the reader: "You is feeling like you was lost in the bush, boy? You says: It is a puling sample jungle of woods. You most shouts out: Bethicket me for a stump of a beech if I have the poultriest notions what the farest he all means. Gee up, girly! The quad gospellers may own the targum but any of the Zingari shoolerim may pick a peck of kindlings yet from the sack of auld hensyne."[31] The letter is, of course, dictated to the Word's high priest, the darkling Shem, who stands behind it as a persona for Joyce. In effect Joyce's focus on the process of writing, though less frontal, is very close to that of Sollers. More important, his use of the Letter as a rich and protean image finds its echo in Sollers's use of the auto-biographical/writing system that opens and closes and ultimately controls the form of *H*.

[29]Ibid., pp. 44–45.
[30]See my "Nodality and the Infrastructure of *Finnegans Wake*," pp. 139–43.
[31]James Joyce, *Finnegans Wake* (New York: Viking, 1939), p. 112.

Our analysis of five distinct nodal strategies suggests that, though each may well have been developed in response to the author's designs, they are also and to an important degree products of the text's conditioning. Joyce may have known that the early sketches for *Finnegans Wake* would have to generate a coherent system of references varying in magnitude and scattered systematically throughout the text. He could not have been aware that, in compensating for what was omitted, the approach would spawn a complex of nodal systems controlling every aspect of the presentation. Goytisolo, starting as he did from a vision of the obsessed but powerless dreamer imagining into being the autodestruction of the self-betrayed Spanish psyche through the regeneration of the past, was clearly obliged to deemphasize (decenter?) the realistic framework. That project obliged him to move, not only in the direction of surrealism, but also toward the tactics of *Ulysses*, the crystallization of latent relations, and the reorganization of the emphatically stated givens of the protagonist's day. In *Féerie*, Céline uses nodality to organize a self-exculpatory diatribe, structured by encyclopedic personal reference and the accentuated repetitions appropriate to the pamphlet. One might say that the nodes of this novel are designed less to rationalize than to obscure (brilliantly) the failure of logic under a barrage of affective detail. In contrast, Gombrowicz has deconstructed a genre, the mystery novel, by making clues generated largely in the protagonist's imagination coalesce to compensate for the virtual absence of a rational development in the real world projected by the narrative. Of necessity, he has turned the manifestations of these "clues" into the substance of his text, generating an action from their interaction. Finally, Sollers's novel constitutes the negative for Joyce's nodal structure by basing itself in the real and observable, the perception of which is systematically decomposed. If the text conveys the author in the process of writing himself as an integral part of the historical moment he documents, it does so by breaking up that moment and his personal interaction with it into a limited number of nodal strands. Writing himself as history, Sollers elaborated a structural principle cognate with that of *Finnegans Wake*. Significantly, he too found in Giordano Bruno, Joyce's "Nolan," an exemplary thinker for whom paradox was the crux. One is reminded of Shaun the post's jaundiced description of his artist Brother Shem's act of "writing the mystery of himself in furniture."[32]

[32]Ibid., p. 184.

Like paratactics, which deliberately breaks and even fragments rhetorical flow by what could be called instrumental means, nodal procedures contribute by substantive means to the rhythmic dimension.
They do so not purely formally but also and perhaps primarily in the
distinctive manner first outlined by E. M. Forster in his *Aspects of the
Novel*, that is, by introducing motival rhyming. The result in most
cases, however, is far more complex than the sort of rhythmic marking
outlined by Forster, since the structure depends for its impact on the
preponderance of nodal systems that can stand in for other nonsym-
bolic expressive components fleshing out a species of parametric
experience.

This statement is most true, of course, in *Finnegans Wake*, where
nodal interaction informs every aspect of the book, from the largest
narrative unit through the syllable, from the imposing Letter system
through the microsystem generated by references to "The Charge of
the Light Brigade," "Do Ye Ken John Peel," the Dublin city motto, or
words drawn from specific exotic languages. The net rhythmic impact
on the alert reader capable of "mastering" or even attending to the
entire text would approximate that of a monstrous and imperfectly
heard symphonic composition orchestrated for variously accented
nodal instruments. Though the *Wake* is the most ambitious of our
examples and the most rigorous, this metaphor also applies to the other
books, each of which foregrounds not only the writing process but also
the process of perception or reading/hearing, making the reader, as
partial perceiver, a vital component of the textual identity.

It is important that we recognize the extent to which the exposed
sensible surface of these texts resists full recuperation. True, the nodal
component invariably contributes significantly to the textual superstructure, being a major source of coherence and hence of accessibility.
On the other hand, though it is seldom occulted, as are the image,
theme, and symbol complexes of more traditional fictions, the developing macrostructure is usually far too rich to be fully perceived at any
given moment. What could be a coolly mechanical procedure thus
acquires an aura of mystery, a curious combination of magic and
humanity, eliciting from its authors a variety of approximate process
metaphors: being compared to weaving and a web by Sollers and
Goytisolo and the kaleidoscope by Joyce.

It should follow that the fully articulated nodal macrostructure, the
superpattern produced by the work perceived as the sum of its nodal
parts, is, with the possible exception of Gombrowicz's *Cosmos*, vir-

tually irrecuperable. Still, with some imagination or with considerable labor, we might conceive of or produce a computer-generated three-dimensional image composed of a nonuniform network of interacting clusters, the medical circulation chart for a fabulous literary beast or the topographical map of some unknown country. The result, even when properly color-coded, would be more decorative than useful. Still, our image may convey not only the impact but the appeal of artifacts employing nodal means to shape what could be qualified, half-sardonically, as an encyclofiction for the postindustrial era. More important, it may suggest the degree to which such texts make manifest and vital the subliminal components of more conventional works.

4

Self-Generation, or The Process Text

"You are writing a book of course?" said Byrne.
"He is," said Brinsley, "and the plot has him well in hand."
Flann O'Brien, At Swim-Two-Birds

"J'y pense, j'y pense, un livre quelle prétention dans un sens, mais quelle extraordinaire merveille s'il est raté dans les grands largeurs."
Robert Pinget, Mahu

Book 18 of the *Iliad* contains what may be the earliest example of a strategy that has become one of the hallmarks of extreme modernity, a fictional passage that makes manifest the origins of a significant portion of its own material, devolving transparently from the manner and matter of what has preceded it. Homer's unforgettable evocation of the Shield of Achilles is particularly startling when seen in this light; for it illustrates how much of this text, and by extension any text, is the product of its own processes of generation, how exposed such procedures can be, and how tolerant listeners and readers are and always have been of narrative play.

The description of course functions to elevate both the object and its possessor by showing off the lifelike and ingenious craftsmanship of Hephaestus. This is therefore a portrait of splendor[1] in which the material bases are expanded to encompass not only the depiction of scenes from life but also the animation of those scenes by virtue of a

---

[1] We may wonder at the deliberate irony: the most splendid of artifacts is given over to the depiction, not of pomp, but of homely, everyday life in rural Greece.

subtle projection of the inanimate surface into the animate universe, the intervention of real time, real sound, and real motion within the frozen temporality of the object.[2]

> On it he wrought in all their beauty two cities of mortal men. And there were marriages in one, and festivals. They were leading the brides along the city from their maiden chambers under the flaring of torches, and the loud bride song was arising. The young men followed the circles of the dance, and among them the flutes and lyres kept up their clamour as in the meantime the women standing each at the door of her court admired them. The people were assembled in the market place, where a quarrel had arisen, and two men were disputing over the blood price for a man who had been killed. One man promised full restitution in a public statement, but the other refused and would accept nothing. Both then made for an arbitrator, to have a decision; and people were speaking up on either side, to help both men. But the heralds kept both men in hand, as meanwhile the elders were in session on benches of polished stone in the sacred circle and held in their hands the staves of the heralds who lift their voices. The two men rushed before these, and took turns speaking their cases, and between them lay on the ground two talents of gold, to be given to that judge who in this case spoke the straightest opinion.[3]

The key to Homer's method is a softening of outlines that licenses the intrusion of increasingly plastic details. This characteristic enables us to move smoothly from the description of still action to an evocation of stilled action to the intrusion of sounds and social attitudes that would normally accompany such action to the full animation of the actors and the scene. The process is as natural as it is strange; for the associations latent in the original picture generate details that in their turn generate and activate others. We might say that the imagined object is the original text upon which the mind of the singer played or that the process through which that object evolved led to the genera-

---

[2]At a much later date Jerome Bosch did something similar in the depiction of the armor of one of the Magi in his painting of the Nativity now in the Prado. There, by the simple addition of organic coloration, the metallic animals on the king's shield and crest are vivified in a context where such grotesquery is acceptable but not the rule. Rabelais may have had Homer in mind when, in his *Cinquiesme livre*, chapters XXX-VII-XL, the mosaics of the battle of Bacchus against the Indians are brought to the vividness of life. My thanks to Glyn Norton for calling this example to my attention.

[3]*The Iliad of Homer*, trans. Richmond Lattimore (Chicago: University of Chicago Press, 1951), p. 388.

tion of an image radically unlike its still-visible source. In textual terms something has been created out of nothing under our very eyes.

Homer's description is an extreme case of the self-generative effect, and his goal may have been as much to show his hand as to magnify his object. We might even say that it is an extreme case pointing toward the awareness that every text is to some degree self-generating. Having put together a few words with an eye to writing or speaking a message, evoking an experience or sensation, spinning a fiction, or simply making a pattern, the creative person is immediately bound by a set of rules that gain in interest and effectiveness to the degree that they are artfully stretched or even broken. Within a New Critical frame of reference, Murray Krieger applies the term to poetry that is "characterized by a self-generating play of words which maximally exploits all that is potentially in them, exploding them into its meaning."[4]

Such a perception would seem to invalidate any effort to create a separate category for self-generating texts as a peculiarly modern phenomenon, a category that would not, for example, consist largely of texts that give accounts of their own writing. I refer to the thematic convention explored by Steven Kellman in *The Self-Begetting Novel*,[5] one evident in books like Proust's *Remembrance of Things Past*, or even Günter Grass's *Tin Drum*, instances of the dramatization of writing. On the other hand, it would not completely exclude Beckett's *Molloy* Céline's *Féerie*, both of which exhibit themselves as writing that turns itself into text, disclosing itself as distinct from any outside generating presence or force.

What concerns us is neither a discreet quality nor a heavily thematized or dramatized one but, rather, the overt *insistence on* self-sufficiency, the *pointing up* of an ability to elaborate text out of its own matter, a mode of verbal perpetual motion. Thus there is an overdetermination of the inner necessity that shapes texts rather than the conventional claim to derive substance from history, from the phenomenal environment or even from logical procedures. Self-generation in this sense is partly the new myth of the text, the account it is obliged to give of itself to its readers. It is also in part a reaction against complacent

---

[4]Murray Krieger, "Literature vs. Ecriture: Constructions and Deconstructions in Recent Critical Theory," in a special issue of *Studies in the Literary Imagination* (titled "Critics at Work") 12, no. 1 (1979), 9.

[5]Steven G. Kellman, *The Self-Begetting Novel* (New York: Columbia University Press, 1980).

conventions that see the text as pure product. And it remains partly the recognition of the degree to which all texts do indeed contain the germs of their own generative principles.

Like the surrealists' ideal reproduction of the subconscious, Mallarmé's "livre instrument spirituel" as reflected in Paul Valéry's *Monsieur Teste*, like the concept of the fully impersonal text postulated by Flaubert and Mallarmé and like Joyce's view of the dramatic work that digests rather than exhibits its author's motivating presence, the totally self-generating text is a goal rather than an achievement. In each of these instances writers strive for the unattainable: the production of a vitality that is absolutely self-contained and self-sufficient, a project that presupposes a Promethean overreaching and an ultimate failure: a Mallarméan shipwreck. Nevertheless, in a sense such texts, by pretending to abdicate authority, seemingly giving themselves over to chance, evoke an extreme of abnegation that takes us back to literary prehistory, to an age before authorship.

Self-generation, as defined here, implies a more or less deliberate and ironic return to the divinely inspired text of religious and classical literature. This Mallarmé evokes in his *Un coup de dés*, where he permits the *Néant* to speak through him, spiritualizing the word as a cosmic utterance but secularizing the resulting text. Joyce was aware of it when he identified as scripture the famous letter dictated by the analphabet ALP, whose word is ultimately indistinguishable from the "nightbook" itself. Beckett installs it in his books through the admittedly ironic but incessantly reiterated references to the occulted source of inspirational prodding: the mysterious Youdi, Knott, and Godot. In short, certain twentieth-century works are extensions of earlier attempts to equate the text with an ultimate and ineffable shaping force.

One thing missing here is the (perhaps essential) sense that contact has actually been made, that the actual Word has in fact spoken through the artist's voice/pen. It is partly to an emphatic sense of dislocation, of a lost connection with such a "reality" or "truth," that these later texts owe their rigorous *formal* honesty—their deliberate self-distancing *in fact* from what, *in theory*, is unattainable. What earlier periods accepted as a sign of humility, the idea that the Word speaks through the singer/writer, has come to signify a tension between self-assertion and abnegation and a declaration of the powerful weakness of language in relation to experience, belief, and, above all, desire.

The earliest and most fully articulated instances of self-generation include the novels of Raymond Roussel, which can be seen by hindsight as growing out of his distorted verbal matrices. Much has been made of how *Impressions d'Afrique* derived from the modification of the phrase, *Les lettres du blanc sur les bandes du vieux billard* to read *Les lettres du blanc sur les bandes du vieux pillard.*[6] Indeed it is remarkable that so slight an alteration, when rationalized, could result in a polished and engaging fiction, that the author's express intent was to develop works rooted entirely in his imagination, that he wrote about contexts and events he had not experienced. The reader of Roussel's meticulous justification of his "readings" of the nonsense words may be equally impressed by the highly idiosyncratic choices he makes, by the way in which he buttresses those choices with arguments in his posthumous *How I Wrote Certain of my Books*. Referring to the sentences cited above, Roussel claims that, in

> the first, "lettres" was taken in the sense of lettering, "blanc" in the sense of a cube of chalk, and "bandes" as in cushions.
>
> In the second, "lettres" was taken in the sense of missives, "blanc" as in white man, and "bandes" as in hordes.
>
> The two phrases found, it was a case of writing a story which could begin with the first and end with the second.[7]

To some extent this procedure resembles the children's game that dictates the production of a tale from a random group of objects: say, a chair, a rabbit, and a bowl of corn flakes. A more likely source is Poe's singularly influential account of the writing of his "Raven" ("The Philosophy of Composition"), itself a prime source of the symbolist aesthetic enunciated by Mallarmé. If both Mallarmé and Poe stand behind Roussel, however, his project is of a different order and magnitude: to demonstrate the writer's total control over a narrative rather than a poem and his absolute freedom from the constraints of *conventional* verisimilitude. He believes that only the first step of his procedure is truly aleatory.

Doubtless Roussel's choices, like those of Poe, were far less objective than he claims. As the surrealists noted, though before the ap-

[6]Raymond Roussel, *How I Wrote Certain of My Books*, trans. Trevor Winkfield (New York: Sun, 1977), p. 3.
[7]Ibid.

pearance of *Comment j'ai écrit*, he was remarkably close to free-associating.[8] Still, the principle of self-generation is operative here as in Poe. The author *feels* that his text is growing out of its own procedures rather than simply out of control. Again, unlike Poe and Mallarmé, Roussel is deliberately alogical. Making no effort to create a simulacrum of a real context, he actually frustrates our efforts to discover credible activities being performed by well-motivated characters. In fact, he resists even the tug of fantasy, subverting, as we have seen, the conventions that would justify the suspension of disbelief.

None of this prevents Julia Kristeva, following the methods of Victor Shklovski and Philippe Sollers, from choosing to center this fringe figure, this total literary eccentric, making his procedures a test case for the production or dynamic of verisimilitude, that is, of a credible rhetoric. In "La productivité dite texte," she shows how Roussel devised his *Impressions d'Afrique* by "doubling," or lining, as one does a garment, the textual process,[9] turning it into the locus at once of reading (*lecture*) and writing (*écriture*) but eventually covering its productive traces:

> By means of this procedure which divides the book into productivity and product, into *action* and *result*, into writing and word, and weaves the bookish substance into an uninterrupted oscillation between two permanently separated surfaces, Roussel is able . . . to follow step by step the development of the translinguistic labor, this movement of word toward image which takes place on the other side of . . . the discursive image, that static effect of the verisimilar. The verisimilar takes over the work: rhetoric doubles (or lines) the overt productivity and this doubling or lining is available as a discursive structure. The dynamic fluidity of the action, "impression," cannot incorporate itself into the enounced except in terms of the static rigidity of the impression as remainder, effect. So the productivity remains unreadable for the public *impressed* by the verisimilar (effect).[10]

[8]This insight is implied by the fact that André Breton and his circle read Roussel as a precursor and that Breton included a sample of Roussel's work in his *Anthologie de l'humeur noire* as late as 1966.

[9]The term "doubling" is taken from Roussel's first novel, *La Doublure* (1896), but the concept is developed in Michel Foucault's *Raymond Roussel* (Paris: Gallimard, 1963), pp. 27–28 and passim.

[10]Julia Kristeva, "La productivité dite texte," *Communications* 11 (1968), 65, my translation.

If we limit ourselves to the product of the original generative procedure to which Kristeva alludes, her observation is correct. As our study of impossible objectivity has shown, however, and as Kristeva is quick to note, Roussel's completed text of *Impressions d'Afrique* was more open to the exhibition of self-generation as process and effect than his posthumous volume suggests.

Though hardly privy to the originary procedure, the reader is privileged to follow a parallel process, a secondary mystery, through the overt subversion of verisimilitude accomplished by the text when it pretends to rationalize the incredible gadgetry that constitutes, during the novel's first half, at once the pretext for the "action" and the action itself. It is through ingenuously bogus and ingenious explanations that this text, which we now know to have been completely self-generative, presents itself as partially self-generating and openly "doubled." The book's second half reveals its "lining" as an echo of its surface and thus dramatically doubles/lines the original subversion that produced verisimilitude out of nonsense. It is as though, while pursuing the concealment of his arbitrary procedures, Roussel was constrained to disclose their trace. Even before he wrote *Comment j'ai écrit certains de mes livres*, he felt obliged to let his reader participate, however partially, in the process of making and unmaking images from and through words.[11]

A similar impulse is operative in other, more contemporary works that present themselves as growing out of their verbal substance, belatedly taking up the banner of those painters and musicians who have found ways of incorporating the generative procedure in their finished product, joining process and perception. We are unlikely, however, to find a model quite so transparent as Roussel has proved to

---

[11]Though I am stressing the primary and secondary self-generation of *Impressions*, Roussel makes an even more transparent use of the procedure (foreshadowing the innovative use of footnotes in William Gass's *Willie Masters' Lonesome Wife*) in his *Nouvelles impressions d'Afrique*. In that text multiple parentheses are used to indicate material generated by the associative procedures. (For a sample of this text, see Kenneth Koch's translation of a canto included in Roussel, *How I Wrote Certain of My Books*, pp. 67–71.) We may see a parallel procedure in the generation of asides and parenthetical structures within many of the sentences of *Finnegans Wake*. Though the procedure is less blatant in that case, the effect is strikingly similar. The basic clause has accreted satellites that at once bury it and reveal it; the language has been enriched and encumbered by puns.

be, so lavish with its hidden and revealed procedures. Nor are we apt to find so complete an example of the text making itself.

Writing about Samuel Beckett's fiction, Allen Thiher correctly notes an "allegorization of the work's autonomous status" and the rejection of a "transcendental signified." Despite his insight, by limiting himself to consideration of the "play of travesty narrators,"[12] he may be over-looking a crucial new component: the tension activated by a discourse that leads the reader through its procedures and engages him/her directly in its production. The point is that, having accepted the onerous freedom perpetually to make/unmake/remake themselves through the procedures of a language that expands to fill semantic space, procedures that imply a congruence between écriture and lecture, Beckett's mature fictions articulate a self-generative program. Most particularly, in his trilogy we are surreptitiously engaged in language that produces events from the stuff of words during the moment we call creative. This engagement pertains whether or not Beckett actually believes in the myth projected by his tripartite record of a retreating creativity, an ever-deepening identity for the writer's shaping and projecting impulse.

We could say that Roussel's novel subsumes its producer in its production. In contrast, Proust uses his self-reflexive but not self-generative *Remembrance* to rationalize its own derivation, attaching it to rather than severing it from the phenomenal world. Despite his early cult of Proust, the author of the trilogy seems closer to the Céline of *Féerie*, who places himself in the midst of his proliferating rage. The Irish author, however, goes further, drawing the writer/speaker into texts that are producing his presence on the page, a presence that may have no referential validity outside the reading mind. Thus thematized, thus animated, the Beckettian word becomes more autonomous, more mysterious and troubling, but then, Kafka and Joyce are among Beckett's mentors, and Flaubert was godfather to his reluctant muse.

The adventure begins in *Molloy*, where two equal-opposite "writers" produce equal-opposite quest narratives in a transparently parodic vein. Both tales derive overtly from the conditions of their telling. We know (or rather, we are permitted to believe), for example, that Molloy

---

[12]Allen Thiher, *Words in Reflection: Modern Language Theory and Postmodern Fiction* (Chicago: University of Chicago Press, 1984), pp. 106–7.

is writing his tale at the behest of an unnamed task master. His memory is woefully inadequate, and he admits to numerous incapacities and enormous ignorance, though occasionally he displays surprising knowledge. From the start, the place usually occupied by narrative is usurped by the incompetent writing accomplished by a figure of fun driven by irrational forces and deprived of subject matter, a presence that puts words on paper as they come, fixing the evanescent, testifying. Committed to shaping a sense of the experienced, he is isolated from but bound by what he records: his lies.

Like Kafka, Beckett begins with a problematic, a vision from which narrative must evolve, but we are struck by how deprived that vision is, how far it has carried Sterne's and Flaubert's self-denial, and how it stretches beyond recognition the realist's implied rejection of pretense and illusion. If it is to be consistent with its own preconditions or decorum, such a narrative must be less than true to a lived experience it begins by discounting. It must call attention to itself as an elaborate embroidery not only on experience but on knowledge and the nature of discourse. It must become an object in its own right and a vehicle for awareness, eventuating in the pre-*cogito* darkness of Descartes, whose project it inverts. All of this is done while playing to and subverting the reader's acquired sense of the orderly, the logical, and the credible but making no attempt to exit to either the fantastic or the dream. Moreover, to succeed as narrative, it must retain and constantly reassert its capacity to surprise and amuse, to renew itself in terms of a manifest system of (admittedly eccentric) rules.

Despite the vitality of the illusion or perhaps because that illusion incorporates its contradiction, this self-perpetuating textual event is, of course, not drawn entirely from textual substance. As readers we sense a controlling hand behind the ones it posits. Like the magician's rabbit, the details have their *locus* in the experiential context of the implied creator and his audience, a shared universe of intertexts, if not of objects, of stimuli that elicit predictable responses.

Here, as in Roussel, two functions combine to convey the illusion of self-generation: association and permutation. Since they appear to dominate just about every verbal procedure, however, something else must also be in place. That something is their transparent and foregrounded mode of operation. The reader is constantly reminded that this text is being built in large measure by association. Permutations of structures, ideas, or images already present or subtly insinuated into the verbal texture help expand, fill out, and differentiate aspects of the action. The narrative must display by conscious and persistent iteration the struggle to create and the limited means at the disposal of the fictional creator. If more conventional narratives foreground events or situations or characters, this and other self-generating texts foreground equally the process of the elaboration of a verbal surface: the stringing together of words, the making of a statement that will withstand the maker's critical scrutiny and test that of the reader.

The reader of *Molloy* waits not for something to happen so much as for something to be said, something that can pass for an event on the page. This tendency is perhaps clearest in the monologue that purports to be the narrative coerced from the recumbent cripple, Molloy. Taking the movable parts of his memory, his background, his vocabulary, his intuition, or his experience, Molloy is positioning them creatively so as to make halfway satisfying arrangements of meaning as well as a totally satisfying arrangement of sounds and images. We may follow this process in the opening "episode," the projective account of a walk taken in opposite directions by two men (A and C in the English version, implying a triangulation with the voyeur Molloy as B) on the road outside Molloy's unnamed hometown:

> It's not goodbye [for me], and what magic in those dim things to which it will be time enough, when next they pass, to say goodbye. For you must say goodbye, it would be madness not to say goodbye, when the time comes. If you think of the forms and light of other days it is without regret. But you seldom think of them, with what would you think of them? I don't know. People pass too, hard to distinguish from yourself. That is discouraging. So I saw A and C going slowly towards each other, unconscious of what they were doing. It was on a road remarkably bare, I mean without hedges or ditches or any kind of edge, in the country, for cows were chewing in enormous fields, lying and standing, in the evening silence. Perhaps I'm inventing a little, perhaps embellishing, but on the whole that's the way it was. They chew, swallow, then after a short pause effortlessly bring up the next mouthful. A neck muscle stirs and the jaws begin to grind again. But perhaps I'm remembering things. The road, hard and white, seared the tender pastures, rose and fell at the whim of hills and hollows. The town was not far. It was two men, unmistakably, one small and one tall. They had left the town, first one, then the other, and then the first, weary or remembering a duty, had retraced his steps. The air was sharp for they wore greatcoats. They looked alike, but not more than

others do. At first a wide space lay between them. They couldn't have seen each other, even had they raised their heads and looked about, because of this wide space, and then because of the undulating land, which caused the road to be in waves, not high, but high enough, high enough. But the moment came when together they went down into the same trough and in this trough finally met. . . . They turned towards the sea which, far in the east, beyond the fields, loomed high in the waning sky, and exchanged a few words. Then each went on his way. Each went on his way, A back towards the town, C on by ways he seemed hardly to know, or not at all, for he went with uncertain step and often stopped to look about him, like someone trying to fix landmarks in his mind, for one day perhaps he may have to retrace his steps, you never know. The treacherous hills where fearfully he ventured were no doubt only known to him from afar, seen perhaps from his bedroom window or from the summit of a monument which, one black day, having nothing in particular to do and turning to height for solace, he had paid his few coppers to climb, slower and slower, up the winding stones. From there he must have seen it all, the plain, the sea, and then these selfsame hills that some call mountains, indigo in places in the evening light, their serried ranges crowding to the skyline, cloven with hidden valleys that the eye divines from sudden shifts of colour and then from other signs for which there are no words nor even thoughts. . . . He looks old and it is a sorry sight to see him solitary after so many years, so many days and nights unthinkingly given to that rumour rising at birth and even earlier, What shall I do? What shall I do? now low, a murmur, now precise as the headwaiter's And to follow? and often rising to a scream. And in the end, or almost, to be abroad alone, by unknown ways, in the gathering night, with a stick. It was a stout stick, he used it to thrust himself onward, or as a defence, when the time came, against dogs and marauders.[13]

Without cataloguing all of the effects in this superficially simple but actually complex passage, we can outline some aspects of the generative process available to the reader. The expression "when next they pass," with its tail of "goodbyes" leads us from the thoughts of a comprehensive "you" to the first-person reflections beginning with "I don't know." The "yourself" in the next sentence is no longer a generalized second person but now the discouraged first person, who proceeds to invent or put into language people who can be distinguished

[13]Samuel Beckett, *Molloy*, in *Three Novels: Molloy, Malone Dies, The Unnamable* (New York: Grove, 1965), pp. 9–11.

from himself. A and C are spawned by the "dim things" of our opening sentence and by the need to "distinguish" people "from yourself";
their passing is a concrete instance of lost activity. Once the "things"
have been personified, though one may question the degree of indi-
viduality bestowed by two capital letters, there is no turning back.
Molloy quite naturally invents a road on which they may pass. To
keep it simple, he removes "hedges" and "ditches," which are consequently present in the reader's mind, but he proceeds to invent completely unnecessary cows that, true to cliché, chew their cud, for
which process they need fields. At this point, he seems to relax into his
task, giving a "scientific" account of the cud-chewing process before
pulling himself up short and, characteristically, surprising us by punc-
turing a cliché. We expect his "Perhaps I'm" to precede an uncharacteristic apology for digressing. Instead, he compounds the surprise by
insisting on the accuracy, not of his account of the scene, but of his
description of the process. Two sentences of beautifully phrased digression are followed by another surprise sentence, "But perhaps I'm
remembering things." This last is designed to put the impatient reader
on guard, invalidating the whole narrative project. It also forms a
pendant to the preceding aside, however, and prepares us for a further
digression. There follows a lyrical treatment of the road, a description
full of Flaubertian animation: "[it] seared the tender pastures, rose and
fell at the whim of hills and hollows." Two touches, the road that
"seared" and the whimsical "hills and hollows," constitute the originality of this otherwise pedestrian sentence filled with pastoral jargon.

   At this point, Molloy makes bold to conjure up a music hall pair,
"one small and one tall" and a town from which they would have to
depart and return. Circumstances are beginning to accumulate, blocks
for the builder to toy with as he convinces us and himself that the tale
is actually lived experience. Accordingly he begins to construct a
human situation and motivation: weariness and chill. At the same
time, he proposes the spatial dimension from which he will derive, by
way of the wave/sea metaphor, the seashore he later visits. Eventually,
the need for a perspective from which a "realistic" narrator would have
to view the action obliges Molloy to posit a hillside perch where he can
see and not be seen. He must then find a strategy for moving his
crippled body: crutches and a bicycle. Throughout, the emphasis is on
the generation of rational and "realistic" discourse to justify and pro-
long an irrational and seemingly unmotivated narrative.

Objects and actions are not enough, however. It is clear from the rhythms, the alliterative and other sound patterns, and the clichés of mood, in short from the verbal gestures, that the text is being shaped by its own echoes and ticks as well as by its apparent substance. Our antepenultimate sentence seems to have grown from its "s" and "n" alliterations just as effectively as the "stick" in the penultimate sentence sprouts from the fear and darkness that precedes it. Since Beckett collaborated in the translation of this book, we are at liberty to see these as calculated effects.

Molloy's text becomes no less self-generative as it progresses. In a segment filled with the repressive alien presence of Moran, who under similar circumstances imagines his own version of Molloy,[14] our speaker recalls what it was like to have been cleaned up and stowed away in a well-furnished room in Lousse's house or asylum:

> I woke up in a bed, in my skin. They had carried their impertinence to the point of washing me, to judge by the smell I gave off, no longer gave off. I went to the door. Locked. To the window. Barred. It was not yet quite dark. What is there left to try when you have tried the door and the window? The chimney perhaps. I looked for my clothes. I found a light switch and switched it on. No result. What a story! All that left me cold, or nearly. I found my crutches, against an easy chair. It may seem strange that I was able to go through the motions I have described without their help. I find it strange. You don't remember immediately who you are, when you wake. On a chair I found a white chamber pot with a roll of toilet-paper in it. Nothing was being left to chance. I recount these moments with a certain minuteness, it is a relief from what I feel coming. I set a pouffe against the easy chair, sat down in the latter and on the former laid my stiff leg. The room was chock-full of pouffes and easy chairs, they thronged all about me, in the gloom. There were also occasional tables, footstools, tallboys, etc., in abundance. Strange feeling of congestion that the night dispersed, though it lit the chandelier, which I had left turned on.[15]

Though they function much as do those of the earlier citation, these lines seem more dependent on what is to come, the narrative of Moran, which will retrospectively give and then discount an aura of coherence

[14]Ibid., pp. 151–58, but especially 154–55.
[15]Ibid., pp. 50–51.

to Molloy's "experience." For at moments like this one, Molloy is most clearly "possessed" by the settled, but for him unsettling, spirit, identity, and "experience" of his counterpart. How, otherwise, could this disconnected, asocial, and avowedly ignorant "writer" understand the intimate nature of furniture, even if he could "recall" it? Elsewhere we find him incapable of understanding even common objects such as a bicycle or a knife rest. Is he imagining real space, or has he inhabited this overfurnished room? Needless to say, only during a second reading of the entire novel does that particular interpenetration become available to the reader. In effect, Beckett has introduced a curious suspense, one hinging not on the evolution of the action or its plot but rather on the nature of all claims to validity.

To fulfill its decorum, the self-generating text we are describing must, like Beckett's novel, simultaneously and repeatedly affirm and disown itself. That is, it must present itself, first, as a process and ultimately, as the result of verbal substance visibly generating substance. Though we are repeatedly invited to respond to it as verisimilar, we are also continually reminded that it derives from the necessities of narrative, a given that implies not only a hidden narrative agenda but also an external or implied authorial will beyond the purview of the narrative proper, one that dictates and validates the results of that agenda. In Beckett's case, the implication is seemingly endless regress of authority. Indeed, by means of such an antithetical presence of absence, together with the appearance of randomness and an actual disaggregating irony, the self-generated fiction makes mock of the convention so accurately described by Patricia Tobin:

> The ambition of story is to eliminate risks to its own autonomy through the setting up of limits beyond which the element cannot stray into alternate relations of adequacy, juxtaposition, reversal, or repetition. Narrative supremacy depends upon such mastering strategies, essentially antierotic, which constitute an aesthetic defense against desire, against the random couplings encouraged by passion or play.[16]

To return to our citation, Molloy is once again generating his account from scraps of nothing, drawing upon a bank of unmoored

---

[16]Patricia Drechsel Tobin, *Time and the Novel: The Genealogical Imperative* (Princeton: Princeton University Press, 1978), p. 68. The reference here is to the theoretical position of Jean Ricardou.

perceptions, those of an outward-oriented awareness alien to everything we have seen thus far. Here we are made inescapably aware of his total otherness. Abandoning the realistic premise, the text presents him as an embodiment of a hidden essence, the inner man, the mind, the instincts, the id, even the muse: allegorical/real identities far removed from the everyday to which his narrative clings so tenaciously. (As Molloy's opposite number, Moran becomes, in this reading, a figuration of the superego, the social or outer range of Molloyness occupying the same psyche or psychic complex, engaged by the same range of philosophical discourse.)[17] Key sentences in our passage are, "It may seem strange that I was able to go through the motions I have described without help [from my crutches]. I find it strange. You don't remember immediately who you are, when you wake." This amusing inversion of the Proustian opening, besides moving us beyond Molloy, points up a characteristic pattern of behavior: the failure or refusal to erase. Molloy/Moran, the writer, lacking the means or will to delete inappropriate phrases, simply writes around them or, as in this case, shrugs them off. The next sentence, by revealing an uncharacteristic hygienic impulse, also prefigures Moran's anal fixation. Throughout, the reader oscillates between the sense that a genuine moment is being recounted with extreme precision and remarkable good humor and the suspicion that the action is being spun out of a fabric of words and emotions anchored in the void. The inconsequential detail enlivens the surface of an account that is at once mysterious and trivial. In effect, Molloy plays with narrative temporality and creates verisimilitude while desolving both in a verbal flow that pretends to hypotaxis (or the rhetoric of the verisimilar)[18] but repeatedly degenerates into an apparent randomness and inconsequence. His play in turn screens the fact that, within the structure of this work, there is little or no inconsequence or randomness, the whole being compounded of echoes and programmed as though by inexorable forces.

Both citations project creative options that are carefully restricted. Once a circumstance has been established, the protagonist proceeds to flesh it out according to a logic dictated by the words used to state it.

---

[17]For an early statement of this by no means widely held view, see my "Molloy: The Quest for Meaninglessness," in *Samuel Beckett Now*, ed. Melvin J. Friedman (Chicago: University of Chicago Press, 1970), pp. 129–56.
[18]See Kristeva's "La productivité," p. 71 and passim.

In our first example, we are faced with a nonevent and a minimal circumstance that progressively raises questions that must be answered or avoided. On the other hand, certain questions are characteristically left unasked. Thus we do not know, nor does Molloy, why he is on the hill. We never learn anything about C, though we imagine things about A. We do not question the sudden appearance of the stick or, later, of the dog. In short, Molloy's is a limited mock-realism of a very special sort, one that persists in leaving blanks where other narratives would offer details and vice versa. The arbitrary becomes the rule. Still, the typical situation will raise questions that cannot be avoided: What is the context? How does one react to what he sees? And so forth. Around such elementary questions the tale evolves, frequently more by means of asides than as a linear progression. It is the asides that most effectively subvert verisimilitude by putting the narrative procedures and the rhetoric in question.

Molloy's second half is dominated by a figure whom Bakhtin might have described as "monologic," one who delights in limits. Lacking the apparent insouciance of Molloy, Moran is anchored in the trivia of life, given to positive assertions (and hence to error). On the surface of it, his circumstances and narrative stance would seem to rule out the possibility of self-generation. As every reader of the book recalls, however, not only does his increasingly unlikely tale conclude with a statement that puts his whole narrative in question; it too is larded with irrelevant-seeming but ultimately significant asides. Furthermore, a careful reader of part one should, like the reader of Roussel's *Impressions*, be aware of the generative principle behind part two: every aspect of the first half must in some way be countered by a randomized equal-opposite re-presentation in the second half. Moran's tale is a parallel antinarrative to Molloy's, the counterspinning wheel of the bicycle. Thus what appears to be a new set of events and a new cast of characters becomes on inspection simply *the* version that Moran, the embodied impulse-complex, is able to give us. We should not be deceived by the fact that Moran's tale appears to be more nearly a recognizable version of our own experience. The further and the more closely we read, the more obvious and necessary the narrative procedures become, thanks to our engagement with the traces of the first narrative *and* our reading habits, all of which are repeatedly displaced by the logic of this discourse.

The third novel of the trilogy, *The Unnamable*, confirms what I have been saying about the fundamental strategies of *Molloy* by carrying them to their logical extreme and approximating their ultimate source. Here there can be no question of observed detail or verisimilitude, since the protagonist or speaker declares himself as an essence in search of an existence (to borrow from a terminology often too literally applied to Beckett). The agony of the incorporeal performing voice derives from the need to represent through narrative, unwillingly, as though under command, a corporeal being whose nature approximates (allegorically) that of the "unnamable's" generative (non)presence. The narrative is no more than a record of the voice's attempts at the behest of other voices to fix its sense of selfhood by imagining what sort of being its nature could motivate.

Though perhaps not immediately evident to the reader, this need to embody becomes increasingly clear as we are dragged into and through the life fragments of two versions of Mahood (first as a crippled quester, then as a basket case in an urn) and one of Worm (a wriggling and persecuted innocent).[19] It follows that the details of these narrative accounts, aborted fragments though they may be, are all overtly self-generated. The speaker itself is transparently the creature of its prose, generated as much as generating.

Each of Beckett's chronicles of falling off exhibits an equal and opposite awareness on the part of the reader of a formal ascendency, a building toward shapeliness that inheres in the very sentences with which decay and deadliness, to say nothing of absence of joy, are conveyed. That is, the same text that portrays despair conveys joy as inherent in the procedures of its own making. This joy derives not only from the abundant (if sinister, sly, and ironic) humor but also from the power of the prose to make something out of absolutely nothing, as in the following description of Mahood in his jug outside the restaurant opposite the horse butcher's shop: "For a collar, fixed to the mouth of the jar, now encircles my neck just below the chin. And my lips which used to be hidden, and which I sometimes pressed against the freshness of the stone, can now be seen by all and sundry. Did I say I catch flies? I snap them up, clack! Does this mean I still have my teeth? To have lost one's limbs and preserved one's dentition,

---

[19]We should equate these figures with avatars of Molloy, Moran, and Malone/ Sapo/MacMan, personifications that have earlier been generated by this questing voice along with others from the Beckett menagerie.

what a mockery!"[20] With alacrity we greet the treatment of a life, physical sensations, and a narrative development, any development, in a text that at times resembles a desert of unfocused and unrelieved language. Here we are struck by the plastic quality given to an existence that is purely verbal. We may also note the traps laid for us, however, and the almost childlike insistence on springing those traps. It is no wonder, then, that we find ourselves snapping up a fly in the person of the unpersonifiable voice. What is more important, the very words that impose their message of being on the nameless presence appear to grow from the words that precede them and, by extension, from the *Word* that is the nothingness. Thus "mouth of the jar" leads inevitably to "my lips," if not to the particular shift into whimsy evident in "Did I say I catch flies?"

It could be said that Beckett's texts are near-perfect examples of applied modernism in that they are characterized by complete control, incessant adaptation, and what could be called authorial absence. Clearly if they are also to achieve the appearance of writing themselves out of their own essence, such texts must be rigorously overseen.[21] As Flaubert would have it, the manner, which changes from text to text, must be fine-tuned to its matter. A reading of Beckett, however, obliges us to reinterpret the post-Flaubertian dictum that the author should abstract himself from his work, becoming Joyce's indifferent artist-god "paring his fingernails." Behind the narrative is the self-effacing author who, by virtue of his active self-effacement, becomes increasingly self-engaged. (The image of a masturbating deity comes to mind.) What results is a text that takes its subjective quality not so much from the matter it treats or from the narrative presence of an authorial persona as from underlying patterns, the systems of personalized rhythms and attitudes that constitute what might be called its gestural vocabulary. The powerfully personalized gesture gives birth to and ultimately sustains the self-perpetuating and doubly narcissistic text, Beckett's reluctant "I am because I say I am not."

---

[20]Beckett, *The Unnamable*, in *Three Novels*, p. 332.

[21]For a different perspective, focusing on the narrator rather than the author and text, see Eric Levy's suggestive view of the "pure narrator," whose "whole being is contained in the act of trying to tell a story" (*Beckett and the Voice of Species: A Study of the Prose Fiction* [Totowa, N.J.: Barnes & Noble, 1980], p. 6).

The procedures of these novels pretending to tell themselves through the medium of a self-engaging narrator may be grounded in a Joycean precedent: the secularization of Loyola's meditative procedure as Joyce's "composition of place," whose locus classicus in *Ulysses* is the development and aura of the "Parable of the Plums" told by Stephen Dedalus in the "Eolus" chapter. This view takes on weight when Beckett makes a direct allusion to the circumstance of the parable during his own first transparent use of self-generation.[22] Allowance made for the usual reversal of details, the single man dubbed C, who pays to climb the circular staircase of the tower in an anecdote generated spontaneously out of the language of Molloy, may well be a tip of the hat to Joyce's account of Stephen's oral textualization of two old women whom he imagines doing the same thing.

The telling and derivation of the "Parable" enable us to see Stephen's creative mind making something out of nothing more than language itself, journalistic and literary conventions, and half-digested experience or memories. For us, however, the importance of the "parable" resides less in its role as an illustration of Stephen's gifts and preoccupations or even as a chronicle of the creative process than in the eventual incorporation of that process in the very texture of the narrative. That is, Stephen's seemingly instinctive appropriation of St. Ignatius's rules will eventually dictate certain aspects of the novel in which he appears: not only the rendering of the Shakespeare argument in "Scylla and Charybdis," but also the form of such later chapters as "Eumeus" and "Ithaca."[23] We may add that the project explicit in Stephen's utterance and behavior will become part of the implicit

[22]An argument could be made for *Watt*'s autogeneration, since the novel is narrated by a character named Sam from the account given in a variety of codes by a demented Watt. In that novel, however, the strategy is only belatedly made more or less clear, whatever the intent, and the universe depicted is far more open than the one elaborated for the trilogy.

[23]In "Scylla and Charybdis," Stephen calls openly for aid in his attempt to render his argument "realistic": "Composition of place. Ignatius Loyola, Make haste to help me!" James Joyce, *Ulysses* (New York: Random House, 1986), p. 155. The reference to the cry for aid at the end of *A Portrait of the Artist as a Young Man* is inescapable and the change in father figures crucial. *Portrait* was under the sign of Daedalus; *Ulysses*, in what concerns Stephen, may well be under that of Loyola, ironically portrayed as the spiritual father of realistic discourse.

project of *Finnegans Wake*, where the true source of words within the larger conceptual frame is, generally if not invariably, language itself.

Having followed his development through *Portrait*, "Telemachus," and "Nestor," we have acquired by "Proteus" a body of experience that can justify what Stephen does with the vision of the two "midwives" walking splayfooted across the strand. We are also with him as he accumulates images elsewhere: in the tower, at the school, on the beach, and in the newspaper office. Still, the deliberate shaping of an aesthetic object from these shards constitutes for us a new sort of experience. It *makes explicit and transparent* the process by which a text can grow through association and recombination, a process mainly *implicit* in *Portrait*. Simultaneously, the account of that shaping makes the recombined materials as engrossing as the process itself while engaging us in a further procedure: justifying the new text with reference to prior givens. That is, as insiders provided with privileged information, we can disarticulate the finished parable as it is being put together, giving it a triple validity as product of the hero's mind, as a reflection on his/our experience, and as a part of an ongoing logical and dramatic development.

To illustrate this point we need examine only two passages, the first from "Proteus":

> They came down the steps from Leahy's terrace prudently, *Frauenzimmer*: and down the shelving shore flabbily, their splayed feet sinking in the silted sand. Like me, like Algy, coming down to our mighty mother. Number one swung lourdily her midwife's bag, the other's gamp poked in the beach. From the liberties, out for the day. Mrs Florence MacCabe, relict of the late Patk MacCabe, deeply lamented, of Bride Street. One of her sisterhood lugged me squealing into life. Creation from nothing.[24]

Once Stephen's self-preoccupation has been interrupted by the appearance of the women, the image is fixed in his mind by metaphorization, a symptom of his cosmological itch. It is realized by his terse positioning of them as historical beings, done with the aid of a few journalistic specifics in a plausible referential but wholly fictive context. "Creation from nothing" indeed!

This combination of pragmatic detail and symbolic reading enables

Stephen to react creatively to the rhetorical overkill of the journalists in "Eolus," producing for a limited and unstable audience the most memorable of his literary achievements:

DEAR DIRTY DUBLIN

Dubliners.

—Two Dublin vestals, Stephen said, elderly and pious, have lived fifty and fiftythree years in Fumbally's lane.

—Where is that? the professor asked.

—Off Blackpitts, Stephen said.

Damp night reeking of hungry dough. Against the wall. Face glistering tallow under her fustian shawl. Frantic hearts. Akasic records. Quicker, darlint!

On now. Dare it. Let there be life.

—They want to see the views of Dublin from the top of Nelson's pillar. They save up three and tenpence in a red tin letterbox moneybox. They shake out the threepenny bits and sixpences and coax out the pennies with the blade of a knife. Two and three in silver and one and seven in coppers. They put on their bonnets and best clothes and take their umbrellas for fear it may come on to rain.

—Wise virgins, professor MacHugh said.

LIFE ON THE RAW

—They buy one and fourpenceworth of brawn and four slices of panloaf at the north city diningrooms in Marlborough street from Miss Kate Collins, proprietress. They purchase four and twenty ripe plums from a girl at the foot of Nelson's pillar to take off the thirst of the brawn. They give two threepenny bits to the gentleman at the turnstile and begin to waddle slowly up the winding staircase, grunting, encouraging each other, afraid of the dark, panting, one asking the other have you the brawn, praising God and the Blessed Virgin, threatening to come down, peeping at the airslits. Glory be to God. They had no idea it was that high.[25]

Stephen's vision is clearly a reaction to that of John F. Taylor, whose invention, the Egyptian high priest's address to the young Moses, was declaimed earlier. Like his aesthetic in chapter 5 of *Portrait*, the para-

[25]Ibid., p. 119.

ble is delivered under adverse circumstances, but the impulse here is of a different order. No academic exercise, this narrative is a vital test of Stephen's powers as a shaper of word-objects. "On now," he urges himself, "Dare it. Let there be life."[26] Lucifer-like, he is conscious of rivaling God by creating from nothing, just as we are conscious of his reshaping *some*thing, especially when we rediscover Florence McCabe. Thus the myth of generation is countered by the fact/effect of self-generation (however primitive) by which this bit of text grows out of textually available substance. Given our privileged position in relation to the details, we are apt to be as engrossed by the procedure of creation as we are by the reactions of the hearers, the context, and the presentation of the text on the page.

Establishing before our eyes a complete setting for what is obviously an imagined action, this inconclusive mininarrative is at once a self-contained object, an action in its own right, and a figure for the text as action and activity—a symptom of the book's method. It stands out from the rest of the treatment of Stephen by anchoring itself in the context of his mind, without, as in other instances, fully exposing the mental operation as random thought. Since, in this highly dramatic moment, the particulars of that thought are passed over in silence by the otherwise loquacious text, the job of reconstituting that process is clearly left up to us readers making and performing our own *Ulysses*. Our effort enables us to recognize and accept the parable as a product of previous experience organized by a permutational process to serve new ends: we must ascertain how it grows organically from the context and from Stephen's relationship to it.

In contrast to the parable, we have the far more prolonged rhetorical exercise known as "Eumeus," a chapter assigned to a Bloomish voice and called by Joyce "Monologue Old."[27] There the material being generated is almost pure excess verbiage: maundering sentences larded with qualifying clauses that proliferate as though by some slight of hand to fill dead space with dead ideas enlivened only by the occasional nugget of information and a sly wit. Like Beckett's *Unnamable*, this chapter seems at times to be running quite out of control. If the "Parable" inspired an aspect of *Molloy*, "Eumeus" may, along with

[26]Ibid.
[27]See Joyce's "schema" reproduced in Richard Ellmann, *Ulysses on the Liffey* (New York: Oxford University Press, 1972), pp. 186–88.

"Penelope," have inspired the verbal flood of the later novel. As we see in the following sentence, the Bloomian discourse of the chapter bursts like a mushroom from the moist subsoil of its own language:

> *En route* to his taciturn and, not to put too fine a point on it, not yet perfectly sober companion Mr Bloom who at all events was in complete possession of his faculties, never more so, in fact disgustingly sober, spoke a word of caution *re* the dangers of nighttown, women of ill fame and swell mobsmen, which, barely permissible once in a while though not as a habitual practice, was of the nature of a regular deathtrap for young fellows of his age particularly if they had acquired drinking habits under the influence of liquor unless you knew a little jiujitsu for every contingency as even a fellow on the broad of his back could administer a nasty kick if you didn't look out.[28]

These circumlocutions, ungrammaticalities, nonsequiturs, and clichés function as gestural markers, underscoring Bloom's discomfort as well as his pride at being with a young man whose intellectual gifts overwhelm him. The text reacts as a correlative not only for fatigue but also for a complex array of states. To those states we can ascribe the leavened language, but it is to the cliché as automatic discourse and to the mimetic habits of the novel that we may ascribe the impression of words being spun almost out of their own substance in the void.

A similar procedure shapes portions of "Ithaca," in which the encyclopedic catechistic responses grow at times exponentially from their questions, and the format may at times be the message. On another level, the evening and night chapters as a whole, controlled by the seemingly autonomous arranging presence,[29] represent a counterstatement to the hyperrealism of the daytime opening. This initially secondary but eventually dominant nonreferential system of meaning enables the text to abandon what Roland Barthes calls referential verisimilitude.[30] Though not precisely self-generative, since it focuses our attention not on textual production but rather on textual procedures, this aspect of *Ulysses* permitted the text to slip its moorings. The manifestly free-floating, arranged portion of the book, by licensing artifice, established language and style as signifying events and the

[28]Joyce, *Ulysses*, p. 502.
[29]See David Hayman, *Ulysses: The Mechanics of Meaning*, pp. 88–104 and passim.
[30]See Roland Barthes, "L'effet du réel," *Communications* 11 (1968), 86.

page as an arena for their activity, foreshadowing the proliferating word-hoard of *Finnegans Wake*.

A book that is recreated each time each reader touches its surface, *Finnegans Wake* may be the century's prime self-generating text. Given Joyce's straining after the absolute in controlled aesthetic expression, this statement may seem paradoxical, but the record stands, if not complete, at least voluminous. In a way unmatched in previous literature, its words did and do beget words. Now that we have both the generative and the postgenerative volumes on our shelves, we can see for ourselves that the pretextual and paratextual manifestations surrounding this seminal work necessarily partake in the process. The treatment of this interaction demands a book, but by relying on existing materials to fill out our position, we can illustrate it briefly, leaving the bulk of the proof to the perceptive reader and to history.

What, then, is the impact of Joyce's procedures and the accumulation of text upon the reader and student of *Finnegans Wake?* In what ways are the process of the book's development and the details of its history reflected in the procedures of apprehension? Is a text that is to such a degree self-generating perceived and experienced as such? Since these are more than rhetorical questions, they defy firm responses and invite speculation.

To backtrack a bit, we may say that Roussel generates rhetorical structures to accommodate the products of an analysis born of and perpetuated by rhetorical choices but ultimately shaped by needs beyond the limits of authorial control. Beckett's books are exercises in the generation of words from the terror of the void in terms of cleverly manipulated personifications of absence whose vital rhetoric enables us to perceive and accommodate a universe of meaninglessness. In contrast, Joyce's *Wake*, which posits a plenum of experience through a polydimensional history, is an exercise in the generation of substantial language from a minimal synthetic statement of existence, one that is less threatening than reassuring. Joyce's vision of a universe deriving from archetypal minima, however fanciful, elaborates its verbal substance from a need to follow the trail of ramifying existences, to disclose it, rather, through a self-perpetuating language. Implicit in every line and syllable of the *Wake* is a universal Book of Genesis and an eternal engagement with father Adam, the bestower of names, and his progeny.

More than simple apprehension, the *Wake*'s goal is immersion and the ultimate in imitation. Readers are surrounded by a gesturing medium that under their eyes seems to bring new textual dimensions into being. This effect is of course partly a matter of focus. The phrase that, from one perspective, will elicit a given attitude and convey a given context and action, will generally, from a slightly different optic, express several complementary and even contradictory experiences. The delightfully unstable result Joyce himself called a "collideorscape."[31] To what is actually a function of the reader's increasing awareness of facets latent in the language we may ascribe the pleasurable sense of creating the *Wake* as well as possessing it. One recalls Mallarmé's revealing view that the Parnassians of his day, by naming objects and thus delimiting them, withdrew the mystery and "deprived [readers] of the delicious joy of believing that they are creating."[32] On the surface of it, then, the illusion that the text makes its meaning from its own substance under our eyes and through the medium of our privileged reading, the sense of the text as *host* or *hosti* (in all of its possible senses) justifies our use of the term self-generation.

There is evidence in the manuscripts that the composition of the *Wake* was, for Joyce, an equivalent experience, that, to a limited but crucial extent, the text continually and repeatedly grew from its own substance, being confined mainly by aesthetic considerations of balance, rhythm, and proportion. We know that, when he began writing the *Wake*, Joyce turned back to his earlier efforts, writing in the famous *Scribbledehobble* notebook the titles of books, chapters, stories, and scenes upon which he planned to elaborate.[33] The cannibalism was by no means simple and direct. For the most part Joyce was letting his mind play associatively over the surface of his early work. Still, even at that stage, before the ink on the pages of the Shakespeare and Company edition of *Ulysses* had dried and while he was still considering a revised edition of that book, he was producing his new text from his old ones.

---

[31]James Joyce, *Finnegans Wake* (New York: Viking, 1939), p. 143.28.

[32]This quotation is from an interview with Jules Huret "Sur l'évolution littéraire," reprinted in *Mallarmé: Oeuvres complètes*, ed. Henri Mondor and G. Jean-Aubry (Paris: Gallimard, Pléiade, 1965), p. 869.

[33]See *The James Joyce Archive*, vol. 28 (Danis Rose, ed., Buffalo Notebook VI.A), and Thomas Connolly's imperfect but still useful transcription in *Scribbledehobble* (Evanston, Ill.: Northwestern University Press, 1961).

Under "Exiles," for example, we find an elaboration on the theme of Tristan and Isolde, beginning with notes on the Wagner opera.[34] Since the Tristan theme is explicit in the notebook for *Exiles* but only latent in the play itself, we may have in this example a paradigm for Joyce's use of his early work in the formation of *Finnegans Wake*.[35] Afterthoughts on the problematics of the published texts became a source for fresh treatments. Thus the *Dubliners* tale "After the Races" concealed the Wildean homosexual motif Joyce developed briefly under that story's title in the "Scribbledehobble" and finally built into an aspect of the "crime" of his father Adam, HCE. Under "Evelyn," a narrative treatment of the "electra" complex, we find allusions to "Pop," who later, as HCE, is an object of incestuous longings and exhibits them. From such jottings grew the early sketches for the *Work in Progress*.

Almost every basic motif and theme and all of the major protagonists in the *Wake* can be traced back to early notes and to the primitive sketches drawn from them. That is, the movable parts were in place even before the writer knew the shape his new book would take and long before he had molded its language. However indirectly, they derived from earlier work that must be considered as essential to the understanding of the *Wake*.

In 1923, Joyce was able to assure his benefactress, Harriet Weaver, that the brief fragments he had written by that time would eventually be joined by the text. In the event, the sketches were to constitute its armature, generating in a surprisingly coherent way its two dominant systems of meaning: (1) the active male chapters concerned with the fall of man, its causes, and its consequences; (2) the account of man's defense and resurrection by the "passive" force delineated in the female-dominated chapters. This is, of course, a radical oversimplification, since there are male aspects in the female chapters and vice versa. Given the limits of the book's themes and the procedures of autogeneration, there is bound to be a total interaction in the infrastructural level, as the systems outlined in the chapter on "Nodality" attest. Still, the concept that the book grew from sketches that

---

[34]*Archive*, Ibid., pp. 89, 95–96 (Connolly, *Scribbledehobble*, pp. 271–331); David Hayman, "Tristan and Isolde in *Finnegans Wake*," *Comparative Literature Studies* 1 (1962), 93–112. For a possible source for this theme, see my account of the Lucia Joyce papers: "Shadow of His Mind," *Library Chronicle of the University of Texas*, n.s. 20/21 (1982), 70, 76–77.

[35]James Joyce, *Exiles* (New York: Viking, 1961), p. 123.

grew from notes that evolved from a reconsideration of the early work can stand as a schematic vision of the actual textual autogenerative process as opposed to the illusion of autogeneration.

My insistence on the text's autonomy is more than rhetorical; for though Joyce wrote the *Wake* and solved the technical problems we are discussing, he was inevitably caught up in the rules imposed by the monster that he was making. The fiction of the text engaged in its own production is useful as a means of underlining a very real aspect of the composition of the *Wake*. As we shall see, it also figures importantly in the history of the composition of Sollers's fictions—and as we have already seen, it is the central fiction of Beckett's novels.

In terms of its macrostructure, the *Wake* to some degree generated itself during 1923, even before Joyce, the first reader, could measure its potential. On the microstructural level, the process was strikingly similar but considerably more transparent. Even a cursory study of the manuscripts will show that at least five subprocesses obtain through-out and that all of them reflect the essential nature of each aspect of the text as presented in each of its several published manifestations and many draft versions. First, there is the tendency for one pun or allusion to generate more language from the need to exploit its latent implications. Second, the *Wake*'s decorum requires that basic thematic content, seminal actions, and core characters be made continuously manifest. Third, in different contexts these characters must undergo appropriate permutations in relation to, for example, the time of the night and the historical system of Vico. Fourth, the passage must pick up echoes from other passages and contribute to the grid of meaning, the internal allusive texture. Finally, the encyclopedic impulse makes each textual moment rich in implications and intertextual allusions to the point of approximating the universal.

Taken together, these requirements place us in the double domain of writing and reading. That is, every attribute of the process of the development of the manuscript will find its analogues in the process of unweaving and reweaving that is reading. The writer's accomplishment and the reader's accommodation are alternative procedures that approach the condition of reversibility. Even if, as readers, we do not actually write the *Wake*, we do experience a disclosure of process and engage in a selecting and shaping when we "wipe our glosses with what we know."[36] That all readers of the *Wake* are glossators is sug-

---

[36]Joyce, *Finnegans Wake*, p. 304, n. 3.

gested by this famous paragraph from chapter I.5, which evokes our
reception of the text under cover of a treatment of the letter's impact
on the archeologist hen:

> Well, almost any photoist worth his chemicots will tip anyone asking him
> the teaser that if a negative of a horse happens to melt enough while
> drying, well, what you do get is, well, a positively grotesquely distorted
> macromass of all sorts of horsehappy values and masses of meltwhile
> horse. Tip. Well, this freely is what must have occurred to our missive
> (there's a sod of a turb for you! please wisp off the grass!) unfilthed from
> the boucher by the sagacity of a lookmelittle likemelong hen. Heated
> residence in the heart of the orangeflavoured mudmound had partly
> obliterated the negative to start with, causing some features palpably
> nearer your pecker to be swollen up most grossly while the farther back
> we manage to wiggle the more we need the loan of a lens to see as much
> as the hen saw. Tip.[37]

The subprocesses of generation can be illustrated briefly, though
their universal application will have to be taken on faith by the reader
unfamiliar with the *Wake*. All of them have contributed to the development of this amusing and not particularly dense sentence from chapter
5:

> Midwinter (*fruur or kuur?*) was in the offing *and Premver a promise of a pril*
> when, *as kischabrigies sang life's old sahatsong,* an *iceclad* shiverer, mere*st of*
> bantling*s* observed a cold fowl behav*iouris*ing strangely on that fatal *mid-*
> *den or chip factory or comicalbottomed copsjute* (dump *for short*) *afterwards*
> *changed into* the orangery when in the course of deeper demolition *unex-*
> *pectedly one bushman's holiday* its *limon* threw up *a few spontaneous* fragments
> of orangepeel, the *last remains* of an outdoor meal by some unknown
> sunseeker *or placehider illico way back* in *his* mistridden past.[38]

During the postfall dark ages, a small boy watches a hen scratching in
the kitchen midden or a dungheap that could also be the grave mound
of the fallen hero and/or a battlefield. The orange peel she uncovers
may be the letter, a memento of a picnic, and/or a relic of a battle
between Protestant and Catholic Irishmen (and so on). In this, its final
form, the basic sentence is enriched by rhymes, alliterations, puns,

[37]Ibid, pp. 111–12.
[38]Ibid, p. 110, my italics except for "illico."

and asides. Otherwise, its form and burden are roughly those of the first version. (We may note in passing that this is the kind of writing one might expect from the young Stephen Dedalus intent on producing a secular composition of place.) I have italicized the major variants, but we should begin with the earliest draft, to which Joyce added only the word "unexpectedly": "Midwinter was in the offing when a poorly clad shiverer, a mere bantling, observed a cold fowl behaving strangely on the fatal dump at the spot called the orangery when in the course of its deeper demolition it threw up certain fragments of orange peel, the remnant of an outdoor meal of some unknown sunseeker *illico* in a mistridden past."[39] One major change in the second version is the scientistic term "behaviorizing" for the straightforward "behaving." We may trace that change to the action of "observing," which suggests psychological research and is reinforced by the fact that its object is a hen. Another change introduces archeological jargon: "the fatal dump at the spot called the orangery" became "that fatal midden (or call it dump, for short) afterwards changed into the orangery." The last part of this alteration adds a touch of ironic elegance to our sentence, pointing up the suggestion of the royal orangeries of Europe. Finally, "remnant" became "the only remains," adding a slight suggestion of and reinforcement for the word "fatal," which occurs earlier in the sentence.[40] The changes in the third draft are not numerous, but "Offing" became temporarily "onning" in a simple associational reversal; "poorly clad" became suggestively "iceclad", and "the only remains" became "the last remains," firming up the association latent in the previous change.[41] The process was continued through the various

[39]*The James Joyce Archive*, vol. 46 (*Finnegans Wake*, chapters 4–5, ed. David Hayman), pp. 235–36.

[40]Ibid, pp. 244–45.

[41]Ibid, p. 251. A fine essay by Jean-Michel Rabaté makes a similar point concerning the genesis of a paragraph from *Finnegans Wake*, pp. 264.15–266.19. Explaining that the passage grew from a simple listing of locations in the town of Chapelizod, Rabaté shows how Joyce elaborated a setting for HCE's pub, interweaving all manner of cultural, historical, and thematic materials. He concludes, "Joyce imposes strict formal constraints illustrated by the drafts which bear witness to the ingenious solutions he found for veritable mathematic problems. Joyce is not all that far from the Oulipo of Queneau and Perec when he sets himself the task of writing what appears to be a banal but jolly description in which he uses little more than proper names taken from the Chapelizod annual directory and when he allows himself no more than the modest liberty of multiplying an actual [mileage] figure." (Jean-Michel Rabaté, "Pour une cryptogenèse de l'idiolecte joycien," in *Genèse de Babel: Joyce et la création*, ed. Claude Jacquet [Paris: Editions du CNRS, 1985], p. 70, my translation).

proofs, pages and galleys, leading to the final version, but it is already clear that the method, even in this relatively simple example, was to let the sentence control its own growth.

This sentence, then, brings together in a predictable but amusing fashion the components of the fall and resurrection or regeneration. Winter contrasts, accordingly, with the youth of the observer; the midden contains relics of a vibrant past; the cold hen stands figuratively for the warm, nourishing female responsible for the letter; a battle is suggested by the orange (faction's) remains in a Dublin suburb; the solar implications of the orange reinforce the outdoor meal or picnic and evoke a sunset, and so on. In short, the gestures of rising and falling, together with the fraternal battles and maternal gifts, are reaffirmed as constants in a variety of ways.

The principles applied here could be elaborated upon were we to examine adjacent sentences, but it is already obvious that the text is using its own thematic material as the compost from which flowers of association will rise and flourish and the reader will derive a sense of engagement with proliferating images. The simple, readily accessible scene accretes supplementary and contradictory shadow contexts. This constant replaying of a limited number of themes is perhaps more consistent with musical procedures than with narrative ones, even though the aggregate is pervasively novelistic, being perhaps the ultimate "masterplot." Joyce, for all the expansiveness of his later muse, is, like Beckett and Mallarmé, a minimalist on this level. Like Beckett, for whom repetition is the ultimate ploy and only escape from and assurance of a necessary silence, Joyce found permutation ("repetition with a difference") the ultimate in pained pleasure. Both of these writers are fully aware of the impossibility of making a statement or fixing "reality" without destroying it. Like Flaubert, both are addicted to paradox as a mode of assertion as well as an act of avoidance. Still, despite his freshly minted language, Joyce is more open in his use of repetition and permutation, more insistent in his use of association, less bound by the exigencies of plot character and setting, more given to constructing his novels as one would an argument.

With paradox as a ground, we may expect to find an insistence on negative markers, imposed not only sequentially but simultaneously, and a consequent rejection of the temporality of assertion. Our sentence begins with a contradiction: both winter and spring are in the offing. Reading on, we discover that *primavera* brings a promise of a peril, an echo of T. S. Eliot's dour commentary. Life's old sweet song has become "Life's old sahatsong," or sad song. The hero of this episode, saintly Kevin, an avatar of Shaun, is a "bantling," or brat, while the hen is a "cold fowl," a term often used to describe a cooked and cooled (hence dead) chicken. Furthermore, we may recall that a bird picks among the spoils of battle in chapter I, where the "gnarlybird"[42] is seen "on her behaviourite job of quainance bandy." Thus the hen of life who recovers the past for mankind is one with the bird of death, but then, even that dismal bird, after the fall of Humpty-Humphrey-Chimpton-Finnegan, is a continuer who provides "iggs for the brekkers come to mournhim, sunny side up with care." It is therefore fitting that the reader of our sentence look back on "some unknown sunseeker . . . in his mistridden past."[43] Furthermore, if "orangery" suggests elegance and sweetness, it also suggests lemons or the French *limon*, which means both lemon and the sort of mud found in the delta of the Nile. We are dealing with primal facts, which include the association of woman with the creative slime and particularly with the triangle/delta of fertility. Also keyed to chapter I.1 is a reference to a buried past or the grave of the hero, this time associated with the dialogue between two prehistoric plebes, Mutt and Jute, avatars of Shem and Shaun, meeting at the hallowed site where they begin mingling their languages. Here in the "comicalbottomed copsjute," the Jute is linked with the Scandinavian manservant Siggerson, who, in a later chapter, doubles as the cop on the beat. The allusion to primitive man is reinforced by the "bushman" in "bushman's holiday." This interpretation by no means exhausts the burden of the sentence or rather the wordplay in which the reader, trapped by liberally scattered ungrammaticalities, is enmeshed, but it may suggest the degree to which the text feeds on its own substance.

Joyce deepened and broadened his book less by adding more basic ingredients than by discovering ways to expose and conceal simultaneously the simplicity of his basic design and its components. Not only did the process disclose the reflective associations and permutations that enable the hen to stand in for Woman in her creative, destructive, and preservative phases, that permit the grand male to be embodied in the lesser and symbolized by the letter as well as by the tumulous/dump/midden that shows how the fall and the rise can be

[42]Joyce, *Finnegans Wake*, p. 10.
[43]Ibid., pp. 12, 110.

generated from a single image. It also enlivened the surface with humor, rhetorical devices, narrative details, and allusions to other passages. As Joyce wrote, it wrote. That is, the words he wrote with one purpose inevitably opened the text to accommodate others limited by the frame of reference but responding to pressures inherent in their language. The process of revising or simply rereading other passages led, and still leads, to the disclosure of previously unregistered echoes and from these to their amplification.

The reader, like the writer, will proceed by imposing upon the text its own reflexivity. That is, as we read, we find hidden in the tapestry the furniture of our textual lives. The text enforces our reading by generating out of its own substance the items we learn to expect from it, disclosing first, by the shadow of an arm and then, by the movement of a head, the presence of the hero or his sons; evoking the crime and its aftermath by a reference to urination or to song. (The scandalous "Rann" composed by Hosty [chapter I.2] is among other things the "sahatsong" of our sentence.) Through this process of embedding and unveiling, the writer and reader coalesce to make, unmake, and remake the text to which they are ultimately atuned: the dream text— the world dream. Yet like the dream of the individual, this universal dream is, as Freud would have it, complete under its disguises (read "condensations" and "displacements").[44] Everything needed for the understanding of the universal word is present in the book that is life as well as dream, since our present is a palimpsest of our multiple pasts. It only awaits the "photoist"-reader capable of looking back through to the "horsehappy values," to see the norms beneath the distortions in the closed system of "Doublends Jined."[45]

Though tending to be as distinct as the writers who have bound themselves over into their service, self-generating texts share certain traits. In addition to making textual autonomy overt and continually reaffirming it through explicit statement or discreet allusion, they tend to involve the reader in their production by refusing to guarantee the credibility and viability of a vision that the reader is obliged finally to

[44]Joyce alluded to Freud's *Interpretation of Dreams* in the *Wake* and in the *Wake* notebooks.
[45]Joyce, *Finnegans Wake*, pp. 111, 20.

establish. All of them recognize that their autonomy is tenuous at best. To reinforce it, they devise both thematic and mechanical procedures, often calling upon the practices and messages of illustrious predecessors (or accessible conventions) for substance and support. It is symptomatic that, long before he began work on his own process book, *Paradis*, Philippe Sollers perceptively read Dante's *Divine Comedy* as "a text in the process of writing itself, and beyond that the first great book to be thought and acted integrally by its author."[46]

Sollers's study of Dante coincided almost precisely with his composition of his breakaway novel, *Drame* (1965), which treats the procedure of writing in ways reminiscent of Gide's project in *The Counterfeiters* but premonitory of his own later and more integrally self-generative fictions. In an essay devoted to *Drame*, Roland Barthes claims that in it "the actor and the narrator, united under an equivocal *I*, Sollers becomes precisely a single actant: his narrator is entirely taken up in a single action, that of narrating: transparent in the impersonal novel, here, becoming opaque, visible, filling the scene."[47] According to Julia Kristeva, this was the moment when writers at *Tel Quel*, whose original mission was, among other things, the promulgation of New Novelistic credos, were attempting to "return to and enrich the technique of the new novel, to force it to attempt an interior experience which was precisely painful, ecstatic or dramatic, one that the rather protestant austerity of the new novel had discarded."[48] Kristeva may well be alluding to *Nombres* rather than to the transitional, austere *Drame*, which Sollers took pains to characterize in his jacket copy as a

> novel writing itself under the reader's eyes. . . . Here, on the paper, in and between the words, perception, dream, sleep, waking, eroticism, death, "reality" etc. reciprocal transformations are given as equivalents. . . . If there is a tale, it tells finally how a language (a syntax)

---

[46]Sollers, *Literature and the Experience of Limits*, ed. David Hayman, trans. Philip Barnard with David Hayman (New York: Columbia University Press, 1983), p. 12.

[47]Roland Barthes, "Drame, poème, roman," in *Sollers écrivain* (Paris: Seuil, 1979), p. 20, my translation. It is interesting to note that Barthes is projecting the novel as in reaction not only to Flaubert's avowed practice but to that of all traditional mimetic narrative.

[48]Julia Kristeva, "Mémoire," *L'Infini* 1 (1983), 45.

searches itself out, invents itself, making itself at once transmitter and receiver—experience of the living violence resulting from the act of speaking, of being spoken.[49]

Self-generation is obviously a factor here, but in practice it is more thematic than real.

By contrast, we have the more exuberant and vital *Nombres* (1968). Quite apart from its declared project to develop a four-sided progression, *Nombres* is a novel at once fixed and in motion, one that is generated by its four prime positions through a series of twenty-five sets. Repeatedly, the reader (though usually in the guise of the writer) is placed in, engaged by, witness to, and source of situations that can be described as frontally polyvalent and autogenerative. The following illustrative passage derives in large measure from the interior citation, an enigmatic utterance, deliberately included as the visible instigator or *amorce:*

2.14 . . . 'so that we have there, under our eyes, within us, an absolutely impenetrable margin': I saw the hall, the audience, and the one who spoke standing in the central alley, turned toward the windows struck by the sound. . . . A picture was hanging on the wall and the bottom of that picture, in a deeper blue, was therefore the space for additions and divisions. . . . And I saw myself rise, open the window, and, turning, noted that the meeting was proceeding behind the window where someone was speaking my name. . . . The street, the city were in fact those which I had left. Nevertheless, I saw them as street, as city, only through a transposition backward whose prospective elements could not be stated. Just like, now, this engraver who, one hundred years before the event, showed the beheading of a king even though the mechanism did not exist. . . . It was easy for me to relive the scene: the discomfort of the participants, the sense of confronting an unprecedented act, the unconscious crowd, conscious more than ever of belonging to the sky and air of this day, to the taste of crime in each throat, and the symbol of his majesty, the body of his majesty dressed in silk cut in two in the cold and crowded square, cut and drowned in blood and cutting time. . . . The drum roll that finally drowns out that voice before the blade sends the organ that produces it into the basket though not before the head has been brandished as proof of a sacrilegious diminution, soiled. . . .

49Philippe Sollers, *Drame* (Paris: Seuil, 1965), jacket copy, my translation.

Unique act having no equal aside from the massacres of priests permitted at last, or again, the parading of that flayed head affixed to a pike through the shouts.[50]

The allusion to marginality generates an instance of external margin when the "I" is projected first as outside a hall, distinct from the audience being addressed. Then, through the medium of a picture with a reversed and open field, his position is altered. Though still on the margin, he is now looking out rather than in, surveying a city that recalls its identity with the Paris of an earlier revolutionary moment. We note that the marginality has been extended to distinguish the "I" from his movements. A further *amorce* is provided by the description of an engraving premonitory of the decapitation of Louis XVI. The mere idea of that "transgression" brings about a further composition of place and a curious identification of audience and victim through the affective "taste of crime in each throat." Like Homer, Sollers procedes to bring life to the content of a print from a different period. The latter, in turn, extends the internal citation through its marginality and doubles the enigmatic "picture." Clearly this text is less a poem than the self-generating (and self-reflecting) narrative process that the narrating "I" describes in part in an earlier passage, "1.13 . . . The account had begun abruptly when I had decided to change language within the same language, when the first knot of resistance imposed itself, when the repetitions had invaded their outlines."[51] Any translation of this text is risky, removing ambiguities essential to its movement, but clearly Sollers's speaker is beginning a description of a textual procedure *and* a physical encounter both with war and with language as joy and distress. The movement is toward an identity of

[50]Philippe Sollers, *Nombres* (Paris: Seuil, 1968), pp. 28–29, my translation. Jacques Derrida includes some of this passage in his discussion of castration in "Dissemination," in *Dissemination*, trans. Barbara Johnson (Chicago: University of Chicago Press, 1981), p. 302 and passim. Like the essay, Derrida's book takes its title from the Saussurian concept of the anagram, but it occurs in a phrase in *Nombres:* "la dissémination sans images" (p. 61), which refers as much to numbers (*chiffres*) as to words or rather reverses the field, turning a page of letters black on white into a column of numbers, an account of the war dead among whom *we* inevitably figure, as does the writer who donates himself to his words. Much of the argument presented here is taken from my introduction to Sollers's *Literature and the Experience of Limits.*

[51]Sollers, *Nombres*, p. 27, my translation. For another reading of this passage, see Derrida, *Dissemination*, pp. 325–26.

the speaker, and by extension the reader, with this "procedure": "1.13 . . . By the completion of a procedure during which I had passed by disfigured flesh, skinless and speaking by ejaculations of blood, by the mashing of nerves and blood become [casualty] figures detached and devalued by the exchange, I became this overturning."[52] In short the experience/text began/begins as decision/s and proceded/proceeds as a self-established decorum in which language and activity (to say nothing of spaces and temporalities) become variously interchangeable. Repeatedly, the body of writing mingles with the body of the writer:

> 3.43 . . . I was therefore ordered to move about in my own shape knowing that I would end up losing it, deserted by it . . . , that I'd end up losing myself in it. . . . Nothing could withstand the story thus released, and the other thus becoming a black fire imposing itself on a white fire, a visible fire on an invisible fire, and the curves and the points—vowels, consonants—bodied forth the mouth of the procedure, 'ink on parchment,' the lowest river, the spring. . . . Silence and activity. Production using me as its base, mirror, filter, thrust, me producing it, in my turn, in its permanent reserve of wellsprings.[53]

By elaborating upon that translation, this text underscores and vivifies the result, a discourse crossing incessantly between the world of its processes and the trompe l'oeil of its consequences, engaging the reader in the double, triple, troubling ambiguity of Sollers's research. Simultaneously, it introduces into its very texture intellectual, aesthetic, and political concerns that make it, however obliquely, one with its time, placing it within history that it produces as language and internalizes.

No wonder this intensely written text stimulated Derrida to write the difficult concluding section and title essay of *La dissémination*, a piece that should be read as a mirror text for *Nombres*. "La dissémination" (first published in 1969) opens with a classic Derridian description of Sollers's method as it relates to the readerly presence:

> The text is remarkable in that the reader (here in exemplary fashion) can never choose his own place in it, nor can the spectator. There is at any

[52]Sollers, *Nombres*, pp. 27–28, my translation.
[53]Ibid., p. 59, my translation.

rate no tenable place for him opposite the text, outside the text, no spot where he might get away with *not* writing what, in the reading, would seem to him to be *given, past;* no spot, in other words, where he would stand before an already *written* text. Because his job is to put things on stage, he is on stage himself, he puts himself on stage.[54]

Speaking of the demise of the "realist" project that characterized the revolutionary climate of the late nineteenth century, the art historian Linda Nochlin claims that mid-twentieth-century artists reveal an obsessive

preoccupation with self-consciousness about the *means* of art: the formal demands of paint and canvas, the self-generating power of the structure of language whether literary or visual. The very aspirations of realism, in its old naive sense, are denied by the contemporary outlook which asserts and demands the absolute independence of art from the world of reality and, indeed, disputes the existence of any single, unequivocal reality at all.[55]

Consistent with this view, each of the novels we have been examining is drawing obviously upon its own inner resources to create a new kind of literary surface. Each is rigorous, controlled by an internal consistency that seems to a remarkable degree to exclude the realist illusion, even the modified or exacerbated realism that enabled Joyce to evoke the outer and inner aspects of a Dublin day and project it out into eternity among the stars of "Ithaca." Still, though Nochlin is surely right about the preoccupation with the writerly surface and the practices that it implies, modern writers tend to return by the back door of the allegory of difference to a recognition that experience too is a form of language. Their texts suggest that nothing is more real than the signs with which we express our existence. Hence the repeated, almost obsessive reinspection of the wounds of history and the sense of an endless present that pervades them. Hence, too, the nagging suspicion that what is being conveyed beautifully, artfully, in rhetoric and through sound is what cannot be better said—the complex and contorted nature of even the simplest feeling, the most trivial experience, the eternal functionless moment.

[54]Derrida, *Dissemination*, p. 290.
[55]Linda Nochlin, *Realism* (Harmondsworth, Middlesex: Penguin, 1972), p. 15.

Such works are ex-centric by definition and "open" in the sense given that term by Umberto Eco, for whom openness is a function of the variety of relations that can be established between the work and its "consumer."[56] Typically, they subvert plot and character while supplying the reader with all manner of unexpected verbal effects and a web of allusions. Their procedures differ radically, however. Beckett's "story" line is first attenuated to the point of virtual inconsequence and then set in a vibratory relationship with counterdevelopments that underscore its improbability while enriching its implications. His personae undermine their own credentials (their sources of credence) as existing beings and as narrators in order to reinforce their validity as aspects of or signals for experience and idea, all the while conveying a poignant distress and perverse pleasure. Their movement out into the world is always countered by a withdrawal, a recommitment to the verbal texture from which they struggle to emerge, which they refuse to reject, and which in turn refuses to give them life.

Paradoxes abound in Joyce as well and not only on the thematic levels. *Ulysses* grows out of and outgrows the superrealistic surface of its opening chapters to become a product and a mirror of its own techniques, a showcase for forms masking and revealing the inconsequence and significance of its action. The explicit self-generation of the composition of place serves as a signal of the implicit use of self-generative effects in the later chapters, which by focusing attention on their procedures, seem to detach themselves from the referential frame, making the lively business of textualization a center of interest. *Finnegans Wake*, however, makes the strongest gesture of aversion, burying the "real" in its idiom and through its form but burning offerings to the narrative conventions that invest each moment of its prose and to the human experience that pierces in an elemental form the linguistic screen. The ghosts of plot, character, and situation glow palely, flitting through a scrim of proliferating formal devices. Accordingly, we follow actions and experience gestures that, though fixed by their universal validity, are curiously immediate and somehow transitory. Details and objects are revealed kaleidoscopically before being absorbed by the pattern in the verbal carpet, becoming in effect cloud creations. Meanwhile the words themselves take on special life in terms of self-perpetuating and omnipresent themes, ideas, personae,

---

[56]Umberto Eco, *L'Oeuvre ouverte* (Paris: Seuil, 1965), p. 308.

and actions. Most significant, an inner logic of repetition seems to grow from the very texture of the language; words generate both meaning and other words through association and permutation.

Building on a social vision laced with linguistic, psychoanalytic, and political theory but grounded in literary procedures and an engagement with the semantic and semiologic dimensions of language, Philippe Sollers has produced novels that move from the Spartan abstraction of *Drame* to the proliferating texture of allusion, sound, and verbal activity in *H* and *Paradis*. These novels increasingly engage in a dialogue with literary theory as they derive themselves from the procedures of textualization, a tactic that could easily turn sterile were the language less energetic. In the wake of the New Novelists' refusal of the literary third dimension, they distance themselves from the tendency to mimic and arrange experience, deliberately dismantling the crisp illusions that their syntax repeatedly imposes, dissociating themselves from the very reality upon which they continually draw. Treating their language as a machine capable of digesting all manner of raw materials in all available modes without lending itself to coherent narrative fictions, these novels still remain coherent as fictions in their own right. The result is a tension between the appearance of autonomy and the indispensable and permanent connection with the autobiography of the writer, of language through literary tradition, and even of the species *homo gallicanus,* .

We should, at this point, sort through the various manifestations that might be termed self-generative. On the one hand we have the occasionally splendid effects of the surrealists, who claim in their early phase to use "random" or "free" association, a practice that would appear to be unaffected by conscious aesthetic choice. Similarly, we have the drug culture prose of writers like William Burroughs and Alex Trocchi, the alleged product of mental processes freed by narcotic use. We may of course question both the degree of control and the real source of such utterances, just as we may question whether or not Coleridge actually wrote "Kubla Khan" in the wake of a dream or the degree to which automatic writing generated Yeats's *A Vision*. Again, there are the Oulipo productions, the assembled novels, and the *I Ching*-generated poems, which pretend to bypass the shaping will by resorting to chance generation. All of these must be distinguished from the carefully monitored illusion of openness and the self-contained chaos produced not only in the works we have studied but also, with significant differences, in works by Robert Pinget, Juan Goytisolo, Maurice Roche, Arno Schmidt, Gilbert Sorrentino, and William Gass. The first four categories arguably seem more genuinely self-generative than the last grouping. Even when we question their avowed freedom, seeing it as little more than a metaphor, such productions do, after all, make claims for the elimination of authorial control and the dissolution of retrievable order in their discourse.

The loss of control and order, however, is not the goal of the works we are studying. In self-generated texts, the novelist's hand is always evident, as is the sense that conscious choices underlie the appearance of the random production of discourse, a fact that builds both confidence and interest, if not suspense. It should be noted that suspense is precisely the effect least evident in such texts and that the inadequately understood distinction between suspense and interest is crucial to any appreciation of the experience and nature of these novels. Interest derives not from expectation alone but also, and in these texts principally, from the quality of the writerly play and the quest for unity, coherence, pattern, and perspectives. In short, in this convention illusion moves toward the ideal of practice and aspects of practice are *perceived* as semiautomatic but are *understood* to be controlled.

True to the underlying Flaubertian project, the self-generating text provides yet another instance of the tendency to liberate the modern novel from the hold of mimetic assumptions, to disclose and even glory in word-ness. It does more when it dramatizes the procedures of arrangement as opposed to those of narrative development. Rendering the arranging activity vivid, as a development, it makes the reader privy to the process by which the writer *becomes* as a product of the text he controls—the writer along with his surrogate, the textualized writing or speaking/thinking persona. The result is at once a declaration of writerly humility and a demonstration of pride, a look-mom-no-hands gesture toward the participating reader. Perhaps that helps explain the curious insistence on the name of the writer evident in some of these texts, the unabashed and frontally autobiographical presence and display that we see, for example, in the late Céline, in Maurice Roche, and in the Sollers of *H* and *Paradis*.

Féerie is a peculiar instance, since Céline, the novelist, after insisting with paranoid tenacity on his pseudonym, suddenly, if ambiguously, at the point of what might be called maximum vulnerablity, dropped his mask to expose a devastated but unbowed autobiographical identity. We may ascribe this tactic to political and personal causes and even claim that Céline in exile had nothing more to lose. The strategy may also, however, have dictated the form his narrative took, one so extreme in its paratactic disjunction, its hyperbolic spleen, and its self-generation that it annulled the existence of the "real" Destouches/Céline it purported to portray and defend, presenting instead a complex metaphor for a collective French guilt couched in the language of outrage and cutting through layers of defenses without actually hitting any target. Or there may be yet another motive, though the effect is the same. Having previously, and wrongheadedly, used his own name when writing his pamphlets, Céline may in *Féerie* be placing the postwar novels under the sign of that vituperative pamphleteering personality, creating a halfway stance between his fiction and his diatribes. (After all, he does not abandon his pen name.)

Something similar may be said of Soller's *H*, in which the writer's actual name, Joyaux, is prominently displayed and even toyed with. In this case, however, the accent is so heavily on form that the writing subject is not only protected but, for all intents and purposes, obliterated except when the readers possess privileged biographical information. Joyce's *Wake* raises other problems, since the Joyce it produces (without specifically naming him), though perhaps closer to the authorial psyche than any previous manifestations, is so well shrouded in multifaceted and polysemous language as to blend in with the figure in the carpet.

In short, the writer of such fictions, by insisting on his "real" presence, sacrifices precisely an aspect of his identity, renders himself a figment of the reading mind for which the evolution of his word is more important than his presence. For the reader, as for the contextualized writer, the textual procedures seal the novel off doubly. Since we witness the fact of self-genesis, we must recognize the essential self-containedness of the text. We must also, however, and repeatedly, acknowledge the substantial nature of the fictional text, its role as a product producing only itself. All the stranger, then, our refusal to accept in practice either restriction—our insistence, as prisoners of the conventions of illusion, on the discarded dimensions: on the reality of the writer (and/or his surrogate) and the verisimilitude of the self-negating product. I would suggest that these operative paradoxes lie at the root of such works' appeal.

Characterized by openness, extravagance, nonconformity, and surprise, these texts seem to find modes of enclosure that enable them to distinguish themselves from their surround before and while they internalize it. Indulging in a discourse motivated apparently, if not in fact, by its own procedures, they exhibit themselves as controlled entities in which the reader shares as a shaper of orders. The self-enclosure, this illusion of difference, promotes our sense of the integrity of the seemingly entropic vision.

Thematized or not, self-generation functions as an emblem of control both over the text and over its implied author/reader, supplanting and supplementing other conventions, which usually survive as traces. More important, it seems to be a twentieth-century response to the nineteenth-century dictum of impassibility, a new test of the powers of the fictional word. The impossible withdrawal of the author from his product is now translated into the impossible withdrawal of the text from its signifying universe, which, as we have suggested, finds other ways of imposing itself.

5

Paratactics: The Grammar
of In-Subordination

Though long accustomed to the disjunction occasioned by the manipulation of lines of action, readers of novels, at least through the nineteenth century, were conditioned to a discourse that provided proper subordination and coordination on all levels. The narrative was generally a coherent "chain of events" or a clearly interrelated group of such "chains" that could be followed, despite conventional or rhetorical ellipses, to its "logical conclusions." Such fiction accommodated surprise happenings and hidden motivations so long as the development was smooth (or smoothed over), the mysteries were explained, and the "loose ends" were "tied together." The novel was a dream of order, an ordering that mirrored its readers' complacent idealization of their daily existence and introduced chaos only surreptitiously into its narrative processes. Loose ends of experience were relegated to the dishonorable fields of folly and fun, and the verisimilar took on the status of truth to life. Perhaps, as an upstart form reaching for critical acceptance, the novel needed to establish its credentials before it could begin to proclaim its freedom, if not from rules, at least from rigid mediation. Under such conditions the introduction of what we will be calling paratactics into fictions that took themselves seriously was bound to have revolutionary consequences.

According to the *Oxford English Dictionary*, parataxis is the "placing of propositions or clauses one after another, without indicating by connecting words the relations (of co-ordination or subordination) between them." Since elevated material usually requires hypotactic qualification and elaboration, qualities seemingly absent from paratactic discourse, "serious" literature has traditionally featured hypotactic arrangements in which occasional parataxis occurred mainly and mildly in contexts demanding disjunction or cataloguing.[1] On the other hand parataxis was acceptable in fictional forms that were openly farcical or that constituted strong attacks on established norms.

Defined as an organized chaos and deriving, as Mikhail Bakhtin has claimed, from the carnival tradition and fertility rite,[2] farce is marked by a tendency toward discontinuity and irreverent shock. Forced conjunctions are not only normal but necessary if the expectations of the reader/viewer are to be fulfilled, though such shocks need hardly occur on all levels and the farcical impulse need never be total. Clowning is the vehicle for achieving farcical conjunctions, just as the clown, or the miscreant with whom we are not obliged to identify, permits us to enjoy vicariously indecorous or unacceptable activity and content. In narrative farce (as opposed to the theater or carnival), the clowning is apt to be expressed in part through a choice of "low" themes and activities but also and to a remarkable degree through a rhetoric of disjunction—in short, parataxis. We find an early instance in Rabelais's *Gargantua et Pantagruel* with its famous not-quite lists, accumulations of generally offensive and often inconsistent materials. Beyond the lists there are the arguments with their concatenations of irrelevancies, and beyond them, the tendency to juxtapose "serious" and comic modes in chapter after chapter.[3] Sterne's *Tristram Shandy*, while pretending to impose extreme hypotaxis on a meticulous account of a progress or life, is remarkable for its inclusion of foreign matter, its footnotes, its justaposition of forms, its impertinent narrator—in short, for its deliberate subversion of narrative order and balance. The result is what the Russian formalist Victor Shklovski has described as "defamiliarization"[4] and rhetorically styled the "typical novel," but it

---

[1]Erich Auerbach, *Mimesis* (New York: Doubleday, 1953), pp. 91–92 and passim. The term "parataxis" has been gaining currency in studies of contemporary artistic practice.
[2]Mikhail Bakhtin, *Rabelais and His World*, trans. Hélène Iswolsky (Cambridge, Mass.: MIT Press, 1968).
[3]David Hayman, "Beyond Bakhtin," *Novel* 16 (Winter 1983), 114–17.
[4]Victor Shklovski, "Sterne's *Tristram Shandy*: Stylistic Commentary," in *Russian Formalist Criticism: Four Essays*, trans. Lee T. Lemon and Marion J. Reis (Lincoln: University of Nebraska Press, 1965), p. 57.

is also a fragmentation that infects or seems to infect every aspect of the text—every aspect, that is, except its rhetoric. Thus there is an extensive range of disjunctive procedures even within the category of farce.

For the purposes of this study, "paratactics" will be applicable not only to the sentence and paragraph but also to clustered paragraphs, conjoined structures and larger formal units, to macro- as well as microparataxis. Furthermore, though many twentieth-century texts make use of the conventions and techniques of farce, we will point to the exception as much as to the rule, to the work that has refused to grant its reader the release of untrammeled laughter or to stop there when dealing in the paratactic play of forms and details. In predominantly serious works there is a tendency to use this device to unify and even harmonize disparate elements by creating a dynamic of difference to which farcical attitudes and subject matter may well contribute (especially in Joyce, Eliot, and Pound). In the predominantly farcical novel, we often find difference imposed on the similar through the parataxis of synonymy (see Jules Valles, Céline, J. P. Donleavy, Kurt Vonnegut, and to some extent, Juan Goytisolo).

The simpler the juxtaposition and the briefer the paratactic elements (the components of a sequence), the closer we are to the true list from which parataxis seems to borrow traits. Like the telephone book and the library catalogue, the list appears to occupy space in a timeless domain. On one level at least, novelistic parataxis would therefore seem to be a subversive form within conventionally diachronic narrative structures. Parataxis is more than a list, however, since it occupies both space and time (that of the larger context) while belonging to neither. Whether it is included in or imposed upon narrative, it contributes a static component, a bulk and density that appears to be immobile. In other ways, it may contribute a dynamism, a jagged dance of interacting and even clashing forms. Inserted into the "properly" coordinated and subordinated text (which we will call hypotactic with some misgivings, since hypotaxis is not precisely the opposite of paratactics, the latter being a broadly conceived disjunction), it may shore up the vision of order by establishing a contrasting optic that the text can reject. On the other hand, if sufficiently strong, it can undermine the text's authority, introducing a semblance of disarray and inducing the reader to abandon the passive role in order to reestablish order. We should note that, in all the arts, imbalance and incompletion are both courted and, like the proverbial vacuum, abhorred. Accordingly, when a relationship is not made explicitly by the text, it will be made by the reader, or the resultant disorder will render the text (temporarily or permanently) unreadable.

Radical parataxis generally puts absence in high relief, advertising what the more conventional narrative plasters over. Not only does lack become a positive factor; it becomes virtually a proclamation of the reader's necessary and active, if sometimes unwilling, presence. We discover ourselves through the need to fill gaps that can and often do disclose fissures in the texture of ("lived") experience, opening onto somethin akin to Mallarmé's *abîme*, if not to his *azur*.

It follows that in many cases paratactic effects constitute frontal attacks on the reader's expectations and desires, imposing disorder on the verbal field we depend upon to orient our reactions. This statement is especially true when grammatical parataxis is accompanied by logical paratactics: disorienting gaps in the development of a thought or an action (or the sort of aphoristic structure imposed by certain philosophers). Though, in some texts, such ellipses may in fact be arbitrary, a mode of deliberate disruption, most commonly associative linkage constitutes a bridge, if not between parataxis and hypotaxis, at least between the paratactic elements. Such associative leaps are often metaphorical in quality even though the metaphors may be muted or ironic. That is, the logic of the collocations is controlled by an unstated but accessible relationship similar to that discernible between the seemingly random reflections that compose the thought stream of Joyce's Leopold Bloom. The same tends to be true for the logic of changes in style, typography, and rhythm.

Parataxis need not be continuously or radically disruptive. Indeed, Gertrude Stein and early cubism illustrate forcefully not only the interaction of two art forms but also the static pole of paratactic discourse at the beginning of a development to which I will allude frequently but that I will not attempt to document fully here. Stein's relationship to the art and artists of cubism is almost legendary, and the influence of the art form on her writing has been widely treated.[5] For my purposes two aspects of the cubist project are noteworthy: the attempt to present simultaneously, if schematically, all sides of a given

[5]See particularly Marjorie Perloff, *The Poetics of Indeterminacy* (Princeton: Princeton University Press, 1981), pp. 70–73.

object and the tendency to break the object (or the space of the canvas) into components that can be neither conjoined smoothly by the viewing eye nor considered as separate entities. The result is a tension between coherence and fragmentation. By obliging the viewer to consider such fragments as both disjunct and inseparable, since joined by color scheme and internal rhythms as well as canvas, the painter installs time in the painting and displaces space. That is, we experience the canvas as a concatenation of moments and also as a spatial unit, a visual dialectic. The temporal component of the process of apprehending a canvas is here greatly amplified.

In moving from a traditionally spatial mode to one that is traditionally temporal, Gertrude Stein attempts, aptly enough, to freeze verbal time and to spatialize her discourse. Since, in her earlier phase, she wished to render action in a continuous present, it was almost inevitable that microstructural parataxis was central to her method— by implication the freezing of time, the creation of a verbal stroboscope. Like certain cubist canvases that tend to convey a unified and almost impenetrable surface before breaking down into conflicting planes from which objects in a spatial field eventually emerge, Stein's use of multiple but similar paratactic encounters on the sentence level results in a text that demands considerable attention if we are to perceive the topography and progress of her vision. In a typical early text, the sentences overlap in a modified shingle effect so that the absence of connectives and the leveling of subordination is obscured by redundancy and monotony. Paradoxically, the reader has less trouble filling in gaps than discerning difference. Discontinuity in this case is less a function of absence *(manque)*, though narrative ellipses proliferate, than of superfluity. (Stein's later works, departing from cubist practice, tend to make sharper juxtapositions with less shingling and hence more contrast, but because they omit narrative development, they still strike us as spatial events.) Ultimately, the process of perception, the gradual freeing of narrative from the verbal matrix, leads to a full sense of the vehicle as container.

In *Three Lives*, following Flaubert in "Un coeur simple," Stein sought to convey a development (a life) as an object (a rhythmic portrait). There is, however, a crossing of purposes imposed by her need to use a temporal rather than a spatial form. For Stein subverted the by-then conventional realistic or trompe l'oeil portrayal of experience along with the essential temporality of the written word and of narrative. In the following extract, sentences are converted into planes and shadings that, when placed side by side, stop action but suggest substance, the distilled but spatially extended matter of daily existence:

> Jeff never, even now, knew what it was that moved him. He never, even now, was ever sure, he really knew what Melanctha was, when she was real herself, and honest. He thought he knew, and then there came to him some moment, just like this one, when she really woke him up to be strong in him. Then he really knew he could know nothing. He knew then he never could know what it was she really wanted with him. He knew then he never could know really what it was he felt inside him. It was all so mixed up inside him. All he knew was he wanted very badly Melanctha should be there beside him, and he wanted very badly, too, always to throw her from him. What was it really that Melanctha wanted with him? What was it really, he, Jeff Campbell, wanted she should give him? "I certainly did think now," Jeff Campbell groaned inside him, "I certainly did think now I really was knowing all right, what I wanted. I certainly did really think now I was knowing how to be trusting with Melanctha. I certainly did think it was like that now with me sure, after all I've been through all this time with her."[6]

Stein's goals could best be achieved through a form that insists upon distinctions between units of discourse while facilitating a mimesis, less of life than of the painterly approach both to the space of the page and the objective universe it modifies. If hers is a singular perversity, as exacting as it is inhospitable, her work is singularly rewarding, though in terms not usually associated with literature: those of verbal texture as a plastic quality. If, at first, the surfaces broken into innumerable units seem depressingly unrelieved, uniform, monotonous, on inspection her rhetoric reveals subtle variations, shadings, and bulges within the sentence units. Thus her parataxis, like that of the early experiments in cubism, finally engrosses us in its surface, obliging us to make for ourselves definitions that would be made *for us* by more conventional narratives.[7]

[6]Gertrude Stein, "Melanctha," in *Three Lives* (New York: New Directions, 1933), p. 156.

[7]This reading of Stein and cubism as surface manifestations rhymes with that of Marjorie Perloff, though there is little here that can be termed "undecidable" or "indeterminate."

Stein's early work represents one pole of the paratactic practice, the use of extreme microparataxis to spatialize the text and veil the objects it represents. We are already on the road to the sort of abstraction found in her later work. Similarly, analytic cubism, with its stoically limited palette and its refusal of mass and coherence, represents an extreme of painterly parataxis and expressive self-denial. It was almost inevitable that synthetic cubism would introduce collage, breaking with the radical asceticism of the early phase to move toward paratactic diversity. By pasting large and irregular pieces of obviously alien material (wallpaper, newspaper, cigarette wrappers, and so forth) on the painted surface, to which they were joined by penciled or painted lines or planes, the artists mitigated the monotony and subverted unity while retaining the basic principles of the cubist vision. Beyond that synthetic cubism, Picasso, iconoclast of his own icons, produced some striking early examples of a more radical sculptural macroparatactics. Similarly, we can point in the later work of Gertrude Stein to the use of associative gaps that forcefully splinter the text.

No single writer better illustrates the range of paratactics than does James Joyce, whose discoveries began, if not with the broken unity of *Dubliners*, certainly with the calculated concision of *A Portrait of the Artist as a Young Man*. When he abandoned his great baggy Edwardian monster *Stephen Hero*, Joyce made a revolutionary decision: to strip his narrative of all but the crucial aspects of Stephen's development. Though the *Portrait* features episodic juxtaposition, style changes at chapter breaks, interpolated passages, and associative development, though it virtually eliminates transitions, the appearance of disjunction derives mainly from the obtrusiveness of two dramatic instances. The opening and closing sequences function as preparation and countersign for all the other innovations.

As Hugh Kenner has suggested the highly condensed impressions with which the book begins may contain the book in germ.[8] This cluster of infantile moments of awareness ("epiphanies"?), crudely juxtaposed and lacking both setting and explicit justification, is drawn from the child's first years:

[8]Hugh Kenner, *Dublin's Joyce* (Bloomington: Indiana University Press, 1956), pp. 114–16.

ONCE upon a time and a very good time it was there was a moocow
coming down along the road and this moocow that was coming down
along the road met a nicens little boy named baby tuckoo. . . .

His father told him that story: his father looked at him through a glass:
he had a hairy face.

He was baby tuckoo. The moocow came down the road where Betty
Byrne lived: she sold lemon platt.

> *O, the wild rose blossoms*
> *On the little green place.*

He sang that song. That was his song.

> *O, the green wothe botheth.*

When you wet the bed first it is warm then it gets cold. His mother
put on the oilsheet. That had the queer smell.

His mother had a nicer smell than his father.[9]

On inspection, though listlike, a seemingly random assortment of impressions, this passage becomes a logical and chrono-logical, though
rudimentary and associative, narrative development. If in itself it is
not hard to read, still it obliges the reader to fill in the conceptual gaps
and supply the appropriate Victorian settings. Even then, we can fully
understand it only after we have acquired an overview of the novel. In
fact, the opening is best understood in terms of the diary with which
the book ends. In contrast, though each diary entry is dated and each
detail is anchored in events recounted earlier, the book's conclusion is
both stubbornly random and extremely various, both distinct from
and subordinate to what precedes it. (One of its prime functions is to
reopen the structure it seems to close.) Though a case can be made for
its structural inevitability, the diary comes as a shock to the reader
trained by the final chapter in another sort of intellectual discipline.
We strain against its fragmented presence to rationalize its function, to
fill in the associative gaps and control its impact as an emotional,
intellectual, and thematic unit, and to determine what it foretells and
how it can be read as the conclusion of Stephen's emotional development.

Joyce's framing of the novel by means of complementary passages of

---

[9]James Joyce, *A Portrait of the Artist as a Young Man*, ed. Chester Anderson (New
York: Viking, 1968), pp. 7–8.

radical paratactics is both daring and unique. As a procedure, it can best be explained not so much by tradition as in terms of the project outlined in the early essay/sketch, "A Portrait of the Artist": "A portrait is not so much an identificative paper as the curve of an emotion."[10] What better way to indicate schematically the nature of a life or vital curve, a shape that is ever changing but always constant to its own identity, than through the use of a convention that dramatizes change and a structure based on that convention, one that underscores repetition-with-a-difference through the imaginative use of ellipses?

Any number of modernist novels use degrees of paratactics, both micro and macro. Earlier in the century there were Rilke's bildungsroman *The Notebooks of Malte Laurids Brigge*, which achieves lyrical concision through the diary form; Virginia Woolf's trilogy and particularly *The Waves* with its intrusive lyrical interludes, its associative musings, its juxtaposed monologue sequences, and its absence of narrative guidance; Alexander Döblin's *Berlin Alexanderplatz* and John Dos Passos's *Forty-ninth Parallel* with their radical juxtapositions of large chunks of raw prose in different modes and voices; and Oswald Andrade's *Seraphim*, a Brazilian novel constructed entirely of brief and heterogeneous entries. More recently, there are books like Michel Butor's novelogue *Mobile*, whose disjunct form Roland Barthes defends in "Literature and Discontinuity,"[11] and Günter Grass's *Tin Drum*, with its abrupt changes in perspective, mode, tense, and style. *Ulysses* remains the most comprehensive example, however, and merits even closer study than I can give it here.[12]

It was Joyce's practice, conscious or not, to reverse his procedures as he moved from novel to novel. Since *Portrait* begins and ends with its most extreme moments of disruption, we need not be surprised (in hindsight) to find the most radical discontinuity toward the middle of *Ulysses* in the ragged and disconcerting overture to "Sirens," the interstitial buffoonery of "Cyclops," and the ribald and Rabelaisian "polylogue" of "Oxen of the Sun."[13] On the other hand, the relatively

---

[10]Ibid., p. 258.

[11]In Roland Barthes, *Critical Essays*, trans. Richard Howard (Evanston, Ill.: Northwestern University Press, 1972), pp. 173–74.

[12]For an extended but still incomplete consideration, see David Hayman, "James Joyce: Paratactician," *Contemporary Literature* 26 (Summer 1985), 155–78.

[13]The term "polylogue," first used by Joyce in his notebooks and *Finnegans Wake* (470.09), is also found in Sollers's *H* (Paris: Seuil, 1973) and is used as a critical tool by

discrete style changes that mark the beginning of each chapter of *Portrait* are replaced in *Ulysses* by shifts that become more striking as the action progresses into the night.

A possible source for these procedures and the generalized parataxis of *Ulysses* may be the theatrical poetry of Goethe's *Faust*. After all, Joyce himself saw the "Walpurgisnacht" as a pattern for "Circe," and both works resort to formal disjunction in order to accommodate an encyclopedic range of human experience. The task set for Goethe's *Dichter* in the "Prelude in the Theatre"[14] could easily have been the one assigned to Joyce's authorial persona. In *Ulysses*, as in *Faust* and far more than in *Portrait*, varieties of contrast and discontinuity function to increase density, to loosen decorum, yes, and even to produce dramatic effects. The same device that, by leaving significant gaps, allows more aspects of experience to be suggested imposes a sense of almost frenetic activity on a nearly static context. Where Goethe, intent on the multiplication of incidents, was able to sketch in only the outlines of character, however, Joyce, who once expressed his dismay at the German writer's failure in this regard,[15] projected against a fixed but timeless and expandable backdrop two fully developed characters within a large gallery of subsidiary figures. On the one hand this character development was facilitated by Joyce's very modernist choice to concentrate on the ordinary and uneventful lives of unexceptional protagonists and on their subtle and various psychological di-

---

Julia Kristeva in her essay on that novel, "Polylogue," *Tel Quel* 57 (Spring 1974), 19–55. Sollers's *polylogue extérieur*, as distinct from a *monologue intérieur* (*H*, p. 42), refers us back to the clatter of undifferentiated voices in the birthday celebration in chapter 5 of Rabelais's *Gargantua*. He could also be referring to the Rabelaisian rout that concludes "Oxen of the Sun," an "exterior polylogue" if ever there was one.

[14]"Don't spare either stage-sets or mechanical effects. Use the big and the little lights of the skies; there's plenty of water, fire, rock-backdrops, animals, and birds. So on this narrow stage show the whole circle of creation, and travel with reasonable speed from heaven through the world to hell" (*Faust*, trans. Carlyle F. MacIntyre [New York: New Directions, 1941], p. 417). In his *Conversations with Eckermann*, Goethe moved at one point from a discussion of *Faust* to some remarks about the text for Mozart's *The Magic Flute*, of which he is reported to have said that, though the "first part is full of improbabilities and jests . . . , we must in all events allow that the author understood, to a high degree, the art of producing great theatrical effects by means of *contrasts*" (trans. John Oxenford [London: George Bell & Sons, 1892], p. 7).

[15]Frank Budgen, *James Joyce and the Making of Ulysses* (Bloomington: Indiana University Press, 1960), p. 16.

lemmas. On the other hand, the encyclopedic range largely reflects his use of suggestion to convey through symbol, allegory, and intertextuality a greatly enlarged allusive dimension.

To this crowded field of complicating factors paratactics contributes mainly on the level of orchestration, making readily visible those rhythms and patterns that might otherwise melt into the narrative fabric. It also serves to foreground the book's structure, itself a function of the arrangement of details and features. In a work of this complexity, mnemonic aids are almost essential, and by marking the gaps and enforcing the leaps, the technique helps make the book's details unforgettable. At the same time, it eliminates space-filling verbiage that could limit comprehensiveness and slow up progress. Furthermore, by making unexpected juxtapositions, it shakes us out of complacent habits of apprehension. Finally, by facilitating diversity, it contributes to the textural impact of the many-sided work, turning language into the prime adventure and making style one of the principal sources of interest and action. In adapting to constant change, the reader becomes a quester for whom knowledge of the text becomes a need to know and experience more of its surfaces, if only to control what has already been experienced. Conversely, the text instructs the reader in modes of apprehension.

The radical opening of *Ulysses* in medias res is a very mild example of Joycean shock tactics, but it sets the tone for what follows. On page 1, a completely unknown character, Buck Mulligan, performs ordinary activities with mysterious and outrageous aplomb. Halfway down the page, our old friend Stephen Dedalus appears, having unaccountably returned to the Ireland he left at the end of *Portrait*. (This opening would be even more startling for a reader unfamiliar with *Portrait*, someone obliged to build a sense of Stephen from scratch, as many of the early readers were.) As the chapter and book develop, we must learn more about Mulligan, just as we must place Stephen in the new context, which is gradually (and dramatically) unfolded as well as established through an unprecedented variety of narrative devices.

Within the chapter, parataxis is accommodated by the microstructure, appearing, for example, in the associative movement of Stephen's stream of consciousness, in the clash between thought and narration, in the conversation, and occasionally in the narrative passages that reflect Stephen's reactions. Thus when Mulligan refers to an incident at Oxford, Stephen's mind produces without transition the following composition of place, a highly fragmented and subjective reconstruction (projection) of events he has not witnessed:[16]

Young shouts of moneyed voices in Clive Kempthorpe's rooms. Pale-faces: they hold their ribs with laughter, one clasping another. O, I shall expire! Break the news to her gently, Aubrey! I shall die! With slit ribbons of his shirt whipping the air he hops and bobbles round the table, with trousers down at heels, chased by Ades of Magdalen with tailor's shears. A scared calf's face gilded with marmalade. I don't want to be debagged! Don't play the giddy ox with me!

Shouts from the open window startling evening in the quandrangle. A deaf gardener, aproned, masked with Matthew Arnold's face, pushes his mower on the somber lawn watching narrowly the dancing motes of grasshalms.

To ourselves . . . new paganism . . . *omphalos*.[17]

Most striking in this oblique foreshadowing of the technique and matter of "Circe" is the variety of devices it employs: the omitted verbs, the unmarked dialogue and unidentified speaker, the sequence of prepositional phrases beginning "with" but not quite in parallel construction, the unmotivated shifts in perspective, and the list of slogans drawn from different contexts. In each instance the reader is obliged to complete a statement, to fill out a vision, but the action is not as a result less startling and dynamic, less immediate. Quite aside from its function as an efficient carrier of characterization and mood, a way of turning conventional exposition into an item of interest and even suspense, the greatly expanded microparataxis of "Telemachus" generates a special sort of reader, one who is able to process or retain quantities of random information, accommodating mercurial shifts, tolerant of ellipses, and unphased or, rather, engaged by an inability to supply missing information.

We may go to school in each chapter, learning how to continue, but we are bound to be unsettled by each new motion of the text. Seemingly unmotivated diversity is our teacher, but even on rereading, we

---

[16]The term "composition of place" is adapted from St. Ignatius Loyola's *Spiritual Exercises*. Don Gifford and R. J. Seidman locate it in "The First Exercise," item 47: "to see with the eye of the imagination the corporeal place where the object to contemplate is found" (*Notes for Joyce* [New York: Dutton, 1974], p. 175).

[17]James Joyce, *Ulysses* (New York: Random House, 1986), pp. 6–7.

may be struck by the audacity of a device, by "Eolus's" headlines or, in "Scylla and Charybdis," by the coy comments in a voice that seemingly mediates between Stephen's and the narrator's positions: "Urbane, to comfort them, the quaker librarian purred."[18] Portraying Stephen as, among other things, the young Christ failing to impress the elders of the temple of Irish learning, "Scylla" is the first chapter that openly, brazenly, displays a noteworthy variety of conflicting discourses: the ambivalent description just cited, typographical intrusions, Stephen's stream of consciousness, interpolated narrative effects, the Hamlet lecture, the conversation of inattentive interlocutors, and the narrator's by now conventional scene setting. Certain of these elements are made to jar with adjacent material; all are interwoven to produce an intricate texture of simultaneous events. Still, perhaps partly *because* of its variety as well as its complex intellectual and psychological content, "Scylla" is relatively discreet in its fragmentation.

This is less true of the cityscape chapter, "Wandering Rocks," in which slivers of Dublin existence are not only randomly juxtaposed but also repeatedly made to intrude on each other's space. With difficulty we may discern a tenuous narrative thread joining the city in a celebration of its own heterogeneity as Stephen and Bloom make their separate ways through the center of town, amplified by surrogates and protected by the ineffectual powers of church and state. The chapter is best seen as a disjunct but chronological arrangement of moments, of snapshots laced with intrusive allusions to simultaneous actions in other locations. It seems appropriate that "Wandering Rocks" concludes with a list of the inattentive (non)viewers of the vice-regal cavalcade. A fine instance of potential parataxis rendered rigorously hypotactic, though marked by significant omissions, this comic catalogue functions as a bridge and a warning.

In a sense "Wandering Rocks" inflates the procedures of the *Portrait*'s opening, lengthening the moments and shortening the time span. By contrast, the "Sirens" overture pushes the *Portrait* procedure to the limits of concision, taking brief snippets culled chronologically not from life but from the body of a chapter we have yet to read (from future time) and violently joining them in sentences remarkable for their tonal effects but incapable of conveying a coherent message. The

18Ibid., p. 151.

result is less disorienting than the process would suggest, for the text teases us with false clues to "poetic" readings:

> Bronze by gold heard the hoofirons, steelyringing.
> Imperthnthn
> thnthnthn.
> Chips, picking chips off rocky thumbnail, chips.
> Horrid!
> And gold flushed more.
> A husky fifenote blew.
> Blew. Blue bloom is on the.
> Gold pinnacled hair.
> A jumping rose on satiny breasts of satin, rose of Castile.
> Trilling, trilling: Idolores.
> Peep! Who's in the . . . peepofgold?[19]

"Sirens" proper, though far less opaque, exhibits a new kind of disjunction designed to prepare us both for the reversal of field that occurs during the evening hours and for the internalized awareness of "Circe." Its unique form enabled Joyce to achieve effects of simultaneity far beyond those of Flaubert's famous macroparatactic comice agricole episode in *Madame Bovary*. Throughout we are privy to and forced to disentangle simultaneous activities in three different public rooms of the Ormond Hotel and in various parts of Dublin. This development, far from being unprepared for, crowns a tendency we can follow throughout the early chapters. We have already experienced the temporal overlapping of chapters 1–3 and 4–6, the complex action of "Eolus," the semisimultaneity of "Scylla," and the intrusions of "Wandering Rocks."

In "Sirens" the procedure is made more immediate, more dynamic, and far more disconcerting. A single sentence or paragraph can carry allusions to several actions accessible to no single participant because they occur in different corners of the narrative space. The impact surpasses that of photomontage just as it approaches that of the musical fugue, its declared model.[20] Overt grammatical parataxis is compli-

---

[19]Ibid., p. 210.
[20]See Joyce's oft-reproduced "Schema," in Richard Ellmann, *Ulysses on the Liffey* (New York: Oxford University Press, 1972), or David Hayman, *Ulysses: The Mechanics of Meaning*, rev. ed. (Madison: University of Wisconsin Press, 1982).

cated by covert phenomena, just as the narrative voice is by turns independent and trammeled (by the imposed presence of a manipulative farceur reminiscent of the puckish persona of "Scylla" but not tied to the attitudes of any persona). The following sequence from the middle of the chapter deals simultaneously with Simon Dedalus's preparations to sing, with Blazes Boylan's jingling progress through town toward Molly Bloom's bed, with Bloom's meal with Stephen's uncle Richie Goulding, with comments in the voice of the puckish narrator, with Richie's voiced reactions to the song as they are filtered through Bloom's consciousness, and with Bloom's reflections on Richie. Each paragraph represents a new rhetorical stance, a different perspective, and a separate strand of narrative. Their juxtapositions, though rational, are virtually transitionless:

> The keys, obedient [to Si Dedalus], rose higher, told, faltered, confessed, confused.
> Up stage strode Father Cowley.
> —Here, Simon, I'll accompany you, he said. Get up.
> By Graham Lemon's pineapple rock, by Elvery's elephant jingly jogged.
> Steak, kidney, liver, mashed, at meat fit for princes sat princes Bloom and Goulding. Princes at meat they raised and drank, Power and cider.
> Most beautiful tenor air ever written, Richie said: *Sonnambula.* He heard Joe Maas sing that one night. Ah, what [sic] M'Guckin! Yes. In his way. Choirboy style. Maas was the boy. Massboy. A lyrical tenor if you like. Never forget it. Never.
> Tenderly Bloom over liverless bacon saw the tightening features strain. Backache he. Bright's bright eye. Next item on the programme. Paying the piper.[21]

Whatever its musical justification, this conglomeration of styles, perspectives, rhythms, and attitudes functions as a total mimesis of Bloom's situation at a moment when he is helplessly anticipating his cuckolding and frantically but only half-successfully trying to fill time with observations of his neutral ambience. In this, virtually the last appearance of what remains of the standardized narrating presence,[22]

---

[21]Joyce, *Ulysses*, pp. 223–24.
[22]The opening chapters all feature a protean but recognizable scene-setting voice, the

we find the most elaborate use of microparataxis, marked not only by the paragraph breaks but also by the internal rhythms of the units. The puck-narrator creates space both by unexpected juxtapositions of particulars (note how the names of places along Boylan's route blend with the sound of his carriage and/or Molly's bed) and by significant omissions such as Boylan's name after "jingly jogged." In addition, he/it simultaneously continues and subverts the associative linkage we expect from more conventional stream-of-consciousness passages.

In "Cyclops" a more emphatic macroparatactics supplants the sort of detailed discontinuities we have been discussing. Concerned about Bloom's fate in the hostile pub context and unaccustomed to not hearing his thoughts, the reader is doubly deprived. Two forms of comic awareness stand between him and the chief protagonist. Not only is the narration confided to a harsh, bitter outsider from Dublin's medium depths, but the dun's slanted tale is refracted and aped by clownish interventions (an extension of the headlines in "Eolus"). The latter, with their parodic commentary in a variety of popular nineteenth-century modes, are designed to harass the narrative, rendering it even more ridiculous than the speaker tries to render Bloom.[23] Thanks to this strategy, though very little occurs, the chapter seems almost slapstick. It is at once perverse and appropriate that sixty years of criticism reveals readers responding according to imposed mind-sets, reading *through* the presentation and against the grain of the chapter in their effort to reconstruct versions of the action and its impact on

---

personification of daylight awareness. A somewhat modified version of this "initial" narrator appears briefly in Bloom's segment of "Nausicaa" only to vanish permanently. The precise nature of this narrator has become a matter of heated debate in Joyce circles and the question will probably not be settled before this book appears. For a selection of now-current opinions see Hayman, *Ulysses*, pp. 88–90 and passim; Karen Lawrence, *The Odyssey of Style in Ulysses* (Princeton: Princeton University Press, 1981), pp. 38–54; and Shari Benstock and Bernard Benstock, "The Benstock Princple," in *The Seventh of Joyce* (Bloomington: Indiana University Press, 1982), pp. 17–18 and passim.

[23]This is true even though Joyce appears to have begun working out his asides during the earliest stages of the chapter's development rather than adding them, as he did the headlines, during the late stages of his revisions. See Phillip Herring, *Joyce's Notes and Early Drafts for Ulysses: Selections from the Buffalo Collection* (Charlottesville: University Press of Virginia, 1977), pp. 124–77; Michael Groden, *Ulysses in Progress* (Princeton: Princeton University Press, 1977), pp. 117–18 and passim; Michael Groden, ed., "Ulysses: 'Wandering Rocks' through 'Hades', *James Joyce Archive*, Vol. 13 (New York: Garland, 1978), including the manuscripts and typescripts of "Cyclops," pp. 81–131.

Bloom, denying themselves the right to enjoy the genuinely funny.[24] Perhaps such ambiguity is an essential ingredient of the fragmented vision, the darkening glass of the cracked mirror held up to reality as the day of *Ulysses* wanes.

It seems consistent, then, that systematic disruption should be introduced just at the moment when Bloom is under the most stress and that its effect should be to strengthen the reader's allegiance. The real feat, however, was to achieve this result through means that are stylistically and thematically farcical. After all, the major cause of Bloom's distress, his probable cuckolding, which the reader may by this time erroneously think should be nothing new for him, is a standard farcical topos. The effect was carefully planned, since, early on, Joyce saw the shift of sympathy from the fancyman and adulterous woman to the victimized husband, from Harlequin, the trickster, to Pierrot, the dupe.[25]

Once we are past "Scylla," not only are the chapter breaks sharper and more surprising, not only do we gradually lose contact with the quirky but dependable-seeming narrative voice that has guided us through the labyrinth of the book's opening chapters, but something happens to our sense of time. In "Cyclops," "Oxen of the Sun," and "Ithaca," where the diachronic development is threatened or overcome by the list effect and the protagonists' humanity is diminished, the reader subsists on the afterglow of documentation and experience stored up from the opening chapters. Still, the refusal to convey time

---

[24]The reactions have been almost as various as the critics, but the remarks made by David Garnett at a seminar session on modernism held in the late 1950s in Austin, Texas, may stand as the most extreme. Garnett was adamant that the chapter was simply not funny, and like S. L. Goldberg, he found the narrative asides self-indulgent. See S. L. Goldberg, *James Joyce* (New York: Grove Press, 1962), p. 95. For more recent discussions, see David Hayman, "Cyclops," in *James Joyce's Ulysses: Critical Essays*, ed. Clive Hart and David Hayman (Berkeley: University of California Press, 1974), pp. 243–75; Hayman, *Ulysses*, pp. 126–27; Lawrence, *Odyssey of Style in Ulysses*, pp. 101–8.

[25]Among the notes taken while he was writing his play, we find the following allusion to Flaubert: "Since the publication of the lost pages of *Madame Bovary* the centre of sympathy appears to have been esthetically shifted from the lover or fancyman to the husband or cuckold. This displacement is also rendered more stable by the gradual growth of a collective practical realism due to changed economic conditions in the mass of the people who are called to hear and feel a work of art relating to their lives. This change is utilized in *Exiles*" (James Joyce, "Notes by the Author," in *Exiles*, ed. Padraic Colum [New York: Viking, 1961], p. 115).

as flow in such chapters, like the insistence on the use of hypotaxis against the grain in "Nausicaa" and "Eumeus," tends to augment reader concern, obliging us to put together an action and/or to approximate the protagonists' reactions with the aid of random clues. In the problematics of reversal and compensation, the manipulation of paratactics in relation to hypotactic procedures is a crucial sign of modernism's declaration of independence.

Intrinsically synchronic, nonnarrative poetry is naturally more hospitable to paratactics than prose narrative, though radical discontinuity in serious verse may well be a twentieth-century invention, or at least a symbolist or postsymbolist innovation. In this context we see T. S. Eliot and Ezra Pound asserting the need for complexity and concision rendered coherent by stringent controls.

Eliot's handling of such controls in his "Waste Land" is, even after Samuel Beckett's extension of it in "Echo's Bones," exemplary. Not only is this esoteric poem divided into segments that differ widely in style and tonality, obliging the reader to make connections, it is also divided into stanzas that intershock. Furthermore, within the stanza, we are apt to find foreign language materials, reworked citations, conflicting voices and styles joined by eccentric punctuation. All of these devices mimetically enforce the theme of moral and cultural fragmentation and decay. The poem's procedures have obliged generations of exegetes to respond to the invitation, "explain me." Constituting a destructive/constructive attempt to eliminate the essential by smoothing over the poem's abrasive texture, their results are a logical, if disjunct, extension of the text, proof of the poem's seemingly endless growth potential.

The macroparatactics of "The Waste Land" should be self-evident, but we may perhaps note briefly its brilliant use of microparatactics:

> Unreal City,
> Under the brown fog of a winter dawn,
> A crowd flowed over London Bridge, so many,
> I had not thought that death had undone so many.[26]

Not only is the concluding line of our fragment with its muted exclamation a dislocation, in sharp contrast to the preceding line, but

---

[26]T. S. Eliot, *The Complete Poems and Plays* (New York: Harcourt, Brace, 1952), p. 39.

both the Dante reference and the opening allusion to Baudelaire, the first great poet of the city, are ungrammatically joined to the basic sentence: "Under the brown fog of a winter dawn, / A crowd flowed over London Bridge" "Unreal City" is clearly an assertion from which the sentence flows. It finds its replique in the modified citation that closes and sums up the stanza: "You! hypocrite lecteur!—mon semblable,—mon frère!" Yet the break between line 1 and 2 is so sharp that the reader may be tempted to place a period after "City." The slide into French and the erratic punctuation of the concluding line from Baudelaire's "Au lecteur" is matched here by the capitalization of "City," which turns the Baudelaire allusion into a pun on the name of London's financial district. In both cases, though in different ways, Eliot is introducing a layered effect, or vertical parataxis, related to that introduced by narrative punning.

On a more immediate level, the passage suggests two sorts of junctures and at least two distinct and complementary readings. The first two phrases could be read as a unit: "[I address you,] Unreal City, Under the brown fog of a winter dawn," in which case the third line is viewed as introducing a break in the rhythm, if not as paratactic. Alternatively, as the spacing suggests, the break could come after the first phrase, so that the second and third units would be joined in our basic sentence. In either instance, the appending of "so many" to the description of the crowd seems to smooth over a shift in the mode of discourse from objective description to subjective exclamation. Furthermore, the brief ejaculation could be punctuated as a question. Ungrammaticality is produced by that shift and reinforced by the Dante paraphrase, which stands out partly because it is not punctuated as a sentence.

The passage continues to alter its mode and focus as it progresses, recalling in a radically different context certain qualities of Stephen Dedalus's interior monologue in "Proteus." But, while Stephen's thoughts skip without warning from topic to topic and occasionally change their mode of address, Eliot's persona follows a single, if suggestive and at times puzzling line. The parataxis that results for the experienced reader from the running together of fresh materials and intertextual citations is muted (along with the potentially farcical humor implicit in Eliot's whimsy and mockery) by punctuation and by the careful modulation of styles at such moments. This obfuscation is in its turn gently undermined by the use of footnotes. Eliot is achieving a balance similar to Joyce's by different means. He is imposing narrative rules on recalcitrant materials where Joyce is subverting serious narrative by introducing a variety of methods superficially inappropriate to it.[27]

It is instructive to compare Eliot's use of stylistic discontinuity and veiled parataxis with Pound's more blatant tactics, since each in his way, as the received ideas of criticism would have it, was producing an epic for his time and each was willy-nilly writing in the shadow of Joyce's book.[28] Briefly, Eliot used paratactics in the service of a satirico-metaphysical statement about contemporary conditions against a backdrop of myth and history. By the rules of satire, he was free to bring in all manner of foreign materials. The trick was not to let this planned but seemingly random medley of high and low become farcical. Indeed, his great accomplishment was to shape a serious aesthetic statement from such materials and in the process to rejuvenate English poetry, inverting or radically modifying its canons.

It is no attack on the poetry of Pound's *Cantos* or on Pound's brilliance as a stylist to say that their discontinuities are a function of the poet's personality, his self-characterization as a clownish rebel and disrupter of conventional (aesthetic) order. It may seem paradoxical to say, however, that the *Cantos* quickly take on a quality of sameness-in-difference, despite radical variations in approach, subject matter, materials, and means. In effect, though Flaubert may have been the "true

[27]For a fuller discussion of the relationship of *Ulysses* to "The Waste Land," which touches on many questions beyond the scope of this study, see Robert Adams Day, "Joyce's Waste Land and Eliot's Unknown God," *Literary Monographs*, vol. 4, ed. Eric Rothstein (Madison: University of Wisconsin Press, 1971).

[28]It is well known and documented how Pound helped in the publication of *Portrait* and how he followed the progress of *Ulysses*, objecting to the use of Bloom along the way but modifying his stand. See Forrest Read, ed., *Pound/Joyce: The Letters of Ezra Pound to James Joyce* (New York: New Directions, 1967), pp. 131, 139, and passim. We also know that Eliot read *Ulysses* in manuscript and even wrote on it. Furthermore, Pound contributed greatly to the shaping of "The Waste Land." The question of impact or influence is less important, however, than the fact that both writers make brilliant and characteristic use of paratactics. For an illuminating treatment of these aspects of Eliot and Pound, one that distinguishes between their methods and in some ways extends and parallels the discussion given here, see Marjorie Perloff, *Poetics of Indeterminacy*, pp. 156–77. Interestingly, while emphasizing parataxis in her discussion of Pound, Perloff overlooks the important precedent found in Joyce, whose work, incidentally, seems to combine the two tendencies that she outlines and may even undermine her argument.

Penelope" of his Mauberly, Pound himself seems to have rejected or severely modified the concept of impersonality by the time he established his epic life-book. The more rigorously Flaubertian Joyce and Eliot retreat from their texts, continually nuancing their disruption, modifying their materials, keeping the reader off balance with parry and thrust, covering their tracks, and making different and differently ambiguous points.

In contrast, Pound is advancing a limited range of arguments with materials that, though varied and rich, are repeatedly reintroduced for rhythm and emphasis. His is an "epic" with social, moral, and economic as well as aesthetic theses that are stated and developed by rigorous and parsimonious, if eccentric, poetic means. This statement is true, even though satire of the harshest sort and caricature (satire's plastic arts cousin) of the sort bound to freeze the smile on the reader's lips repeatedly collide with extracts from letters, substantial economic treatises, and lambent airs as delicately nuanced as the brushwork on an ancient Chinese scroll.

The effect of such rough encounters, though often humorous, is seldom farcical at least partly because, even when particulars are puzzling and conjunctions shocking, the associative linkages are accepted as a given of the poetic procedures and the overarching development is everywhere implied. The reader is too concerned with rationalizing, too convinced of Pound's mastery and seriousness of purpose to laugh even when the poet resorts to clownish behavior. On the other hand, the method applied, however discreetly, to both small and large units enlivens the poetic texture as could no other, introducing concision, reinforcing urgency, and making possible the widely varied dictions and exciting shifts in tone and mood, the overt and insistent encyclopedism.

These lines from Canto XL are characteristically uncharacteristic of a poem whose impact is cumulative and whose disruptive effects are quickly accepted and unyielding both to readerly ignorance and to the impulse to allegorize:

> Esprit de corps in permanent bodies
> "Of the same trade," Smith, Adam, "men
> never gather together
> without conspiracy against the general public."

Independent use of money (our OWN)
toward holding OUR bank, own bank
and in it the deposits, received, where received.
De banchis cambi tenendi. . . .
Venice 1361,
62, shelved for a couple of centuries . . .
whether by privates or public . . .
currency OF (O, F, of) the nation.
Toward producing that wide expanse of clean lawn
Toward that deer park toward
the playing fields, congeries, swimming pools, undsoweiter:
Sword-fish, seven marlin, world's record
extracted in 24 hours.
Wd. make the loan, sterling, eight hundred thousand
n Peabody wd. quit business.
England 1858
IN THE NAME OF GOD THE MOST GLORIOUS MR.
D'ARCY
is permitted for 50 years to dig up the subsoil of
Persia.
'62, report of committee:
Profit on arms sold to the government: Morgan
(Case 97) sold to the government the government's arms . . .
I mean the government owned'em already
at an extortionate profit
Dollars 160 thousand, one swat, to Mr. Morgan
for forcing up gold.
'Taking advantage of emergency' (that is war)
After Gettysburg, down 5 points in one day—
Bulls on gold and bears on the Union
'Business prospered due to war's failures.'

'If a nation will master its money'[29]

The obvious and fundamental strategy of this text is to take absolute
liberties in the name of the presentation of evidence. Thus, its first line
joins a French cliché to a technical term without supplying a verb. The
second line procedes to define the term through the medium of an

---

[29]*The Cantos of Ezra Pound* (New York: New Directions, 1956), pp. 47–48 (of "Eleven
New Cantos").

Adam Smith citation disrupted in its turn by the use of the document formula, "Smith, Adam," a play on Pound's frequent use of Adams, John. In line 5, a second "sentence" relates implicitly the "conspiracy" of the Smith citation to the suspect practices of banks that equate money deposited with money owned. After that, it is possible, though hardly natural, to cite Venician regulations dating from 1361, beginning with a fragment in Latin. To this point Pound's presence has been felt in the choice of citations and the manner of their joining and in the parenthetical "our OWN," with its characteristic use of capitals for emphasis. Now Poundian rhetoric intervenes more pointedly, though in small ways, as in the anachronistic term "shelved" and the familiar "couple" in a context that purports to translate the document. (His procedure here echoes that of Joyce's "Nestor" where the substance of Mr. Deasy's letter is conveyed by recording only a few significant fragments. It is the pretense of scanning.)

Pound has only begun his argument against the banks' use of public money, but reader engagement must be maintained, so we quickly turn from documents and Poundian asides to a stenographic narrative of the uses to which the rich bankers put their ill-gotten gains. There is drama in the harsh accounting of rich men's pleasures, the sort of excitement that adheres to lavish expense and waste, an appeal like that of the human interest story or the juicy item in a gossip column. The emphasis throughout is on the use of money as power, and criminal behavior sanctioned by that power, as in the case of Morgan's manipulations. Even today, we may recoil from the idea of the resale to the government of its own arms, but the real force of the poetic statement derives from the role forced upon the willing reader, who is obliged to fill in gaps in the discourse, to draw conclusions. From that process, from the harsh beauty of the verbal collage, the surprise occasioned by the word choices, the choice of citations, the interjections, and the display of so much determinedly prosaic material on the poetic page comes much of our enjoyment (and even *jouissance*) in Pound's text. The poetry of the *Cantos* also derives in large measure from the traces left after the deliberate exclusion of superficial vestiges of the poetic past. To some degree it emerges from the perverse disclosure of echo and meter in the transparently prosaic, the meter imposed by radical breaks in the discourse, by the idiosyncratic emphasis, and by the ingenious use of the natural pauses of prose discourse. It is a metrics against the poetic grain, but its impact, like that

of Alban Berg's music, is undeniably aesthetic and even dramatic to
the degree that the concluding line of our passage comes close to
achieving lyrical intensity and genuine pathos.

By yoking together fragments relating to his topic and letting the
reader rationalize their conjunction, Pound has elaborated a multidi-
mensional assemblage reminiscent of certain cubist works. (He himself
would call it an ideogrammatic approach, patterned after the procedures of Chinese written language.)[30] At times it seems that just
about anything can serve the driving need to make points that are in
themselves hardly poetic: integral and fragmentary citations, documentation, typographic effects, passages in foreign languages, and
even the Chinese ideogram itself. Against the radical discontinuity of
this arrangement, Pound poises the quality of his choices and his own
active, if interstitial, discourse as the cement and animating principles
that keep the *Cantos* from resolving themselves into catalogues or falling into chaos. Yet the juxtaposition of such a wide range of relatively
unmodified (or raw) materials and the use of a distinctive and abrasive
discourse brings us perilously or (as the French might say) deliciously
close to the extreme of total parataxis. That risk is, here and in many of
our other examples, undeniably a factor contributing to the aesthetic
appeal.

The quality of affrontery and conviction embodied in both the tone
and the form of the *Cantos* is carried over into Pound's correspondence
and even more into his infamous and damaging, if at times witty and
even profound, wartime propaganda broadcasts from Italy. It seems
almost fitting that he would have used in those broadcasts not only the
grammatical parataxis of his *Cantos* but also the related principle of
ideogrammatic assemblage, but then, Pound was nothing if not consistent. It is therefore beside the point to wonder whom he thought he
could convert by means of encyclopedic harangues filled with mis-
directed innuendo, libel, slang, arcane knowledge, poetry, literary
criticism, racial slurs, and theories designed to attack the monetary
policies and economic principles of England and America.

The broadcasts are particularly interesting for what they tell us

---

[30]As everyone knows, Pound's source is Ernest Fenollosa's famous essay "The Chinese Written Character as a Medium for Poetry," which Pound edited, publicized, and
published. See *Instigations of Ezra Pound* (New York: Boni & Liverright, 1920), pp. 357–
88. For recent discussions of the method, see Laszlo Géfin, *Ideogram: A History of a
Poetic Method* (Austin: University of Texas Press, 1982).

about paratactics as an instrument of conviction, a mode of incite-
ment—less to action than to commitment to the text. The following
extract is from broadcast 33, which opens with an attack on the Tal-
mud as "the dirtiest teaching any race ever codified":

> ALL right, now what does your Bible tell you about SOCIAL organi-
> zation? It tells you the Jews went into captivity, that is, into a state
> wherein they had NO CIVIC responsibility, in great part a slave condi-
> tion. As to their own organization it consisted in what still survives in the
> kahal system. There was a LAW, NOT an ethical system. This law was
> a set of finnikin prohibitions, and there was little distinction between the
> transgressions; what there was, was related mostly to the MAIN purpose
> of the law; namely to provide FINES, payable to a gang or tribe of
> allegedly religious superiors, who seem to have had no particular ethical
> status.
>
> IRRESPONSIBLE taxation, taxation to and for the benefit of a gang
> of exploiters.
>
> Just like the Bank of England or the Morgenthau, Warburg system in
> the United States. Taxing the people TWO dollars for every dollar spent
> by the government.
>
> That is BASIC; all particular grafts and swindles over Army contracts,
> or contracts in peace time are EXTRA, over and above the main wheeze.
> I leave out all questions of detail, questions as to what Moses learned in
> Egypt, what the kikes picked up in Babylon. I ask you WHY WAS
> CHRIST crucified? He was crucified for trying to BUST a racket.
> There had been mystic sects in Palestine before the ZERO year of the
> Christian era. Some say they had been there for 200 years.
>
> I am not considerin' the religious and mystic question. I am asking
> WHY the Sanhedrim and the Priests and Levites were so dead set on
> Crucifixion. Pontius Pilate couldn't make it out. He wasn't interested in
> having a revolt on his hands. So he washed 'em. BUT what stirred up the
> big men in the kikery?[31]

Clearly, even though the formal parataxis is intermittent, the language
of outrage and urgency lends itself to a cumulative approach to argument, a literal piling up of (plausible?) assertions that are to be taken as
evidence. The larding of these assertions with slang, slur, and asides
contributes to the zest and discontinuity. The result, despite Pound's

---

[31]*Ezra Pound Speaking: Radio Speeches of World War II*, ed. Leonard W. Doob (West-
port, Conn.: Greenwood Press, 1978), p. 118.

use of a rational framework and "facts," may not be wholly convincing, but who would deny that the impact is powerful?

Like the *Cantos*, but for obviously different reasons, the broadcasts differ radically from one another in topic, style, sources, and use of evidence. Though we should probably not put too much weight on the resulting macroparataxis, it is worth noting that Pound is sufficiently in control to vary his approaches with an eye to modal balance. He repeatedly demonstrates his ability to create through modulation a mix of the positive and the negative, the light and the ominous, cajolery and attack. Here too we are close to the *Cantos* (one of which was actually included), what with the piling up of raw data mixed with opinion, the bald assertion, the calls to authority, which themselves often boil down to assertions. In fact, Pound is using orthodox propaganda tactics modified by his own wonderfully idiosyncratic procedures and voice. The broadcasts are readable today thanks to that voice.

As we read through them we may be struck less by the paratactic grammar than by the juxtaposition of subject matter with an eye to connecting what are generally perceived as opposites: Jewish religious codes with financial ethics, Pound's coven of Jewish financiers with the Comintern, his Rapallo peasants with the Chinese. We can also point, however, to pure (and bombastic) paratactics in broadcast number 33's concluding paragraph or in the harsh but clevery modulated negative litany (a procedure with distant roots in the *Egyptian Book of the Dead*):

> I also respect it. I consider it part of civilization against which you have a horde of bloody barbarians financed by a bunch of skunks. Meet a few Mongoloid or Tar Tar communists. Meet a few of Baruch's importation, of Warburg's importation, meet the lower strata, not merely the Willie Wiseman's who have been given directorates. Meet a few of these dirty swine, out to destroy Bach's music.
> Bach? OUT.
> Shakespeare? OUT.
> Destroy everything that is conducive to civilization. Damn civilization. The Kike is out for all power. The Kike and the unmitigated evil that has been centered in London since the British government set the Red Indians on to murder the American frontier settlers. Has hurled the Slav, the Mongol, the Tartar OPENLY against Germany, AND POLAND, and Finland and Romania. And SECURELY against all that is

decent in America. Against the total American heritage. This is my war all right, I have been in it for 20 years. My Grandad was in it before me.[32]

Once established, the flow will carry surprising flotsam, such as the sudden and passionate assertion that Jewish financiers are out to destroy the music of Bach and the literature of Shakespeare (counters or synecdoches for Germany and England but doubtless also for Stalin's war against the arts). The Jews, as the prose heats up, are also given responsibility for setting the Indians against American settlers and the Russians (seen as a Mongol horde) against Europe. The effect of this method—the effect of all such catalogues—is to level and equate facts, to mingle and confuse fact and fiction, to equate rhythm with demonstration, and to generate affective but vicarious participation in the reader.

The same device that produced laughter in Rabelais functions as a scourge when, in broadcast 16, Pound accuses the English (and Americans) of selling their birthright and goads them on to the violent expulsion of the Jews. We do not laugh, nor are we meant to, though the passage is larded with absurdities and nonsequiturs. This is, of course, a modified parataxis, just as it is a modified list and litany, but then the modifications are a major source of interest together with the overt clowning that lifts the scurrility a notch above the usual propaganda. We must recognize, however, that the net impact would have been radically different in 1942, before the Holocaust and the State of Israel, from what it is today, far less complex, far more degrading for "right-thinking" Englishmen. There is a bitter paradox here; for Pound's rhetorical strategy inevitably brings to mind the typical ranting of *Old Testament* prophets such as Isaiah and Jeremiah, of which his words are a ghastly pastiche; Whitman turned sour would be a more direct source, but the procedure may best be qualified as paranoid discourse.

Though, as we shall see, Pound and Céline make very different use of discontinuity and fragmentation, it is not surprising to find one and one-half of Pound's broadcasts devoted to a fellow propagandist: "Times like these are times when a writer should git down to bedrock and talk without fuzz on his tongue. Céline does that all right. Time to

[32]Ibid., pp. 119–20.

read Céline for the simple truths that stand there in his writing, expressed with perfect lucidity—and simplicity."[33] Beginning a few years before Pound but writing out of a similar rage (and anxiety) and an equivalent fear/hatred, Céline, that other explosive autodidact, was busy getting himself into hot water. Less well read but no less gifted verbally, he shared Pound's views and even his methods, though without officially joining forces with the Fascists or being accepted by them as an advocate.[34]

Between Céline and Pound there are of course important differences in technique, if not necessarily in goals. Pound uses a field gun where Céline prefers the hand-held automatic weapon, the incessant chatter of small arms fire designed to wear down the reader/enemy/target. His units are smaller and his imaginative vigor at times seems greater. Pound has the renaissance mind-set, while Céline, though he has frequently been compared to Rabelais, has a preeminently medieval thrust. The pamphlet to which Pound refers, *Bagatelles pour un massacre* (1937), calls to mind Bruegel's dark humor in the splendidly macabre *Triumph of Death* in the Prado. There we see animated skeletons in every conceivable position and action, even in the act of disguising themselves behind the mask of life. Like Bruegel's proliferating metaphor, Céline's anti-Semitic statements explode into discrete units of meaning, all pointing up the same message while anatomizing their topic. In Pound, there is often the shadow and scaffolding, if not the substance, of a logical development to which parataxis contributes relief and an aura of activity. Céline prefers the rhetorical barrage to logic, peppering the reader with lists of attributes, profanities salted with harsh irony and bitter spleen, gingery with false sympathy, replete with mass-cultural catalogues that glow with rage and exuberance.

To achieve the impact, if not the precise grammar, of disruption, he breaks his sentences into brief phrases often punctuated with his fa-

---

[33]Ibid., p. 132. On p. 129, Pound is even more explicit in his praise for the anti-Semitic pamphlets.

[34]Although Céline seems to have been eager to be credited with his opinions during the war years, he had difficulty actually joining any group. See the testimony of Karl Epting, "Il ne nous aimait pas," and Robert Champfleury, "Céline ne nous a pas trahis," in *Louis-Ferdinand Céline, L'Herne* 3 (Paris: L'Herne, 1963), pp. 56–59 and 60–66, but see also the more nuanced treatment in François Gibault's biography, *Céline: Délires et persécutions, 1932–1944* (Paris: Mercure de France, 1981).

mous three points of suspension and with exclamation points reminiscent of Pound's capitals. Thus, in a passage designed to counter the image of the Jew as downtrodden and vulnerable, a condition the writer will increasingly ascribe to himself, we find a catalogue of influential Jews. The names of politicians, bankers, actors sail across the page, each on a raft of punctuation. The paratactic impact of the following is accentuated by the ordering and modification of the list, its grotesquely anomalous mix, to say nothing of the qualifying adjectives: "The persecuted arise, emaciated, wan, out of the night of time, centuries of torture . . . Léon Blum, . . . Hayes, . . . Zuckor, . . . Litvinoff, . . . Levitan, . . . Brunschwig, . . . Bernstein, . . . Bader, . . . Kerensky, . . . a hundred thousand Levys, . . . the crucified Chaplin . . . the Marx Brothers tragedians . . . "[35] Clearly, Céline is not so much disproving the past injustices as asserting with a powerful (and vicious) irony that the Jews have now made it, using the stereotype of the rich Jew to downplay the appeal for a reaction against anti-Semitism. His brilliance is clearest in the attack on the Jewish clowns, figures whose theatrical vulnerability should render them immune from the scorn even of a master of joyous vituperation, a fellow clown, in fact. Instead, they are perceived as part of an international conspiracy to control opinion and mask power. Céline uses not one but three paratactic devices to immobilize his target: the sequence of sentimental clichés, the stroboscopic list, and the elevation/denigration of the powerful(?) clowns.

No one knew better than Céline how to mobilize paratactic difference and, in the process, to make inadequation work for him. The effects used in a single page of his diatribe, while not in themselves numerous, permit him to achieve any amount of comic outrage by ringing changes on his single theme. Here, for example, is how he opens his attack on Charlie Chaplin, a man who had been his preferred comedian and perhaps even the model for his treatment of America in *Voyage au bout de la nuit:* "You put together a Joseph Stalin like a Joan Crawford, same process, same gall, same con-job, same outrageous Jews pulling the strings. Between Hollywood, Paris, New-York [*sic*] and Moscow nothing but a perpetual funnyfact factory. Charlie Chaplin too gives his all, splendidly, to the cause, a great pioneer of Jewish imperialism. He's the big secret. Here's to good Jewish whining!

[35]Louis-Ferdinand Céline, *Bagatelles pour un massacre* (Paris: Denoël, 1937), p. 45.

Here's to immense lamentation!"[36] This equation, doubtless stimulated by Chaplin's recent portrayal of Céline's current hero in *The Great Dictator*, rather hamhandedly turns Chaplin's humble mockery back on him and by extension on the "powerful" Jews. Clearly, the intent is *comic* outrage, though it is unlikely to be seen as such. In the absence of verifiable facts, rational arguments, and polished syntax, the text makes its points by multiplying myths and extrapolating from details, generating not-quite-synonyms, inventing side-issues. Like the good propagandist, Céline knows how to settle real and imaginary scores, how to seem righteous when attacking the weak.

The obvious effect of such verbal barrages is to immobilize the argument, turning a development into a landscape or at the very least an important heap. No matter, the impact is never neutral. The master clown achieves the incontrovertible effect of a prolonged fit of rage, a release of tension, a display of wild gestures implicating the reader in language as action. Like Pound, he uses an imposing mass of "facts" as weapons to stun us, though affective rhetoric is the necessary adjunct. Redundancy works *for* him precisely because he has "a way with words." He can even manage through his attacks to uphold the "right" by defending the defenseless majority against the conspiratorial minority. Typically, the more outrageous his position, the more doubts he can raise. We are treated for example to an assault on the sacrosanct French wine industry at once for diluting the wine and for stupefying the weak-willed French public. It is "a gigantic cess pool of Jews and watered wine . . . Hasn't anybody caught on? . . . No one in on the sting? . . . Not just a padlock, an Alcatraz on the lips of the big Jews!" (In this instance, even Céline is forced to pull back a bit, speaking of the viniculturists "Jews or not.")[37]

Whereas in other instances of paratactic discourse we have experienced logical gaps, associative linkage, and failed transitions, here no demands are made on the reader other than the insistent demand for allegiance and penance. The gaps exist but they tend to be trompe l'oeil when the language is characterized by superfluity. Indeed the sheer velocity of the words, the unmediated flood of images and allegations, anesthetizes the intellect, contributing to the text's power to badger us. If we begin by being amused by inventiveness, by the

[36]Ibid.
[37]Ibid., p. 126.

writer's ability to generate a seemingly boundless mass of particulars and metaphors, we may soon experience a mild anxiety, a dizzyness, a need to conciliate, to mollify the speaker or his speaking text. This reaction is similar to what one might feel in the actual presence of an unreasonable but well-directed rage of which we are not necessarily, or not at this moment, the target.

At some point, by virtue of the energy and persistence of the discourse as well as of our admiration for the skill and resourcefulness of Céline/Destouches,[38] we may slip into a tacit if not an emphatic agreement, becoming in the process coconspirators. I am speaking, of course, of the reflective reader, the most difficult to sway, and not of the less imaginative or already committed, who may instantly echo the text, finding in it substantiation for clichés that have long been in the public domain, salve for perceived injuries. The latter reader, like Pound, will readily join to the text's seductive voice his or her own. In either case, the dynamic pause is a significant emotional weapon at the crossroads of paratactic discourse. For at the same time that it cuts the discourse into manageable units, it denies the reader the right to stop and contemplate.

Another important aspect of both the Poundian and the Célinean texts, one which has been developed and repeated in more contemporary works (see for example the novels of Henry Miller, William Burroughs, Kurt Vonnegut, Juan Goytisolo, and Philippe Sollers in *Lois* and *Femmes*), is its aggressivity. Both Pound and Céline are attacking not only their shared and declared "enemy" but also that potential ally the reader, who is seen as both ignorant of and collaborating in evil. The technique, a familiar one, does not depend only on parataxis; nor is the tactic unusual if we bear in mind the traditional farcical assault on the audience and its values. Still, parataxis, as a mode of collision and surprise, can readily become a basic tool of the self-righteous verbal clown, a means of reproducing and prolonging the farcical catastrophe, the explosive moment during which order is demolished only to reappear in the aftermath.[39]

---

[38]Much could be said about Dr. Destouches's use of a nom de plume and the process by which, once unmasked, he went public, accepting the role of target and potential victim of his own victims, rationalizing his fears.

[39]We may point to it repeatedly in Joyce's "Circe" chapter and particularly in the following highly mimetic evocation of Stephen's drunken dance: *"(He wheels Kitty into Lynch's arms, snatches up his ashplant from the table and takes the floor. All wheel whirl waltz*

Though Céline's discourse is fundamentally farcical, though his words are a form of action complete in itself, and though we may construe his covert intent as not only entertainment but also emotional liberation, or catharsis, the overt intent of the pamphlets, like that of the broadcasts, is destruction in the real world. The reader and the reader's values are to be construed as vehicles for that destruction, if not as its target. The clown, refusing to be content with laughter, has broken into the world of his audience. We need hardly be surprised, then, that, like Pound's prosecutors, Céline's reacted as much to manner as to matter, lifting the clownish mask and demanding the maximum punishment for the verbal crime.[40] Neither should we be astonished that Céline was consistent in reading attacks on his books as retaliatory attacks on his person.[41]

Even in the purest, most outrageous farce, there are moments of repose, calms before the ejaculatory storms, and though he is always testing the frontiers of formal chaos in search of the most efficacious utterance, Céline as novelist is a master of modulation. If the pamphlets fail to convince and often even to entertain, it is because the author seems to forget that pure rant, like pure cant, is acceptable only in small quantities, that a prolonged explosion finally deafens and

---

twirl. *Bloombella Kittylynch Florryzoe jujuby women. Stephen with hat ashplant frogsplits in middle highkicks with skykicking mouth shut hand clasp part under thigh. With clang tinkle boombammer tallyho hornblower blue green yellow flashes Toft's cumbersome turns with hobbyhorse riders from gilded snakes dangled, bowels fandango leaping spurn soil foot and fall again)"* (*Ulysses*, p. 472).

[40]A polemic by Julia Kristeva gives the equally valid opposite side of the coin, that paratactic outrage is far less dangerous than hypotactic persuasion. Speaking out against the resurgence of French anti-Semitism and the rehabilitation of a right-wing writer like Drieu La Rochelle, she writes: "And, *in terms of literature*, it would not be the radical and dramatic experiments of Céline or of Pound that would be advanced but rather the 'fine sentences' of a Drieu, bearing witness to the misty stirrings of a soul that, if it lacks a heaven, at least does not deny itself earth, a visceral being capable of justifying its irrationality" (*Art Press* 26 [March 1979], 6–7, my translation).

[41]See the preface Céline added after the war to his *Voyage au bout de la nuit* (Paris: Gallimard, 1952): "Vous me direz: mais c'est pas le 'Voyage'! Vos crimes là que vous en crevez, c'est rien à faire! c'est votre malédiction vous-même! votre 'Bagatelles'! vos ignominies pataquès! votre scélératesse imageuse, bouffonneuse! La justice vous arquinque? garrotte? Eh foutre, que plaignez? Zigoto! Ah mille grâces! mille grâces! Je m'enfure! fuerie! pantèle! bomine! Tartufes! Salsifis! Vous m'errez pas! C'est pour le 'Voyage' qu'on me cherche! Sous la hache, je l'hurle! c'ęst le compte entre moi et 'Eux'! au tout profond . . . pas racontable . . . On est en pétard de Mystique! Quelle histoire!" (p. 10).

blinds its audience, producing a continuous blur rather than a sequence of sharp images. Shock and delight give way to boredom and distress.[42] Furthermore, radical parataxis is inimical to rational thought and even conviction, verging as it does, on the one hand, on stasis and, on the other, on unmotivated motion. Even the inclusion of a handful of ballet scenarios in *Bagatelles* fails to right the balance.[43]

Given the polemic's obvious weaknesses (mixed with whatever strengths), especially the excess of disruptive paratactics on the microlevel, we may wonder that Céline could regain his balance and write viable postpamphlet novels. The London sequence called *Guignol's Band*, written during World War II but concerned with World War I, shows that he could. On the other hand, the extraordinarily innovative but critically unsuccessful *Féerie* sequence (1952) would seem, at first glance, to demonstrate the dangers of pamphleterring, its adverse effects on the novelist. Before arguing for the paratactic virtues of these neglected books, we should glance at the rhetoric of what most consider his best work: *Journey to the End of the Night (Voyage au bout de la nuit)* (1933) and *Death on the Installment Plan (Mort à crédit)* (1936).

Journey is most remarkable for the mild and generally engaging macroparatactics of its "picaresque" first half, the section evidently modeled after Voltaire's *Candide*. In these pages, the novel jolts its hapless protagonist, with little or no transition, from Paris to the battlefield and back before shipping him off to Africa and then by galley to America, an adventure that culminates in a surreal vision first of New York and then of Detroit. Unlike Joyce, Céline does not shift styles as he shifts locales, though he alters his modes somewhat as he moves from episode to episode. While we may point to some feverish prose characterized by microparatactics, the tonality of the narrative and its pace remains throughout fairly stable. In contrast to the bitter satiricocomic tone, the emphasis on traditional farcical tropes,[44] and the gen-

---

[42]The error has been repeated by William Burroughs in some of his later work, if not in *Naked Lunch*, and Burroughs is by no means alone.

[43]Louis-Ferdinand Céline, "Scandal aux abysses," in *Ballet sans musique, sans personne, sans rien* (Paris: Gallimard, 1959).

[44]Céline had from the start a tendency to present in a favorable light fringe types belonging to the farcical community of outcasts. These, with the aid of a clownlike suffering persona and in the voice of a punishing clown, he set off against the satirized norms. In addition, without freeing us to laugh as a more conventionally farcical treatment might, his handling of human situations emphasizes the ridiculous.

erally fluid world-weary monotone of *Journey, Death on the Installment Plan* provides us with a vista of periodic and catastrophic change, exposing us to extreme variations in pace and tone, making ample use of grammatical breaks. The prose is potentially disruptive, its delivery staccato even when the overriding anguish is muted, as in this treatment of little Ferdinand's dog and the joys of the cinema:

> It didn't give me any pleasure to beat him, / I'd much rather have kissed him. / In the end I'd fondle him / and he'd get a hard-on. / He went everywhere with us, / even to the movies, / to the Thursday matinee, at the Robert Houdin. / Grandma treated me to that too. / We'd sit through all three shows. / It was the same price, / all the seats were one franc, / one hundred percent silent, / without words, / without music, / without titles, / just the purring of the machine. / People will come back to that, / you get sick of everything except sleeping and daydreaming. / The *Trip to the Moon* will be back again / . . . I still know it by heart.[45]

The calm tone of this passage is undermined by a latent disruption carried in part by the nervous discontinuous rhythm reminiscent of the flickering cinematic image, the metronomic beat of the short assertive phrases (indicated here by slashes and available in the French). Thus, despite the fact that we are in the presence of Ferdinand's grandmother, the book's most cherished and least flawed character, a mute discontinuity shapes the rhetoric. What interests me is the fact that, in such a passage, Céline's parataxis conveys a complex tenderness even while retaining its spring-steel tension. Significantly, the conceptual gaps are small, there are few points of suspension, and we experience almost none of the farcical proliferation of synonyms and hyperboles.

Thanks to his control over rhythm, Céline is able to maintain interest and generate surprise, thanks to it and to his resourceful use of variations, the mixing of action and reaction, the proliferation of engaging detail, the narrator's salty idiom and irreverent asides, and what we soon register as an overriding narrative periodicity. Texture and substance, pressed into the service of interest, repeatedly contribute to the gradual development of a tension that is inevitably crowned

---

[45]Louis-Ferdinand Céline, *Death on the Installment Plan*, trans. Ralph Manheim (New York: New Directions, 1966), p. 68.

by a climactic explosion. It is the latter, the moment approaching the intensity of pure hilarity and intense rage, that foreshadows and overshadows the style of the pamphlets. Take, for example, the following extract from Ferdinand's half-hallucinated epic attack on his splenetic father.:

> I'm caught up in the dance . . . I stumble, I fall . . . That does it, I've got to finish the stinking bastard! Bzing! He's down again . . . I'm going to smash his kisser! . . . So he can't talk anymore . . . I'm going to smash his whole face . . . I punch him on the ground . . . He bellows . . . He gurgles . . . That'll do. I dig into the fat on his neck . . . I'm on my knees on top of him . . . I'm tangled up in his bandages . . . both my hands are caught. I pull. I squeeze. He's still groaning . . . He's wriggling . . . I weigh down on him . . . He's disgusting . . . He squawks . . . I pound him . . . I massacre him . . . I'm squatting down . . . I dig into the meat . . . It's soft . . . He's drooling . . . I tug . . . I pull off a big chunk of moustache . . . He bites me, the stinker! . . . I gouge into the holes . . . I'm sticky all over . . . my hands skid . . . he heaves . . . he slips out of my grip. He grabs me around the neck. He squeezes my windpipe . . . I squeeze some more. I knock his head against the tiles . . . He goes limp . . . he's soft under my legs . . . He sucks my thumb . . . he stops sucking . . . Phooey![46]

Not only are the phrases shortened, but the intrusive dots multiply, the action swells with catalogues. A frantic stutter infects the prose. Typically, several pages are devoted to exploiting and expanding upon more than describing the action,[47] purging bile without releasing the reader's tension or resolving Ferdinand's conflicts. The ellipses are fundamentally a pacing mechanism, turning even regular discourse into a tissue of pauses, a "lacework" that is resolutely harsh, but the pace is deceptive. While seeming to speed up the action, it slows it down by introducing impediments (see the stroboscopic cinematic impact that I mentioned earlier).

---

[46]Ibid., pp. 316–17.

[47]We may list a dozen or more structurally and thematically parallel passages strategically located to provide animated climaxes, passages that combine to constitute the book's dramatic armature. Individually, they motivate transitions into fresh contexts and new stages of the protagonist's anxious pilgrimage through a world of inverted values.

That does it.
I've got to finish the stinking bastard!
I'm going to smash his kisser!
I'm going to smash his whole face
That'll do.
He's disgusting[48]

Characteristically, such extended hallucinatory rampages resolve themselves into analytical renderings, extended anatomies of a multi-faceted moment, but their impact on the reader is hardly static. What marks the exceptionally rigorous paratactics of *Mort à crédit* is the way it modulates from mild to extreme manifestations within a narrative context structured by repetitions. What sets it off from the hate-filled frenzy of *Bagatelles* is the coherence of that development, the continuous and rigorous control of tone and pace, the subtle and con-tinual variations as well as the adherence to a carefully established plot structure and well-delineated, if highly conventional (to both farce and melodrama), characters. Yet in this novel in which Céline achieved full maturity as a writer, we have ample warning of things to come, just as, in the pamphlets, we may see the foreshadowings of the later fiction.

Féerie (1952), Céline's breakaway postwar novel, was written during his Danish exile as he awaited extradition to France, where he ex-pected to be tried for treason. The frantic tone and eccentric structure of the two volumes may in part be ascribed to that situation. (He claims to have written it in jail, "cell 84 during the winter of 1947.")[49] There are other, more organic reasons, however, for a strategy that places Céline once again in the vanguard of experimental fiction. Whereas in *Bagatelles* the question was what to do about the "Jewish conspiracy," here it is how to defeat those who, though they share in his "guilt," would "wrongfully" inculpate Céline/Destouches. Given this function, we need not be surprised to find the text ordered (or disordered) in a similar manner. The rhetoric is once again frenzied, vituperative, redundant; the argument is often convoluted, less open to

---

[48]Céline, *Death*, p. 316.
[49]François Gibault, *Céline, 1944–1961: Cavalier de l'Apocalypse* (Paris: Mercure de France, 1981), p. 71. Céline scholarship on this neglected novel has been of late particularly rich. See the remarkable issues of *Lettres Modernes, L.-F. Céline*, nos. 3 and 4 (1978, 1979), ed. Jean-Pierre Dauphin.

logical presentation than to the accumulation of associatively generated details. Narrative content is minimal, and as is usual in such cases, the structure is nodal.[50] This text, which makes so few concessions to the reader, constitutes an attack and a challenge to which we must respond on its own terms. It is as though the circus or music hall clown had suddenly turned serious behind his mask and assaulted us directly with his slapstick, using bitter rather than good-natured ridicule. As readers, we must somehow make that rhetoric our own, control its frenzy by attuning ourselves to the voice without becoming its real victim, Céline/Destouches's scapegoat. One can readily understand the book's unpopularity in postwar France.

Roughly two-thirds of the first and better volume of *Féerie* is given over to the ruminations and fulminations of the imprisoned Dr. Destouches (at once the historical person and a literary persona, hence neither one nor the other). We are bombarded with his preoccupations: the conditions of his flight from France, prison life, anal complaints, legal problems, his book and its publisher, his hallucinations, and so on. Everywhere there is a need to arrange, assemble, and naturalize the shards, most of which have been wildly distorted by the speaker's feverish imagination. It is the urgency of his situation as reflected in his discourse that must capture our interest in the absence of coherent action or narrative suspense. Céline/Destouches is reconstituting his literary and social identity. (Readers of Beckett may detect a forerunner of *The Unnamable*.) Since the treatment is consistent, on the level of detail as well as of development, though the material is various, one or two brief samples should suffice to illustrate what might be described as the parataxis of aggressive self-awareness.

The book opens with a description of the treatment accorded the pariah Destouches toward the war's end by former friends attuned to his vulnerable status as a collaborator in about-to-be-liberated Paris:

Creatures act in the same way at the same time . . . the same ticks . . . Like the little ducks around their mother, in the parc Daumesnil, in the Bois de Boulogne, all together, head right! . . . head left! whether they be ten! . . . twelve! . . . fifteen! . . . same thing! all heads right! synchronized! Clemence Arlon sideeyes (askances) me . . . its the ep-

[50]See above, chapter 3.

och . . . Had she ten . . . twelve . . . fifteen sons . . . they'd sideeye
(askance) in the same way![51]

The passage continues, amplifying the image, developing the motive
of threat but in terms of ducklike and therefore seemingly innocent
and harmless, if stupid, antagonists. As presented, the situation is
fundamentally farcical: the poor clown put upon by a mass of inoffen-
sive normal citizens, the shepherd mowed down by a herd of sheep.
Céline is not portraying any such event, however. Instead, he is letting
language carry the farcical charge: in the image of ducks, in the enu-
merations, in lists of traits, in words like "biaiseraient," which is
generally used in a figurative sense, but most clearly in his use of real
and mock parataxis. The passage, a very mild example of his discontinuous rhetoric, is deliberately chosen to show how pervasive the
technique is and how it can be used to convey the ominous as well as
the explosive. When he wishes to heighten such effects, Céline simply
reinforces and sharpens his images, introducing obscenity, absurdity,
shortening sentences, multiplying detail, innovating argotic turns of
phrase and gestural asides which distort the syntax of otherwise hypotactic sentences.

Here, in a self-reflexive paragraph predicting how *Féerie* will be
received by press and public, we have a moderate example of the
procedure:

> Need another sort of laugh now . . . sidesplitter like the hops of hip-
> pos! To your health Gugusse![52] so many assassinated all over the lot, so
> long as it isn't them, they yawn! . . . [53] They'd see the lake in Daumes-
> nil chock full of last night's corpses, the hundred guillotined by the
> Party, they'd say: it stinks! That's it! No more! total disdain! . . . so talk

[51]Louis-Ferdinand Céline, *Féerie pour une autre fois* (Paris: Gallimard, 1952), pp. 11–
12, my translation: "Les êtres se comportent presque tous en même temps de la même
façon . . . les mêmes tics . . . Comme les petits canards autour de leur mère, au
Daumesnil, au Bois de Boulogne, tous en même temps, la tête à droite! . . . la tête à
gauche! qu'ils soient dix! douze . . . quinze! . . . pareils! tous la tête à droite! à la
seconde! Clémence Arlon me regarde de biais . . . c'est l'époque . . . Elle aurait
dix . . . douze . . . quinze fils . . . qu'ils biaiseraient de la même façon!"

[52]There is a running argument between Destouches and his publisher Gaston, or
"Gugusse," Gallimard.

[53]See the postliberation revenge on collaborators with which Céline/Destouches was
obsessed.

about buying my books! . . . so they hug their guts laughing, incoercible fit, explosive, shitting all over, pissing, can't stop, through the salons, the stations, even in front of the tax collector. Come off it, betya they put you away for this one! So there you are, convulsed, brayheyheying at my sallies, filling the Tuileries! . . . so you become obscene! a public show! they stop you, ask what for?
—It's Fay! . . . Fay! . . . Fay![54]

The laughter feigned and prescribed by Destouches is bitter, a baring of the teeth at human cruelty rather than an invitation to shared pleasure. His text is punctuated with accusations, illuminated by challenges issued to a cowed and cowering reader guilty of reading the very words that are being celebrated in this abrasive prose. Characteristically, connective words are omitted and the resulting rhetoric is a swiss cheese of artificial pauses, some signaled by the ellipses, others left unsignaled. The phrase "alors pensez achetez mes livres" contains not one but several possible sentences: "alors pensez que n'import qui acheterait mes livres," "alors, pensez, vous devrait achetez mes livres," "alors, pensez que quelqu'un aurez l'esprit d'acheter mes livres," and so forth. The blanks, though not enormous or profound, leave us with the impression of a floating meaning, while the clear thrust of the text is to attack our status as readers.[55]

We may be struck by the fact that the technique at this point, the

---

[54]Ibid., p. 56, my translation: "Maintenant faut un autre genre de rire . . . les lecteurs à désopiler c'est des sauts aux hippopotames! A la vôtre, Gugusse! tellement d'assassinés partout que pourvu que c'est pas eux ils bâillent! . . . Ils verraient le lac Daumesnil comblé des corps de la veille, des cent guillotines de Partis, ils diraient: ça pue! Pas plus! dédain total! . . . alors pensez acheter mes livres! . . . moi et mes miteux avatars . . . fables, bien entendu . . . , et qu'ils s'en tiennent le bide de secousses, d'incoercible crise, hilares, chiant partout, pissant, pouvant plus, à travers les salons, les gares, sous les regards du Percepteur. Ah, dites, gajure qu'on vous enferme! Que vous convulsiez par exemple, hihahaniez des mes saillies, plein les Tuileries! . . . que vous tourniez obscène public! qu'on vous arrête vous demande de quoi?—C'est *Fée!* . . . *Fée!* . . . *Fée!* . . . "
[55]For another view of Céline's practice, see Leo Spitzer's classic essay "Une habitude de style (le rappel) chez M. Céline," *Français moderne* 3 (June 1935), 207. Spitzer was of course interested in a stylistic detail from which he could draw large conclusions like the following, which puts Céline in his place in relation to Flaubert: "The road followed by Céline is quite short when compared to the one self-imposed by Flaubert: moral despair—something approximating stylistic despair, and nothing more, whereas Flaubert draws artistic polish from his moral imperfection" (my translation).

submergence of the reader in an apparently indiscriminate bog of fragmented discourse, results in a leveling of the rhetoric that could reduce the whole text to uniformity. Céline deliberately works against this potential. Even though the prisoner's diatribe moves us startlingly close to the planar effects achieved by Gertrude Stein, he fills verbal space, while Stein empties it. Maintaining his intricate texture of interruptions, he manages to introduce important peaks of frenzy and deep valleys of repose. A case in point is the passage that follows our citation: a tongue-in-cheek vision of the extravagant rewards he will receive from the runaway sales of his books. Like Beckett after him, Céline knew how to capitalize on even the least promising material, how to bring into play the details of style as actions or gestures, how to mobilize his language without necessarily mobilizing his actors.

In this text, given over almost entirely to the tireless inspection of sores and wounds, we may be shocked to find the last third devoted to pure and outrageous clowning by a successful miscreant, the crapulous legless painter Jules, at once a fanciful embodiment of occupied Paris and an alter ego for the unrepentant collaborator in his Danish prison. With the appearance of Jules the old Céline returns, rediscovering his prewar voice, now tempered in the bile of the interminable overture. After a sudden parataxis break that ushers in the clown and his elaborate act, we read a long slapstick sequence, a classic Célinean moment that repays our patience while paradoxically poisoning our joy. For Jules is not to be confused with the clown of release. His presence finally drives the reader into the camp of the embittered narrator in a book that turns radically upon itself, converting the topos of joy into a weapon with which to flog us for our complacency, inverting accepted morality in order to exculpate the prisoner whose guilt is never really in question.[56] An extravagant bit of special pleading has been saved from bathos by the paratactic storm that blows it our way and denies us a ready purchase on its content. Its maddening mix of outrage, joy, horror, and distress, its intricacy in excess covers the Doctor's whine while putting our own tenuous moral vision into question. The failed

[56]Céline does not hide his collaboration or display repentance, though he may introduce mitigating circumstances. He is not pleading for the reader's love but rather challenging innocence, facing down hatred and questioning good faith. Knowing what we now know about the extent of collaboration in France, Céline's position seems somewhat less unreasonable, takes on that curious shade of off-rightness we find in his contorted portrait of America in *Journey*.

art of *Bagatelles* has been turned to good use by the need to create a climate in which the postwar Destouches/Céline can breathe.

Literary bedfellows, like political ones, can be strange. Somehow, Céline's perverse but rhetorically effective defense of unacceptable behavior foreshadows Juan Goytisolo's splendid and often scurrilous anti-Fascist and philo-Semitic *Count Julian (La reinvindicación del Conde don Julián),*[57] a multifaceted attack on the moral bankruptcy of Franco's Spain. Here too we find a lower-depths monologue garnished with vignettes of action. Like that of Céline's semiautobiographical Dr. Destouches, Goytisolo's voice, shaking a rhetorical fist in helpless rage, is treasonous, as is its alter ego, the legendary Spanish count who betrayed Spain to the Moors.[58]

Count Julian's setting is Moroccan Tangiers, a Spanish-speaking Moorish city directly across the Straits of Gibraltar from Spain, and thus distantly analogous to Céline's prison. This circumstance generates and justifies the style and structure of the narrative: "the life of an émigré of your stripe is made up of a discontinuous series of events that are very difficult to assemble into a coherent whole."[59] From the random or "discontinuous series," the figure self-addressed in the second person (in a continuous present-tense narrative) weaves a fabric of revenge, a project complete in its imagining, devastating in its presentation, ultimately immobilizing and masochistic: namely the rape of the Spanish psyche by words that embody imagined actions.

We might say that, by modulating his pace, diction, and rhythm, Céline restores a measure of hypotactic subordination that counteracts the dominant parataxis. In contrast, Goytisolo uses hypotaxis to generate a discontinuous aura, effectively taming his polemic by undercutting its natural rhetorical mode, but then the polemic conveys less rage than honest distress and disappointment (and a degree of compensatory and not ungratifying self-flagellation). The pain is turned as much inward as out, and the punishment is accepted (as reward?) as much as or more than it is administered. It is as though we were

[57]Trans. Helen R. Lane (New York: Viking, 1974).
[58]For a discussion of the formal implications of this use of treason, see Michael Ugarte, *Trilogy of Treason: An Intertextual Study of Juan Goytisolo* (Columbia: University of Missouri Press, 1982).
[59]Goytisolo, *Count Julian*, p. 11.

confronting the sadist with the masochist in an utterance in which the masochist is singularly and complexly triumphant.

In *Count Julian* as in *Féerie*, the exorcism of dread, loathing, and self-punishing rage is accomplished by a variety of strategems, but whereas Céline's syntax is as discontinuous as the novel's action, Goytisolo is content to generate a chaotic *impression*, the illusion of formlessness conveyed partly through the indiscriminate use of colons to punctuate phrases as well as sentences. Like Céline's ellipses, the colons create an aura of parataxis even when the grammar is rigorously hypotactic. Furthermore, they permit the author to include the patches of parataxis dictated by the emotional pitch, but in general, the blend is mild, as in this extract from the opening, with its description of the desolation that accompanies the protagonist's awakening:

> Eyes still closed, at a distance of barely ten feet from the light: the daily struggle of climbing out of bed, putting on a pair of house slippers, walking across the room toward the bright parallel stripes of light, pulling on the cord of the venetian blinds like a person drawing water from a well: an apathetic sun?: threatening thunderheads?: blinding light rearing in fury?: a dead land, a chimerical sea: mountains along the coast, a monotonous ebb and flow of the tide: range upon range of deserted, arid, bare crests: bleak moors, vast expanses of barren soil: an inorganic realm seared by the fire of the low-water mark, cruelly chiseled by cold northern blasts: lying there motionless, you allow yourself a few brief moments of respite: at times, the cold masses of air moving in from the high-pressure area of the Azores invade the Mediterranean basin and condense between the two shores as though passing through a funnel, blotting out the landscape: a new Atlantis, your homeland has at last foundered and disappeared from sight: a terrible cataclysm, a blessed relief: the few friends you still have were doubtless saved: no need, then, for sorrow or remorse.[60]

There are traces of parataxis in the list, in the erratic punctuation and in the fact that this sequence, dealing with the raising of the venetian blind, is repeated with important differences three times over without explanation. (Such repetition with a difference is perhaps an homage to Robbe-Grillet.) At other points we find that, rather than being divided by colons, whole sequences are printed one phrase below the

[60]Ibid., p. 4.

other to give the effect of discontinuity to a moment of outrage that is actually cast in a very conventional and largely hypotactic mold:

no
that's not the way
death is not enough
his destruction must be accompanied by the most refined tortures
famished dogs
bloodthirsty wolves
leeches
they will drink his young, fresh, pure blood
along with six other young lads and seven young virgins
he will be sacrificed
helpless and defenseless
to the monster shut up in the tortuous labyrinth of Crete by
King Minos[61]

The disjunct impact is due more to the arrangement of narrated experience and to the tone in which it is delivered than to any particular grammatical strategy.

As we have seen, associative linkage tends to disorient the reader sufficiently to create a disruptive aura. Like Céline but more obliquely (and hence more like the Joyce of *Ulysses*), Goytisolo's narrative development is associatively controlled. He frequently imposes a smooth surface effect by letting his run-on sentences grow into superparagraphs, by suppressing capitals and periods, or by permitting his disparate images to flow together, giving the impression of self-generation reinforced by the other narrative strategies. Early on we witness a mock-epic slaughter of bugs accomplished by the bitter exile who will later press the little corpses between the pages of Spanish classics in a library:

the death toll that greets your eye at the beginning of each day: all sorts of different winged species, done in by a powerful insecticide as the inhabitants of Herculaneum and Pompeii were annihilated by the lava pouring down from the roaring volcano: sudden death extending its tentacles through the Forum and Stabian Baths, the Temple of Isis and the House of the Dorati: wings of fine veins, balance mechanisms, suck-

[61]Ibid., p. 171.

ing tubes perfectly conserved amid peristyles with Doric columns, mar-
ble porticoes, Pompeian friezes: awaiting Bulwar's pen to immortalize
them: clumsy thick-bodied flies.[62]

Though we have little trouble following the development, we are
brought up short by a reference to the "fine veins" of the wings and the
other insect traits that follow the list of recovered splendors and frozen
horrors. The contrast in scale and magnitude between dead insects and
the buried splendors of a devastated Pompei, between a man's relatively modest act and nature's catastrophe, is typical of Goytisolo's
method. We may also point to quick and seemingly unmotivated scene
shifts, imaginative leaps justified by the semihallucinated prose. Finally, however, tactics of the sort pioneered by Céline are submerged by
this text, which maintains superficial attributes in the service of their
subversion. Goytisolo's book is very effective as an attack upon established order because of precisely this tension between apparent and
real discontinuity, a tension between the rebel's dream and his inac-
tivity, an attack supported by the book's efficient nodal structure.

In the context of the paratactic and mock-paratactic polemics we
have been examining, it is interesting to look at the language in dissolution that characterizes and vivifies a predominantly farcical novel. J. P.
Donleavy's *The Ginger Man* is more openly and thoroughly paratactic
in its effects, more deliberately and outrageously funny than *Count
Julian* or even *Féerie*, more fragmented both in its structure and in its
discourse:

> In the morning all silence between them. Sebastian heating soup jelly,
> dipping bread in it and drinking a cup of tea. How I hate the fear of it.
> Hate my own hatred. Get out of all this with escape and murder. Poor
> Marion. I have never felt so sad or pained. Because I feel it all seems so
> useless and impossible. I want to own something. I want to get us out of
> this. Get out of this goddamn country which I hate with all my blood
> and which has ruined me. Crush Skully's head with a poker. A green
> Jesus around my neck and this damn leaking ceiling and this foul
> linoleum and Marion and her wretched shoes and her stockings and
> panties and her tits and goddamn skinny back and orange boxes. And the
> black smell of grease and germ and spermy towels. All the rot behind the
> walls. Two years in Ireland, shrunken teat on the chest of the cold

[62]Ibid., p. 10

Atlantic. Land of crut. And the drunk falling screaming into the ditches at night, blowing shrill whistles across the fields and brown buggered bogs. Out there they watch between the nettles, counting the blades of grass, waiting for each other to die, with the eyes of cows and the brains of snakes. Monsters growling from their chains and wailing in the dark pits at night.[63]

Such passages contain a battery of minor paratactic devices (omitted words and missing connectives, isolated words and phrases, and so forth) reinforced by the constant shifting of voice, tense, and subject matter, the erratic punctuation, and the use of sentence fragments. The associative linkage is more implicit yet more openly random, somewhat perversely in the manner of the stream of consciousness. We quickly learn to accept the flow of words and expect the shock of such inappropriate-seeming conjunctions as "Crush Skelly's head with a poker. A green Jesus around my neck." Given the rush of words and effects, there is no time to work out the logic of this juxtaposition or to recover from the double shock of its content before we plunge into new confrontations. The text consists therefore of a headlong scamper through rough rhetoric and sweet reflection toward endless surprises, shocks, and comic delights.

This sort of texture is natural and appropriate, if rare, in a treatment of clownish action. It is, after all, the verbal equivalent of slapstick. We have reason to be surprised, however, when novels making extensive use of disruptive devices, as do *Féerie* and *Count Julian*, turn the farcical tradition on its head. Each uses clownish language larded with unsavory reference, making the reader its victim, employing clownish protagonists in roles that exceed the limits of what we generally accept as farce, moving the farcical impulse toward its dark roots in the primal laughter of destruction and regeneration, something akin to what the Indians symbolize by the deity Shiva. Extending the individual passage in such a way as to simultaneously slow down and magnify the reading, they may well produce more extreme outrage by exposing with graphic insistence functions that are, even in our permissive days, on the verge of the unacceptable. The result is inverted humor, not so much black as bilious.[64] The mode is horizontal para-

[63]J. P. Donleavy, *The Ginger Man* (New York: Berkeley, 1985), p. 80.
[64]We may note that the nineteenth century went part of the way in perverting farce by turning Pierrot into a poet, the grotesque into a heroic protagonist, and the outcast

taxis produced by a variable but relentless accumulation of surface detail. (We are not really far from the techniques of certain impossible object texts that capitalize on unmotivated juxtapositions to achieve disbelief.)

As defined earlier, vertical parataxis employs unmediated allusive levels of discourse, relationships imposed but not explained by the text that demands (rather than requests) explanations and accommodations. Such, for example, are the multiple layers of signification in Eliot's poem, in *Ulysses*, and in Maurice Roche's novels. More urgently, however, such are the relations imposed by the pun texture of *Finnegans Wake* and by post-Wakean fiction in general.

There is no escaping the fact that a word in such books refuses to stay flat on the page, to settle comfortably into one dominant meaning. Instead it exploits and magnifies its overtones. The single word or isolated lexical unit in the *Wake* and in other essentially "open" texts often functions as a pair or "cluster." Such clusters are frequently self-contradictory, polyvalent, and even dissociated. That is, if we settle on one dominant, or prime, sense, we cannot overlook or be unaffected by the other senses and the other verbal forms that impose supplementary and contradictory readings. We are obliged to locate them in the

---

into a speaking and ultimately sympathetic figure. See Nerval, Verlaine, and Mallarmé for the use of the poet-clown, see Hugo's hunchback as the grotesque, and see Dostoievski's underground man and Lautréamont's Maldoror as the bitter outcast. What sets all of these apart from contemporary usage is their rhetoric which is rigorously hypotactic, if occasionally immoderate in tone. Furthermore, we may see in nineteenth-century usage a significant modification of farcical practice: the installation of the clown and outcast as figures worthy of sympathy and even empathy within a romantical or serious context and the presentation of the outcast as the potential rebel. The twentieth century seems to have taken note of the aberration. At any rate it has performed a further operation on the farcical text, reestablishing the clown as a figure of fun but retaining the serious component. Thus Bloom and Dedalus may play comic Pierrots to Boylan's and Mulligan's Harlequins (see my "Forms of Folly in Joyce: A Study of Clowning in *Ulysses*," *ELH* 34, [June 1967], 260–83, for a treatment of this development in Joyce). The clown regains his rags of ridicule, which the reader learns to share. But there is, as we have seen, a further development, one that gives many modernist texts a particular piquancy and poignancy: paratactic procedures regulate the rhythms, contributing the essential farcical or "carnivalesque" gestures, turning literature back toward performance. In the process, hitherto forbidden subject matter has been opened up to aesthetic scrutiny, and the very definition of "literary" has been significantly altered, while the obscure mechanisms of prose meters have emerged to generate what could best be described as a new music.

larger semantic field of the passage and text, and/or we must experience the haunting sensation of incompleteness and impotence, the insistent *resonance*. That resonance (a variant of information theory's "noise")[65] is a constant in such works, a necessary and inevitable component of our reading, for there is no way in which we can accomplish a complete reading, given the essentially vibrant nature of polyvalent irony[66] and the impossibility of maintaining in suspension the cluster of unstable and antagonistic readings and impressions available at any given moment of text. Like our experience of life and our sense of living, such texts are achieved only when finally put down. Even then they demand special procedures; in their kaleidoscopic variety they conform to and confound the vision of whoever reads them.

Before accepting the aura, however, we invariably settle upon the sort of paratactic readings to which I have alluded. That is, we find in the textualized words elements that suggest parallel interpretations, that undermine, complicate, and derail the immediate impression, frequently setting us to musing about other possibilities. In the process, we will find ourselves constructing parallel sentences and parallel conceptual structures some of which Joyce describes in his famous definition of the dream in question 9 of the catechistic chapter I.6 of *Finnegans Wake*.[67] The reader encounters such structures at first with the surprise that is built into them and is renewed by each encounter with the unexpected, then with puzzlement, and finally, if the puzzlement is explored, with a sense of participating in the shaping process.

That vicarious process implies in each instance a persistent awareness of the conceptual gaps among meanings. In the sentence "The playgue will be soon over, rats!"[68] for instance, we readily perceive a number of distinct but interrelated meanings. Suspending our reading, we may try to justify, though not necessarily to conceptualize, the tension between "The play will soon be over, too bad,"; "The playgue will be and soon will be over, too bad—It is produced by rats," and

---

[65]The article "Perception" in *The Encyclopedia of the Social Sciences* (p. 559) alludes to "interfering messages" and coins the term "cocktail party effect." Umberto Eco goes further in applying information theory to the arts, beginning with a theory of linguistic entropy and moving toward a concept of "noise" and "redundancy" or "overdetermination," which he applies to works that rebel against conventions of communication. See *L'Oeuvre ouverte*, (Paris: Seuil, 1965), pp. 76–93.

[66]This may, of course, be intertextual, but it is seldom solely that.

[67]*Finnegans Wake*, p. 143.

[68]Ibid., p. 378.

"The play is a plague or the plague is a play which will soon be over, too bad," or even "Children are subject to plague even in play," and so on. If we consider the sentence in its larger context, the meanings are even richer, but significantly, the interpretations do not advance the argument, and the readings are violently linked by the verbal play. This is clearly a paratactic function and an extension of the procedures we have observed elsewhere, being at once plethoric and elliptical. We may add that such texts also feature varieties of horizontal paratactics and that by a magic associated as much with rhythms, tonalities, and attitudes as with meanings, they finally cohere, conveying experience to the reader willing to contribute to the generative and degenerative venture. Paratactics becomes in this context a necessary semiotic correlative to the signifying process.

Punning may be as old as literature, but there is no precedent for the explosion of puns in serious literature during the post-Flaubertian moment that we are calling modernism. Even before Joyce and quite apart from the word play of a Lewis Carroll, there are the powerful puns and neologisms of Jules Laforgue and the verbal and visual punning in Mallarmé's "Un coup de dés."[69] The eleven pages of that mini-epic poem represent typographically a boat, an inkwell, a feather, a hat, a whirlpool, a wave, a constellation, and so forth, each of which extends and defines while subtly commenting on the text. That is, they are an integral part of the semantic and semiotic statement, a supplementary gesture. They also constitute a semantic statement on a secondary visual level requiring justification and finding its mediation in the mind engaged by the verbal texture.

Since Mallarmé, visual punning has become a common source of vertical paratactics as well as a more immediate gestural component of concrete poetry and fiction. One thinks of the famous concrete poem composed of the word "apple" multiplied and so arranged as to imitate the form of the fruit but containing at its center the word "worm." The impact of that embedded other in the typographical heart of the perfect object/image is dynamically disruptive even though the apple

---

[69]For discussions of Mallarmé's punning, see Robert Greer Cohn, *Mallarmé's "Un coup de dés,"* Yale French Studies (New Haven, 1949), pp. 23–33 and passim. See also David Hayman, *Joyce et Mallarmé* (Paris: Lettres Modernes, 1956), vol. 1: *Stylistique de la suggestion*, pp. 149–78.

itself simply rewrites the sentence, "This apple has a worm in it."[70] That poem may stand as an emblem for much concrete poetry which can be seen as growing out of a group of works by Mallarmé, Joyce, Pound, Cummings, and Apollinaire, whose procedures blatantly combine vertical with horizontal parataxis.[71] It is of course also an emblem of the "concrete" novel, a mixed-media or verbovisual text: Raymond Federman's post-Beckettian work, Maurice Roche's extraordinary sequence of meditation novels (beginning with *Compact*, 1965), and William Gass's ingenious bit of paratactic theater *Willie Masters' Lonely Wife* (1968).[72] Since Roche has pushed the parataxis of illustrative detail and the arrangement of print the furthest, achieving the most intriguing results while demonstrating great competence and tact, we may use his work to illustrate how the device can further expose, enrich, and undermine narrative rhythms.

It is everywhere evident that, however ironically, Roche's prose presentations aspire to the condition of music. What could be more natural in a man who combines remarkable verbal gifts with the abilities of a draftsman and designer and who began his career as a musician and composer?[73] All of his books, through a system of visual pauses and spatial arrangements, of typographical notations and pictorial irruptions, achieve an analogue for music on the page, that, despite a consistently disruptive texture, sustains a reassuring, if tenuous, contact with the conventions of narrative, folk poetry, and the essay. Still, though Roche has consciously integrated the new-musical impulse with those of prose narrative and concrete poetry,[74] the reader who looks for the tonal component in this prose can easily be misled,

---

[70]For a good overview of the concrete poets' theory and practice, see Mary Ellen Solt, ed., *Concrete Poetry: A World View* (Bloomington: Indiana University Press, 1968).

[71]A. de Campos, D. Pignatari, and H. de Campos, *Teoria da poesia concreta* (São Paulo: Duas Cidades, 1975), pp. 17–25 and passim; for a translation of "Un coup de dés," see Richard Kostelanetz, ed., *The Avant-Garde Tradition in Literature* (Buffalo: Prometheus Books, 1982), pp. 257–62.

[72]We find this dimension also in Arno Schmidt's *Zettles Traum* and *Abend mit Goldrand* and in Julián Ríos's multifaceted work in progress "Larva," which features illustrations and layered footnotes. Both of these writers follow Joyce in their use of puns, though both have found further freedoms, generating fresh and engaging disruptions.

[73]David Hayman, "An Interview with Maurice Roche," *sub-stance* 17 (1977), 5–11.

[74]This integration is perhaps most transparent in Augusto de Campos's multicolor poem *poetamenos* (São Paulo: Invençâo, 1973), which is described as a "*Klangfarbenmelodie* with words after Webern."

as were so many of Mallarmé's critics. Like Mallarmé, whom he admires, Roche deals in broadly defined aesthetic rather than simply tonal qualities. Even though he has spoken of the audible dimensions of his texts,[75] the music is always more visual and ideational than tonal. Still, the musical ideal, the composer's instinct, underlies and permeates his discourse; the combined paratactic devices contribute to a narrative surface analogous to the tonal surface and texture of works by Boulez and even Stockhausen.

Faced with the problem of rendering simultaneously a highly personal view of the presence of death in life through universal (and hence often transparent) metaphors and a universalized discourse, encyclopedic in its range, Roche instinctively evolved a musical solution. We can do no more than suggest the contribution of parataxis to that solution. *Compact* (1966), for instance, is composed of eight discursive lines, each in a different type face and ostensibly a different voice or point of view. The voices are juxtaposed in such a way that the book is visually a tissue of typefaces and spaces conceptually twining narrative visions and mininarratives, none of which is actually telling a tale. The reader is obliged to coordinate these disparate and frequently jarring elements much as the listener would the components of a piece of modern music.

In the later fictions, Roche carries his procedures further or in a different direction. Indeed each successive novel adds fresh disruptive procedures while reutilizing the formal vocabulary of the earlier volumes. As a result, what would have been a macroparatactic device in one novel will become microparatactic in a later one, which, however complex its texture, need not be less readable or coherent.

Roche seems capable of digesting disruptions in much the same way that Céline did before him, but there are significant differences. Roche composes his structures, calibrating his spaces, calculating each of his effects, manipulating print and modifying language as would a musician making free with tones and registers. Céline's rage, his sense of language as a weapon to be used to ward off terrors in the flesh, led him to ever more poignant expressions of anguish, anger, and despair,

---

[75]I agree with Léon Roudiez, who finds himself "thwarted by the visual aspects" of the texts ("Readable/Writable/Visible," in *Visible Language* 12 [Summer 1978], 238). In fact, when Roche reads his own work, there is very little evidence of verbal rhythms or of the effects so striking in Philippe Sollers's remarkable dramatic rendering of *H* and *Paradis*.

ever more violent explosions. Though their impact can be varied, these semantically overmotivated displays were not conceived and are not received as arrangements of sound or space. Roche's muted anguish and irrepressible wit leads to subtler and more sophisticated exhibitions of rupture, more elaborately orchestrated texts, more encyclopedic in their formal as well as their intertextual range, more visibly absurd and farcical in their juxtapositions; yet, ultimately, we see them as more rational, filtered by what Inez Hedges has called an "ideology of protest."[76]

The extent and variety of the Rochean forms and formulas is "mind boggling," but we must point to precisely that proliferation, without attempting to catalogue the individual items, if we are to understand his contribution to what is rapidly becoming a tradition. By exhibiting and controlling these effects, by the almost magical generation of changes, Roche establishes an orchestration that requires an awareness of the conventional use of a given technique for a full understanding of the meaning of its revised function but that rewards any reading. When we consider new music, with its insistence on redistributing functions, turning old materials to fresh and even shocking uses, making use of aleatory noise, and so forth, the parallel is inescapable. Roche himself underscored this suprathematic implication of his method when he named one of his novels *Maladie Mélodie* (1980) and larded it with musical citations, pastiches of musical forms, calling one of his divisions a "Duo," subtitling another "opéra comique," including intermezzi and divertissements. This statement pertains even though his thrust is transparently thematic and the musical forms cited are conventional. As he himself puts it, "The *malady* is a presence in continuo whose tempo is established in a mental space by the *melody*. Pain is linked to music; you can't conceive of the latter without acknowledging the existence of the former; love and death participate in both."[77] His use of the word *mélodie* is ironic (bitterly so) in relation to his theme of the relationship between joy and suffering and (comically) as a description of the form of this remarkable volume. His perversion of musical notations in the mock-operatic performance is calculated to upset musical decorums.

---

[76]Inez Hedges, "The Cinematographic Writing of Maurice Roche," in *Visible Language* 12 (Summer 1978), 240–80.
[77]Maurice Roche's inscription in my presentation copy of *Maladie Mélodie* (July 1980).

Perhaps the best account of his approach is given by the aggrieved lover/text in an attack on its (protagonist's) amorous behavior:

parlando
—You forced me to make love while listening to you read from "Opéra bouffe,"[78] a practice fugue—while you wrote it—, a recording of Bach's "Fantasy in sol minor," the "Battle of Tancred and Clorinda" on the radio, a televised report of a rugby match. . . .

      And, you slob, you were recording that stew on a tape recorder because you wanted to turn it into a diachronic/synchronic Hörspiel—. . . just so's you'd not lose any of it, eh?

BLACK[79]

In the *Hörspiel* we may catch the spirit of Roche's macabre play of and upon forms in this image of superimposed and spread out activities on the textual bed/matrix of love and death. We may also see his method in the evocation of operatic discourse in which we find such an unlikely melange of allusions, behavior, and dictions as part of a projected immediate performance. (The action of this chapter is described as "theater," and the instructions following these lines are "NOIR," which suggests the mood of the moment as well as the theatrical lighting of a real stage.) Indeed, the reference to "diachronic/synchronic" activity suggests the horizontal and vertical parataxis that characterizes every moment of this text, that is, the movement or rather leap from expressive form to expressive form, from subject to subject, from voice to voice as well as the disjunct play of

[78]Roche's third novel.
[79]My free translation. *Maladie Mélodie* (Paris: Seuil, 1980), p. 35:
parlando
—Tu m'obligeais à faire l'amour en écoutant simultanément ta lecture d' "Opéra bouffe," une fugue d'école—à mesure que tu l'écrivais—, la "Fantaisie en sol mineur" de Bach sur disque, le "Combat de Tancrède et Clorinde" à la radio, le compte rendu télévisé d'un match de rugby . . .
      Et, salaud, tu enregistrais cette salade sur un magnétophone dans le but d'en composer un Hörspiel diachronique/synchronique— . . . afin de n'en rien perdre, hein?

NOIR

allusions and parodies evident even in this relatively simple passage, which is preceded by a coloratura aria describing a sodomite episode from Sade's *Justine:* "'and to stick up his ass a torch whose flame . . .'" Like a character from Beckett's trilogy, Roche's text/persona is whiling away the hours with light/dark pleasantries born of

ins i

co(s)mic   p ration   (to use two of Roche's favorite games).

des e

What follows this piece of theatre is a "Divertissement" entitled "MOUVEMENT," written like the score for a piece of music. A semipoetic and virtually untranslatable bit of erotic badinage, it seems simultaneously to document a rugby game, a sexual encounter, a conventional and classical musical score, verses from a libretto, commentary on Freud in Italian, and so forth. In short, all manner of parallel texts are juxtaposed in such a way as to suggest simultaneity. The arrangement implies a development; the slashes underscore the play of contrasts, suggesting both poetry and music but moving toward our contemporary modes of antimusicality. To this is added the counterpoint of illustrations that are clinico-erotico-musico-sportive. For all the differences, one is reminded of Pound's ideogrammatic method and his interest in music, but Roche is far more concerned with a playful texture, more enlightened about musical procedures and perhaps more aware of the primacy of discontinuity in his text, as the brief extract overleaf suggests. Here we return to the principle of programmed confusion with the elision of treatments of music and a bicycle race, in a pun-filled false hypotaxis.[80] The discontinuity is reconstituted by the reader's awareness, being, like the pun, an utterance that breaks apart under the strain of conflicting significances. Indeed, Roche, like Joyce in *Finnegans Wake*, bases most of his formal innovation on the pun principle. Consequently, we may read his procedures as an effort to amplify and order random conjunctions or perhaps as an attempt to make the reader rationalize randomness. In the number and range of punning effects, in the sophistication, range, and control of allusions, and in the ultimate return to the textualizing act he excels.

---

[80]The device was also used, though to very different effect, by Joyce in his evocation of a sexual crime/horserace that functions as an entr'acte in the Butt and Taff episode of *Finnegans Wake*, pp. 341–42.

I . . . Introduction and : "Attaboy, Buster!" /
                                  — Leave the scrimmage along
the median line; opening the center. /
                                  Subject to the alto. /
                                                      Depart
by closed side. /
            (Take the slut from behind, twist the pussytwat) /
                                                      . . . Coda,
prolongation of the subject — /
                        Half-turn contact. /
                                        (circumbilivagination
of the side of the pruggarse) /
                        Opening to the center . . . /
                                  Response in the dominant, /
pass to the right quarter wing /
                        the subject "pursued" by the counter-
subject — /
            delaying action, /
                        con le robuste braccia, e altrettante
poi da que'no-di, da que'no-di te-na-ci ella si scinge /
                        but a call of foul. So /
                                              . . . third
                        entry to the soprano /
                                  No-di di fier ne-mi-
                        co e non d'a-man-te. /
                                  kickoff
                        for placement (to follow) to the left wing : /
                        Bass response . . . /
                                        attack from
                        the rear lines /
                                  (excellent exposure) /
                        seems to prefigure a good development . . .
Outflanking of the left wing . . . Pressure on receiver [touche] . . .[81]

[81]My free translation. Ibid., pp. 39–40.

I ... Introduction et : « Allez, gros! » /
        — Sortie de mêlée sur la
ligne médiane; ouverture au centre. /
        Le sujet à l'alto. /
        Départ côté
fermé. /
        (Prendre la gerce à revers, contourner la ménouesse) /
        ... Coda,
prolongation du sujet — /
        Demi-tour contact. /
        (circumbilivagination du
côté de prozinard) /
        Ouverture au centre... /
        Réponse à la dominante, /
passe au trois-quarts aile droit /
        le sujet « poursuivi » par le contre-
sujet — /
        placage à retardement, /
        con le robuste braccia, e altrettante
poi da que'no-di, da que'no-di te-na-ci ella si scinge /
        mais règle de l'avantage. Donc /
        ... troisième
entrée au soprano /
        No-di di fier ne-mi-
co e non d'a-man-te. /
        coup de pied de
déplacement (à suivre) sur l'aile gauche : /
Réponse à la basse... /
        cette attaque partie
des lignes arrière /
        (excellente exposition) /
semble annoncer un bon développement...
Débordement à l'aile gauche... Poussée en touche...

Bearing in mind the difference between the controls of verse and those imposed by a system of sharp and generally irregular breaks in the surface of the narrative, we may say that Roche's work uses paratactics to produce the revealed metrics of prose. Since the latter denies the older metrical formulations, we can also speak of prose "dismetrics," a sort of rhythmical punctuation that declares the breaks in discourse to be signifying moments in its development, part of its essential music, but manifestly *ir*regular, reacting forcefully against the regularity ascribed to and imposed by earlier narrative forms.

The instance of Maurice Roche should help us review and consolidate the major attributes of paratactics. First, the more decided disjunctions accented by their placement on the page often function as rhythmic markers, pauses made palpable, accentuating breaks in narrative continuity. By extension and in the process, they also outline the spatial pattern or skeleton of the text. Thanks to their "concrete" format, these novels expose to the eye what is latent in other texts that make systematic use of parataxis. Thus Joyce's *Portrait*, rather than letting us slide from chapter to chapter or even passage to passage, insists on the breaks by altering style and suppressing transitions, establishing form as a component of meaning and disjunction as the book's decisive formal gesture. When poetic rhyme and meter were jettisoned in favor of free verse, an effect registered clearly by Apollinaire, Eliot, and Pound, poetry was freed from the controls dictated by convention, but poets were individually obliged to improvise fresh controls. Not surprisingly, the randomized poetry and overtly measured prose metrics we are alluding to, inevitably but subversively, brought the organization of much modern literature close to the edge of the domain traditionally reserved for music.

Beyond that, as Roche's practice also shows and as we have observed in our discussion of Stein, there is not only a fresh emphasis on tempo and the temporal reception of the text but also a decisive spatial component, a more emphatic (and limited) version of what Joseph Frank calls spatial form.[82] On the one hand, the page, long the domain of poets, has become increasingly the locus of redefined novelistic

---

[82]"Spatial Form in Modern Literature," in Joseph Frank, *The Widening Gyre: Crisis and Mastery in Modern Fiction* (Bloomington: Indiana University Press, 1968), pp. 54–60.

effects and typographical play. There is increased attention to such supplementary signifiers as the interaction of styles and modes, the arrangement of type, punctuation or its absence, and the text as a field of action rather than as a passive display.

Furthermore, as illustrated by the explosive sequences in Céline and, most recently, by the extended carnivalesque explosion in Robert Coover's novel *Gerald's Party*, proliferating, unhierarchical verbal effects give birth to a verbal landscape that is both in the language and in the field of images it projects. Sequences like the famous channel crossing in *Death on the Installment Plan*[83] with its seemingly endless evocation of vomit or the even more extreme landscape generated by the exploded brain of Courtial des Pereires[84] incorporate all manner of action while conveying the impression of a mass of seemingly undifferentiated verbal matter distributed over a seemingly unbounded verbal space. This is even truer of the bloody shambles that dominates *Normance*, the second volume of *Féerie*.

Another kind of spatiality facilitated by paratactics can be traced back to Flaubert's sequence, in which not only are passages of farcical caricature and pastiche juxtaposed to the ironic flirtation between Emma and Rodolf but the various interludes are spaced to underscore the distinctions. No one extended this attempt to produce the global moment better or in more ways than did Joyce, who employs it as a formal leitmotif throughout the realistic half of *Ulysses*. Indeed, simultaneity, most noteworthy in group scenes, has become a staple in modern fiction, as witness *Gerald's Party*, where the celebration/carnival is conveyed as an infernal/farcical conflict conducted simultaneously all over a well-delineated but fluid context.

An offshoot of the encyclopedic impulse toward comprehensiveness, this sort of radical juxtaposition, a mimesis of the spatial plane, is further complicated by the sublimated vertical paratactics of allusion that characterizes so much early modernist fiction. Its apotheosis is surely the overt and preponderant verticality of *Finnegans Wake*, the post-*Wake* pun-texts, and visual texts like those of Maurice Roche, William Gass, Julián Ríos, and Arno Schmidt. These works render inescapable the metaphorical dimension that imposes synchrony on so much of the modernist canon, producing a three-dimen-

[83]Céline, *Death*, pp. 123–26.
[84]Ibid., pp. 525–29.

sional semantic field based in radical difference as well as in similarity. The more emphatic post-*Wakean* effects must be seen as extensions of the urge to produce the full impact of simultaneity or the sort of sensory overload afforded by lived experience. It is worth noting that this practice of overloading the conceptual as well as the sensory field readily exceeds the disruptive limits of traditional farce, Mikhail Bakhtin's carnivalesque mode, and even those of what Bakhtin calls novelistic dialogism, heteroglossia, and stratification. One might say that, at its most ambitious, the practice extends, reshapes, and reanimates what could be called the encyclopedic/epic tradition.[85] That is, the added dimension of verticality makes possible a previously unavailable inclusiveness, one drawing on the expanded field of knowledge and awareness available to modern man and its concomitant confusions and pleasures. In short, however perverse it may seem, given the obvious antirealism of some of these texts, truth to experience is approximated even through overtly intertextual three-dimensional manifestations that systematically resist recuperation and reject even the pretense of reference.

Nodality, as defined by this study, contributes to the visibility of a novel's thematic and motival structural rhythm while constituting a complex and obtrusive three-dimensional semantic framework or scaf-

---

[85]*The Dialogic Imagination: Four Essays by M. M. Bakhtin*, ed. Michael Holquist, trans. Caryl Emerson (Austin: University of Texas Press, 1981), pp. 426–33 and passim. Though Bakhtin would disagree, the pattern for this still-fertile dialogic tradition is not the early novel but its predecessor, the Homeric epic, and especially *The Iliad*. It is there after all that we are permitted to sense the complexity of battle, the integrity of the cultural context, while accommodating the discursive ranges and distinct modal variations of the four communities. That is, through various modal and perspectival strategies, Homer conveys an integral and dynamic simultaneity. Thus though we may perceive only a corner of the action at any given moment, we are exposed through situation comedy to the universe of the gods, through melodrama and even tragedy to that of the Trojan family and community, and through romance to the world of the Achean men. By a further twist, through the essentially timeless epic simile, we experience the universe of the Homeric singer's audience. These various registers and this modal mixture are not without the dialogic tensions Bakhtin discerns in later, more transparently heteroglossic novels. It is noteworthy that writers such as Joyce, Eliot, and Pound did in fact return to the Homeric muse for something more than thematic materials, that even Marcel Proust's depiction of the Princess de Guermantes's reception in *The Past Recaptured* probably owes something to the Homeric precedent, something not to be found, for example, in Flaubert's rather mechanical rendering of the group scene and the battle: its capacity to shift our attention from one social skirmish to another within a crowded field.

folding upon which readers stand as re-producers of texts perceived as networks of relationships. In contrast, we may conceive of paratactic insistence, mainly semiotic in its nature, as contributing a supplementary (metric) punctuation capable of expanding vertically so as to generate an equally imposing spatial superstructure of isolable masses. Not surprisingly, when the two tactics overlap or interact, as in the *Wake, Féerie*, or *Compact*, the effect can initially be as daunting as it is ultimately compelling for readers obliged to adjust to and fathom fresh and frequently ingenious decorums.

The fact that Roche's heterogeneous procedures have been made to serve a unified cause underscores how, by questioning the need for seamless discourse in serious art, paratactics has made possible undreamed-of textures and forms. By unseating conformity and enthroning change, inverting or recasting in the process the procedures of what Mikhail Bakhtin calls the "joyous relativity" of the carnival, the serious clown who writes twentieth-century fiction has disclosed an almost unprecedented and still unfathomed paratactic potential, one limited only by the artist's imagination and the challenge of order.

From another perspective, a tactic that opens up a potential may also serve to fill a need. It seems obvious that writers in a variety of cultures and epochs have come to paratactics more or less independently in response to their distinct projects and that their practice has set precedents for twentieth-century narrative and poetry. It is equally clear, however, that a climate for discontinuous discursive procedures and fragmented structures preexisted and helped determine the modernist efforts. Nothing else could explain the simultaneous composition of three works like Rilke's *Malte Laurids Brigge* (1909), Gertrude Stein's *Three Lives* (1909), and Joyce's *Portrait* (1914). In *Malte*, the radically disjunct diary entries or macro-units accommodate an encyclopedic range of topics that combine to map the evolution of its protagonist's self-awareness and constitute his identity. *Three Lives* uses extreme but formally limited microparatactics to still and spatialize action, paradoxically minimizing disjunctive effects. Joyce innovates in the service of a multifaceted "portrait" a subtly articulated disjunction designed to accent details and conserve narrative space.

Furthermore, only a climate of change established by intellectual as well as political developments in the late nineteenth century could explain the simultaneous departure in several art forms from norms of integrity and coherence, a development that signals a concerted but hardly conscious effort to respond to and accommodate a sentiment of uprootedness and flux. In the plastic arts, fauvism, expressionism, futurism, cubism, and dadaism all share a tendency to fragment their own presentation while deliberately challenging aesthetic givens. Significantly, each of these movements found literary as well as plastic expression.

Finally, Maurice Roche's use of a polyvalent verbo-musico-plastic approach provides us with an extreme instance of the tendency in our century to achieve through paratactics the effect of the Gesamtkunstwerk. That is, by adding an encyclopedia of forms to other inclusive tendencies, writers such as Joyce, Pound, Eliot, William Gass, Maurice Roche, Haroldo de Campos, Arno Schmidt, Julián Ríos, and Philippe Sollers have found distinct ways to extend through languaged events a spectacular tradition with roots in the seventeenth century, if not in Greek tragic practice, filling the surface of the page with signs that point toward and incorporate traces of the other arts while deliberately juxtaposing seemingly incompatible literary modes. Thus Joyce inserts dramatic dimensions and devices into "Scylla and Charybdis" and "Circe" and musical devices into "Sirens," incorporating a visual component in "Eolus" and music hall effects of the pantomime in "Cyclops" and "Circe" while accentuating elements of the lyric, the epic, the farcical, the melodramatic, and so on. The enabling procedure for this sort of behavior is in each instance a decorum that, by downplaying hierarchies, facilitates the display of difference.

We are now in a better position to assay the formal potential of paratactics, with its emphasis on the list effect achieved by means of unmediated juxtaposition and equation. In practice, one pole of the paratactic list is illustrated by the muted or consistent catalogue achieved when all the elements fit more or less readily into a single category. The opposing procedure plays up sharp distinctions of form as well as content among its members. Thus the typical Célinean catalogue of grotesque detail excels in making unusual and shocking conjunctions but maintains a semiotic and semantic coherence designed to produce a uniformly explosive impact. In contrast, the opening of Joyce's *Portrait* brings together disparate activities without locating them in time and space, and his overture to "Sirens" joins in false concord materials so disparate as to defy repeatedly our efforts to control and order them. On the other hand, Stein's shingled rhetoric paratactically eliminates contrasts by emphasizing redundancy, effectively flattening discourse and diminishing development, and Ezra Pound's arrangements of disjunct particulars are made to constitute meaningful "hieroglyphs." Though all of these texts make use of radical juxtaposition and leveling, their effects are clearly various. We may isolate a paratactics of redundance (Stein), a paratactics of inadequation (Joyce), a paratactics of superfluity (Céline), and a paratactics of total congruence (Pound). There is nothing, furthermore, to stop writers from conjoining such effects or elaborating others.

By attenuating the list, enlarging the paratactic units, or by multiplying and interspersing the listing procedures, writers have achieved astonishing degrees of complexity, energy, and interest. In the process some of them have also created a special kind of wholeness in seemingly endless difference, a trait previously reserved for the extremes of farcical display in literature or the sort of sport qualified by Northrop Frye and Mikhail Bakhtin as Menippean satire. The prime instance of this polyphonal paratactics is still *Ulysses*, in it not only do the chapter styles respond to categories of the paratactic list but also the various narrative approaches taken within a given passage and, though somewhat more discreetly, even the associative strings generated by a moment of experience.

When stressing the operation of paratactic procedures, we must also take in to account the various ways in which parataxis and hypotaxis can be made to interact. We may begin by noting that the writers capable of mastering such procedures tend to be those most conscious of their language and most fully in control of their form; for in order to succeed in subversion, these apparently extravagant works must be meticulous. After all, each detail is doubly on display, thanks to the inevitable formal accentuation. Had the muse so dictated, these writers could have produced conventional work of great polish, masterpieces of hypotactic discourse. Against that potential as well as against the tug of convention they use paratactics, establishing in most instances an unstable balance, a dynamic of subversion made more powerful and complex by the coexistence of conjunction and disjunction. In most cases, such writers use excess not simply to produce shock but rather in an attempt to control a plethora of ideas, impulses, or emotions without castrating them, imposing patterns as bulwarks against the energy of their materials.

This effect is best illustrated not only by the competitive factors in

Joyce's texts or Goytisolo's expression of tension and distress through eccentric syntax and punctuation but also by such failures as the pamphlets of Céline or the broadcasts of Pound in which art collides and colludes with propaganda and even with an underlying insanity proper as much to the age as to the artist. Perhaps such examples and counterexamples help us account for far more than a trace of the discarded conventions in palpably disjunct texts. They explain the need for a range of compensatory hypotaxis sufficient to constitute, more than a reminder of the repressed continuum, an inescapable, if perhaps at times parodic, demonstration of the powers of an illusive order. I have referred to this demonstration in my analyses of Joyce and Céline, but I could as easily have shown parallel effects in any of the others. What should interest us is the manner in which, in the face of even the most radical disruption, varieties of order reassert their hold as the necessary countersign to the antithetical impulse. It should be noted, however, that such countervailing impulses also enhance the vitality of the texts they help structure, contributing or enhancing vertical parataxis.

Surfacing during a period scarred by political upheavals, rocked by cultural shifts, and stirred by technological revolutions, high literary paratactics may be seen as a curiously ambiguous manifestation, superficially supportive of change but deeply anxious about the loss of stability and perhaps vice versa. We may perhaps see it as a power-filled manifestation of insecurity and weakness to which the anxious artist of an angst-full time resorted. Surely, it is significant that, like the great masters of carnivalesque outrage, some of the most able exponents of discontinuous form—Pound, Eliot, Wyndham Lewis, Céline, and even Joyce—have been basically conservative, using manifestations of disorder as charms against the same.

Whatever the source of their impulse, by placing the emphasis on difference rather than on coherence, such writers have put a mirror up to a present reality, one that runs counter to that of the classics of nineteenth-century realism. In the wake of their production we can no longer speak with the confidence of a Stendhal of the novel as a mirror promenading along a road. Today, the concept "walk" has changed, as has the image road and the mirroring potential of language. Not only has "progress" cracked, if not fractured, that famous looking glass, it has also given us new insights into the nature of experience and of the expressive act that relates and relates to it. The introduction of the sense or illusion of the principle of chance, the stepchild of Mallarmé's toss of the cosmic/creative dice, into this century's art has been decisive enough to make us all aware of the deceptions wrought in good faith by earlier generations. Ultimately it has also clarified the nature of chance and difference as native even to the blander work canonized by previous eras.

Paradoxically, once discontinuity achieved a degree of acceptance, which it did with astonishing rapidity, the tendency was (as it still is) to work against it, to treat it both as a convention to be manipulated and as a new tool to be exploited. It was only natural that writers as different as Guy Davenport, Juan Goytisolo, Gilbert Sorrentino, Alain Robbe-Grillet, Robert Creeley, and Frederic Tuten should, each in his way, resort to and conceal paratactics. After all, even Joyce, after multiplying accented difference in *Ulysses*, embeds it in his *Wake*, integrating what are on inspection palpably paratactic effects in the fabric of a tapestry that moves beyond time within a verbal universe of seemingly random but actually calculated repetition. Such procedures take us surprisingly close to the earlier transgressive behavior of Stein. With hindsight, it seems almost inevitable that change and shock, the staples of clowning, would become the matrix from which the new-minted order of "openness," itself a product of the encyclopedic impulse and Flaubertian aesthetics, could emerge.[86]

Perhaps the use of form to mimic disorder that is exemplified by so much that has remained or is becoming current is best regarded as a taming of disorder, a coping with fear of disorder, a prayer for peace, and a candle lit at the altar of orderly existence as well. It is also a statement of the unquenchable vitality of the aesthetic impulse. Despite the occasional violence of its discourse and the antisocial nature of so much of its content,[87] paratactics, like the carnival from which it inherits so much, is above all and increasingly a way of coping, an antitoxin. It is crucial for our aesthetic moment, however, that this remedy find applications in a variety of modes. Of equal importance is the fact that, even when they make us laugh, such applications seldom

[86]If, as Umberto Eco himself insists, "openness" is not confined to moderns, we may say that the emphases highlighted by Eco are hallmarks of the post-Flaubertian developments that characterize high modernism and modernism in general.

[87]See Philippe Muray's comments on the therapeutic value of Céline's prose in *Céline* (Paris: Seuil, 1981), p. 68.

release us but rather, and with astonishing frequency, set us to asking painful questions without hoping to find adequate answers.

Taken together, the five creative options I have discussed, responding as they do to formal imperatives, help account for the astonishing diversity of modernist aesthetic practices. Though they all derive from older manifestations, frequently in neglected or underprized work, they are employed more frequently and are better articulated in the literature of our century. This may reflect the needs of our period, with its more open and favorable critical climate for change. Together with the tendency to foreground stylistic peculiarities and to invest all contexts with a pervasive aura of paradox and irony, these devices constitute important parts of the visible skeleton of modernity, contributing to a body of principles that also have become a carapace. Though perhaps not pervasive, they are obvious and common enough to merit close study. Though distinct, they tend to cluster in the individual work.

To reinforce this view, we may turn to the critical reception of Ezra Pound. Claiming to reflect a consensus on *The Cantos,* Richard Sieburth gives an accurate and perceptive account not only of Poundian parataxis but also, under the topic "capitalism," of a nodal procedure with mnemonic encyclopedic functions. According to Sieburth, this sort of nodality constitutes Pound's response to the tradition of the cultural catalogue.[88] The practice of other writers suggests that Pound's instincts were right; nodality in a paratactic vein enabled him economically to convey the impression of completeness and coherence. Though the strictly encyclopedic function need not be central, our own study discloses that both paratactics and nodality are cumulative, repetitive rhyming devices, giving varieties of coherence to forms that seemingly break the bounds implicit in all formal statements, both restore form while conserving the original disorder.

Had he wished to go further, Sieburth could have spoken of something approximating double-distancing in Pound's manner of cooling and heating his discourse, his generation of an internally tensed reception. In one sense, even, *The Cantos* is a self-generating text, growing out of the logic of association and the rhythms and quirks of an indi-

[88]Richard Sieburth, "The Design of the *Cantos:* An Introduction," in *Iowa Review* 15, no. 2 (1985), 20–21, 27.

vidual existence. My point is not that Pound is the measure of modern man or the progenitor of contemporary practice, despite arguments to that effect in Hugh Kenner's *The Pound Era*. Rather, it seems clear that certain procedures are attuned to the creative priorities of our moment, that they are almost inevitably part of the message.

Pound is not alone. We can see all of these techniques contributing to the shape of *Ulysses*. If we consider the arbitrary procedures attributable to the arranged component, those parts of the book that undermined the hard-won realistic discourse of the opening chapters and unsettled generations of readers, we will see that Joyce was also close to producing an impossible object in a text designed to resist total realistic recuperation. Clearly, no work, not even *Ulysses* or *The Cantos*, can or will or needs to exhibit all aspects of all of these tactics, but the presence of one or more of them in so many modern works, something that cannot be said of the art of the previous century, suggests the presence in our century of a formal imperative capable of generating the rudiments of a period manner, if not a readily perceptible period style. Perhaps we may adduce from this the existence of a still undefined formal imperative beneath the astonishing heterogeneity of the contemporary.

Index

Library of Congress Cataloging-in-Publication Data

Hayman, David.
  Re-forming the narrative.

  Includes index.
  1. Fiction—Technique. 2. Narration (Rhetoric) 3. Fiction—20th century—History and criticism. 4. Modernism (Literature) I. Title.
PN3383.N35H38 1987   808.3   87-47546
ISBN 0-8014-2005-9 (alk. paper)